COMMUNICATION AND COLLABORATION IN THE ONLINE CLASSROOM

COMMUNICATION AND COLLABORATION IN THE ONLINE CLASSROOM

Examples and Applications

Patricia Comeaux

University of North Carolina, Wilmington

EDITOR

ANKER PUBLISHING COMPANY, INC.
Bolton, Massachusetts

Communication and Collaboration in the Online Classroom
Examples and Applications

ISBN 1-882982-50-9

Composition by Deerfoot Studios
Cover design by Delaney Design

Anker Publishing Company, Inc.
176 Ballville Road
P.O. Box 249
Bolton, MA 01740-0249

www.ankerpub.com

ABOUT THE EDITOR

PATRICIA COMEAUX is Professor of Communication Studies at the University of North Carolina, Wilmington. Early in her teaching career, she discovered the value of an interdisciplinary approach to teaching and research when she designed and developed a communication across the curriculum program at Illinois Wesleyan University. Since then, her teaching and research interests have been in observing and examining communication and learning in institutions of higher education. Since the 1990s, her research has focused on the qualitative assessment (observation and examination) of the interpersonal nuances involved with communication and learning in distance education settings. She has served as an outside project evaluator for a number of distance education funded projects. In addition, she has published numerous articles on the topic of collaborative learning in higher education and the impact of interactive technologies on communication and learning.

About the Contributors

JOAN E. AITKEN is Professor of Communication Studies at the University of Missouri, Kansas City. She teaches an array of courses in speech communication and has edited the National Communication Association's (NCA) *Communication Teacher* and coedited *Intrapersonal Communication Processes* with Leonard Shedletsky. Her main area of scholarship is communication education and technology. Her contact information is aitkenj@umkc.edu.

MARY BOZIK is Professor of Communication Studies at the University of Northern Iowa. She has served as editor of the National Communication Association's (NCA) *Communication Teacher,* is currently an elected member of the Central States Communication Association Executive Board, and was a member of NCA's task force that wrote the K–12 speaking, listening, and media literacy competencies. She teaches graduate classes on the Iowa Communications Interactive Video Network and directs the Master's Program in Communication Education. Her contact information is bozik@uni.edu.

DEBORAH BRUNSON is Associate Professor of Communication Studies at the University of North Carolina, Wilmington. She teaches courses on race relations, diversity, and leadership, and has published articles on teaching and learning in *Communication Education, Journal of Leadership Studies*, and *Communication Teacher*. Her contact information is brunsond@uncwil.edu.

ELE BYINGTON is Associate Professor of English at the University of North Carolina, Wilmington. She is former director of the composition program at the university and coeditor of a textbook for college writing and reading courses, *Critical Issues in Contemporary Cultures*. Her contact information is byingtone@uncwil.edu.

SCOTT A. CHADWICK is Assistant Professor in the Greenlee School of Journalism and Communication at Iowa State University. His research interests focus on the use of communication technology in education and how trust is built, maintained, and damaged in organizations. His recent work appears in *Management Communication Quarterly, Computers and Composition*, and the text *Electronic Communication Across the Curriculum*.

He currently teaches courses in organizational communication, communication research methods, and the social effects of communication technology. His contact information is chadwics@iastate.edu.

FRANK FULLER is Assistant Professor of Adult and Continuing Education at Northwestern State University. Before he began his teaching career, he worked for many years as a community college continuing education administrator in Texas and Colorado. His research interests focus on community building and mutual assistance in distance education programs and how those programs can empower their clients. His contact information is fullerf@nsula.edu.

ROBERT GILLAN is Director of the Master's of Education and Educational Specialist degree programs in Educational Technology at Northwestern State University. He edits the *Middle School Online Journal,* manages the LearnNet web site, serves on the editorial board of the *Journal of Technology and Teacher Education,* and edits the Faculty Development section of the *Society for Information Technology and Teacher Education Annual.* In the mid-1980s, he founded the Louisiana Association of Computer Using Educators and led the development of the educational technology program at Northwestern State University. His contact information is gillan@nsula.edu.

RICHARD HUBER is Professor of Science Education at the University of North Carolina, Wilmington. In 1999, he received the Distinguished Teaching Professorship Award. He has published extensively on the use of the Internet for teaching environmental education. He has received two university Innovations in Technology awards and is currently the principal investigator for two externally funded web-based projects, Students as Scientists (http://smec.uncwil.edu/GLAXO/SAS/index.htm) and the Riverrun project (http://www.inttek.com/~dnorris/river/site/index.html). His contact information is huberr@uncwil.edu.

BRIAN KLINE is Assistant Professor of Speech Communication at Gainesville College. He teaches courses in public speaking and interpersonal communication, and is a reviewer for the *Basic Communication Course Annual* and a Governor's Teaching Fellow. His contact information is bkline@hermes.gc.peachnet.edu.

RONALD MCBRIDE is Associate Professor of Educational Technology at Northwestern State University. He has 27 years of experience in education technology and mass communications, with 19 in higher education. He has authored 20 articles in his field and is currently writing a book titled *Teaching at a Distance: The Human Connection.* He is a consultant for distance learning and education technology applications and has a deep appreciation for the role and scope of technology collaboration between public and higher education. His email address is mcbride@nsula.edu.

RICHARD G. MILTER is Associate Professor of Management and Director (as well as one of the original designers) of the Master's of Business Administration's Without Boundaries program at Ohio University. He serves on the executive board of EDINEB, an international network of innovative educators based in Maastricht, the Netherlands, and has delivered seminar courses on decision-making, leadership, business policy, organizational behavior, and strategic management to students in the United States, Malaysia, Sweden, and Hungary. He has presented workshops to educators on action learning strategies across the United States, Sweden, Hungary, the Netherlands, Russia, Japan, and Malaysia. His contact information is Milter@ohio.edu.

MAHNAZ MOALLEM is Associate Professor of Instructional Technology and Program Coordinator and an original designer of the Instructional Technology Master's program at the University of North Carolina, Wilmington. She teaches courses on instructional systems design, instructional technology, and classroom assessment and evaluation. Her main area of scholarship is instructional design theories/models and principles. She has authored many articles in her field and is currently writing a book titled *Instructional Design for Teachers.* Her articles are published in journals such as *Instructional Technology Research and Development, Educational Foundations,* and *Contemporary Educational Psychology.* Her contact information is moallemm.@uncwil.edu.

NINA-JO MOORE is Professor of Communication at Appalachian State University. Although she teaches a variety of communication courses, she specializes in interpersonal and intercultural communication. Her research interests are in intercultural and gender communication. Her contact information is moorenj@appstate.edu.

MARY ANNE NIXON is Associate Professor in the College of Business at Western Carolina University and consults with numerous companies in project management. She teaches full-time in the totally Internet-based Master's of Project Management degree program. Her main area of expertise is legal issues in project-based management. Her current research deals with issues and androgogy of teaching over the Internet. Recent publications are in *Technological Horizons in Education (THE), WebNet Journal,* and *Technology Source.* Her contact information is nixon@wcu.edu.

RICHARD OLSEN is Assistant Professor of Communication Studies at the University of North Carolina, Wilmington. While working as a doctoral fellow at Regent University, he helped to establish one of the initial residency experiences for distance doctoral students. He was the lead producer and instructor for an audiocassette-based course for the master's of art students at Regent. He has also had significant involvement in oral communication across the curriculum programs that are often strongly informed by the larger institutional culture. His contact information is olsenr@uncwil.edu.

BETH RODGERS LEFTWICH is Assistant Professor and Coordinator of the Library of Congress: An Adventure of the American Mind project, a cohort in the College of Education and Allied Professions at Western Carolina University. She teaches computers in education courses to pre-service and in-service teachers. Her main areas of expertise and research are instructional design and student attitudes toward computer technology. She has copublished in *Technological Horizons in Education (THE)* and *Technology Source,* and is a contributing author in *Applied Learning: Introduction to Speech Communication* (1999). Her contact information is leftwich@wcu.edu.

TRACY CALLAWAY RUSSO is Assistant Professor and Director of the Communication Studies' Master's of Arts program at the Edwards Campus of the University of Kansas. Her research focuses on communication behaviors in mediated environments, especially communication between and among teachers and students in online classes and on communication in distributed organizations. She teaches the first completely online class in the University of Kansas's College of Liberal Arts and Sciences and is currently working on a series of online classes. Her contact information is trusso@falcon.cc.ukans.edu.

ROBERT SCHIHL is Professor and Director of Distance Education for the College of Communication and the Arts, and former Director of the Doctoral program at Regent University. He has published five books in television production, an eBook (averaging 15,000 hits a month) on biblical apologetics, and is writing his second eBook on moral apologetics. He created and designed three distance degree programs in the college and directed them through Southern Association of Colleges and Schools accreditation reaffirmation. He consults for colleges in developing courses and degrees in computer mediated communication/education. His contact information is robesch@regent.edu.

LEONARD J. SHEDLETSKY is Professor of Communication at the University of Southern Maine. He teaches intrapersonal communication and other cognitively oriented communication courses, such as Meaning and Communication, Communication and Cognition, and Theories of Language. He wrote a book on intrapersonal communication, *Meaning and Mind: An Intrapersonal Approach to Human Communication,* and coedited a second, *Intrapersonal Communication Processes.* He has written numerous articles and book chapters and presented conference papers and workshops on aspects of intrapersonal communication. His contact information is lenny@maine.edu.

KAREN TRACEY is Associate Professor of English and Coordinator of the Writing program at the University of Northern Iowa. She is the author of *Plots and Proposals: American Women Fiction, 1850–1890* and coeditor of *The Craft of Argument with Readings.* Her contact information is karen.tracey@uni.edu.

FRANK P. TRIMBLE is Professor and Chair of the Department of Communication Studies at the University of North Carolina, Wilmington. His teaching areas include corporate communication and performance studies and has published articles on related topics in journals such as *Communication Education, Theatre Crafts,* and *The Forensic of Pi Kappa Delta.* Original musical stage plays include "Fly Wright: The Story of Two Brothers" and "Ebenezer: A Christmas Carol." His contact information is trimblef@uncwil.edu.

MARY E. WILDNER-BASSETT is Associate Professor of German Studies and a member of the faculty and graduate advisor for the Interdisciplinary PhD program in Second Language Acquisition and Teaching (SLAT) at the University of Arizona. She writes, teaches, and presents papers and workshops on pragmatic aspects of applied linguistic analysis and discourse analysis of learner language; learning styles and strategies; professional development of teachers; and computer-mediated communication and its interface with complexity, subjective and standpoint theories, and second language acquisition and teaching. Her contact information is wildnerb@u.arizona.edu.

PATRICIA WORRALL is Assistant Professor of English at Gainesville College. She teaches courses in composition, technical writing, and literature. She contributed to *Eighteenth Century British and American Rhetoric and Rhetoricians* and *The Late Medieval Age of Crisis and Renewal 1300–1500*. She has also written play reviews for *Shakespeare Bulletin*. Her contact information is pworrall@hermes.gc.peachnet.edu.

TABLE OF CONTENTS

SECTION I: PROGRAM DEVELOPMENT
FOR DISTANCE EDUCATION

SECTION II: PROFESSIONAL COLLABORATIVE ENDEAVORS: TEACHING ACROSS THE DISTANCE

SECTION III: CREATING ONLINE LEARNING COMMUNITIES: A FOCUS ON COMMUNICATION AND STUDENT-CENTERED LEARNING IN THE VIRTUAL CLASSROOM

FOREWORD

Collaboration plays a key role in contemporary higher education's approach to knowledge creation and its ability to leverage its tremendous investment in faculty and staff. Ira Fuchs, Vice President for Research in Information Technology at the Andrew W. Mellon Foundation, underscored the fundamental importance of collaboration to higher education in an interview with *EDUCAUSE Review:*

> I believe that institutions of higher education will be able to sustain our comparative advantage only by working together and that our collaborative environments constitute our version of Archimedes' lever.... Our open, collaborative environments are essential to our nature. (Katz, 2001, p. 19)

Collaboration has long been an essential part of research and scholarship in higher education. The emergence of more constructivist and experiential approaches to teaching has also focused attention on collaboration as a means of learning. In decades past, faculty on the same or nearby campuses collaborated, but long distance collaborative arrangements were severely constrained or slowed down by the geographic dispersion of the participants and the limited means for communicating and exchanging materials. The Internet changed that, of course, first by providing the means for email and later by providing the means to exchange many kinds of media and materials, as well as by permitting direct access to computing resources and software. Today we can collaborate, through mediated communication, with faculty, students, and institutions on every continent. No matter when and how it takes place, if used effectively, collaboration causes a synergistic transformation that enhances the value of the thoughts, activities, and discussions of a group of people working toward a common goal. It creates a final result that is greater than the sum of its parts. To be successful, it requires the right mix of both appropriate process and communication. In today's knowledge economy, much of that communication is enabled or supported by technology.

Technology provides great opportunities for all types of educational and collaborative activities. But many people struggle, knowingly or unknowingly, with a basic question: What is the appropriate role of technology in teaching and learning environments? In my opinion, the answer to that question is that technology is an enabler, both a tool that can be used to construct a knowledge environment and a channel for human interaction that functions most effectively when seamlessly integrated into the environment. Like any tool, information technology can be less effective, or even damaging, if used inappropriately. This is more likely to happen if we have unrealistic expectations of technology or do not understand how different technologies affect process and communication.

Too often we are tempted to focus more of our attention on the novelty of the medium itself, or the bells and whistles of technology, and shortchange our plans for the human process and interaction. In a well-planned collaborative experience mediated by technology, the collaborative strategy provides the process and structure for social interaction and technology provides the channels and modalities for communication. When the collaboration or interactivity takes place within the context of a learning experience, the process must also include appropriate pedagogical strategies. At times, we must rethink our original strategy because the available or cost effective technologies do not support that strategy. In these cases it is even more important to understand how the available technology either helps or hinders us in reaching our goals.

Each chapter in this book recounts an author's experiences struggling with these issues. As you read through the accounts you will see how each dealt with fundamental questions such as:

- What is technology's role in enabling effective collaborative activities in higher education?

- How does technology interact with process to facilitate effective collaboration?

- What are the strengths and weaknesses of various technologies in supporting collaboration and learning?

- When can you use technology to mediate communication and when do you need face to face meetings?

The authors have many important lessons to share with you, but two are paramount. The first is that effective deployment of technology in an educational environment nearly always requires collaboration among a team of people who bring to the planning an appropriate mix of pedagogy and content and technology expertise. The second is that preparation is essential. In face to face communication we can "wing it" more easily because we have the opportunity to get instantaneous verbal and nonverbal feedback and alter our approach based on that feedback. We can ask spontaneous questions. With mediated communication this capability is constrained both by the timing and modality of feedback opportunities. In mediated environments, preparation is important because it provides an opportunity to structure the activities and interactions to provide alternatives for students with different perspectives and learning styles. It provides them with learning strategies and information formats and lets them choose strategies that optimize their chances for success.

One of the unalterable rules of working with technology is that it creates changes in any system to which it is introduced. A corollary is that the greatest return on your technology investment comes from optimizing the process to take advantage of the inherent characteristics of the particular technology. So we make the best use of technology when we select it for its ability to enable the process we need and we examine our processes to exploit the new capabilities of the technologies available to us. Figuring out the complex interplay of cause and effect is not simple. The authors in this book provide a rich casebook with first-hand experience and advice. They offer useful reference points for constructing your own collaborative environments. With their examples to inspire you, and their advice to guide you, go forth and collaborate.

Kathryn L. Conway
Lead Consultant, Strategic Consulting Services Division
Eduprise, Inc.

REFERENCE

Katz, R. N. (2001, March/April). Archimedes' lever & collaboration: An interview with Ira Fuchs. *EDUCAUSE Review, 36* (2), 17–22.

PREFACE

This book is a culmination of almost two decades of my teaching and research interests in observing and examining communication and learning in higher education classrooms. In 1983, as a new faculty member at Illinois Wesleyan University, I was in charge of designing and implementing a communication across the curriculum program at this small liberal arts university. Thus, early in my post-secondary career, I discovered the value of interdisciplinary dialogue (a theme of this collection). I designed the program on the premise that effective communication in the classroom increases the potential for learning. That philosophy and belief remains, to this day, the center of my teaching and research endeavors.

When I arrived at the University of North Carolina, Wilmington (UNCW) in 1991, UNCW (along with several universities throughout the state) was part of a pilot project titled "Vision Carolina" which established video conferencing capabilities via the North Carolina Information Highway. These distance learning classrooms (equipped with cameras, microphones, and television monitors) provide simultaneous audio/video interactions in real time. Competitive stipends were offered to faculty to develop team-taught courses over the distance learning network or to examine instruction in this environment. I took advantage of the latter, thus beginning my observation and examination of communication and learning in distance education environments. In 1998, I expanded my agenda to include online web-based instruction and have been a "virtual visiting professor" in several "classrooms" throughout the United States. My particular interest is in the qualitative assessment of the interpersonal nuances involved with communication and learning in distance education settings. These investigations have been a catalyst for invigorating, critical, and insightful interactions about teaching and learning with colleagues who have been long-time friends and others who have become colleagues and friends through our collaborations.

My experience since 1991, and in editing this collection, has reaffirmed my conviction that effective communication in the classroom increases the potential for learning. Effective communication—as my introductory chapter asserts—is a process in which individuals co-construct and negotiate meanings in a communal space. As the technological revolution unfolds, we must critically assess the characteristics and the quality of instruction. The focus of this book is on the qualitative assessment of the teaching and learning with interactive technologies already taking place.

THE BOOK'S PURPOSE

The purpose of this book is to provide readers with a comprehensive understanding of the human communication issues that must be addressed in higher education as interactive technologies evolve and continue to impact instructional design and practice. The question explored throughout the book is, How have interactive technologies affected teaching and learning in institutions of higher education? The contributing authors articulate the underlying assumptions and theories of collaboration and learning, as well as the challenges faced and benefits realized, in their endeavors to incorporate interactive technologies into their instructional practice or curriculum.

This collection is written for faculty, graduate students, administrators, and scholars in higher education. It is for readers who have a particular interest in the topic of communicating and collaborative learning via interactive technologies. It will also be of interest to those who want to learn about pedagogical applications of interactive technologies across different disciplines and institutions. Because of the multidisciplinary and comprehensive approach to this book, it will prove valuable to a wide range of readers. What is needed at the cusp of this technological revolution is critical analysis of the human communication lessons learned as faculty and administrators plan for the future of teaching and learning in institutions of higher education.

This collection represents faculty from a variety of disciplines across university campuses and with varying degrees of expertise and experience in using interactive technology in their classrooms. Some contributing authors write from a first-time experience with and a healthy skepticism of interactive technologies in their instructional practice. Others write from an experienced perspective and a long history of using interactive technology in their instructional practice. In addition, faculty from the position and perspective of program planners and directors examine the process of developing distance education programs.

The contributing authors describe and analyze their experiences in collaboration and in using interactive technologies as they address, through a case study approach, 1) why (their motivations or incentives) they chose collaboration, collaborative learning methodologies, or particular interactive technologies, 2) what the collaborative experience, program, or course was (what risks and challenges did program planners, faculty, or their students face in their endeavors), and 3) how effective was the program, collaborative endeavor, or course (for example, what worked, what did not, what did they learn, what would they do differently, and what suggestions do they have for others).

The uniqueness of this treatise is that it contains lessons from the field from a human communication perspective. While the contributing authors draw upon theories and perspectives from a variety of disciplines—instructional technology, educational learning theory, social constructivist theory, collaborative learning theory, organizational and leadership theory, small group theory, composition and rhetorical theory, interpersonal communication theory—what they have in common is that they frame their experiences in terms of communication and collaboration.

In addition to the case studies, the foreword provides readers with a frame for understanding the relationships between technology and the processes of communicating and learning in instructional settings. In the introductory chapter, I provide a comprehensive review of the scholarly literature in the disciplines of communication, education, instructional technology, and distance education as they relate to the focus of this collection. And, in the concluding chapter, I highlight some common themes emerging from the case studies and end with my reflections and observations about teaching and learning with interactive technologies.

THE BOOK'S ORGANIZATION

The book is organized around three sections. The first, Program Development for Distance Education, contains four case studies in which the authors describe and analyze their efforts as part of a design and planning team charged with adapting and developing a graduate degree program for distance education. The disciplines represented in these chapters are business (general degree and project management degree), education (instructional technology certification), and communication studies (joint degree with divinity).

In the second section, Professional Collaborative Endeavors: Teaching Across the Distance, the authors describe their motivations and incentives for collaborating in course design and in teaching across the distance with interactive technologies. Four of the five chapters present case studies of faculty electing to teach with colleagues from different institutions across the distance via interactive technologies. The last chapter considers teaching and presentational strategies in an interactive audio/video environment focusing specifically upon the impact that video images have in a teaching environment mediated by technology. Of the five chapters, three describe courses taught in an audio/video environment (sometimes referred to as interactive television), one describes an online team-taught course, and the other describes how two instructors took turns serving as "visiting virtual professors" in each other's classes.

The five chapters in Section III, Creating Online Learning Communities: A Focus on Communication and Student-Centered Learning in Virtual Classrooms, all detail the efforts and pedagogy involved in creating online learning communities. Although the authors in these case studies use different software packages, their educational objectives are similar: to create an online communication and learning environment as an integral part of an online course (Chapters 11 and 12), in combination with the face to face classroom environment (Chapter 10), or as an extension of the face to face classroom environment (Chapters 13 and 14).

The courses and curricula described and examined in this section are Second Language Acquisition and Teaching (graduate level); Instructional Systems Design: Theory and Research (graduate level); College Writing and Reading (undergraduate course); an interdisciplinary general education cluster course combining Oral Communication, College Reading and Writing, American Civilization, and Humanities (undergraduate level); and Public Speaking and Composition (undergraduate level).

As technology's role in instruction increases, it is important that effective communication remains a part of the instructional process. The collaborative learning strategies found in this collection are sure to affect instructional design and practice as interactive technologies continue to evolve.

Patricia Comeaux
June 2001

ACKNOWLEDGMENTS

This project, the writing and editing of this collection, has been a collaborative endeavor with interactive technology. I would like to thank and acknowledge all my contributing authors and collaborators for their responsiveness to our demanding time lines. Electronic communication (emails with attached chapters, chapters edited electronically, documents faxed, etc.) made the process efficient, focused, and highly interactive.

This book is a testimony to the power of communication and collaboration. I approached the editing process in a collaborative style and have strengthened existing collegial relationships and friendships and made new ones. I have said many times throughout this process that I really should title this book, "Pat and Friends: Communicating in the 21st Century." Through electronic interactions with my collaborators, I have grown professionally and personally.

I would like to thank Susan Anker for her valuable guidance, especially at the beginning stages of this endeavor. Carolyn Dumore provided excellent assistance during the editing process. In addition, I appreciate the efficiency of the staff and quality of work of Anker Publishing Company.

Finally, I would like to especially thank and recognize two of my contributors. Ele Byington, my friend and colleague, helped me frame my original ideas for this collection and was an excellent reader and respondent for my two chapters. Richard Huber, my partner, colleague, and best critic, provided valuable feedback throughout the writing and editing process and continually influences my life and my work.

COLLABORATION, COMMUNICATION, TEACHING, AND LEARNING: A THEORETICAL FOUNDATION AND FRAME

Patricia Comeaux

We shall not cease from exploration
And the end of all our exploring
Will be to arrive where we started
And know the place for the first time.
—T. S. Eliot

As Eliot's verse suggests, humans have an irresistible urge to explore, and many of our present-day explorations focus on the possibilities as well as the impact of interactive technologies upon our lives. The question explored in this introductory chapter, as well as the book, is, How have interactive technologies affected teaching and learning in institutions of higher education? The contributing authors make clear the underlying assumptions and theories of collaboration and learning, as well as the challenges and benefits of incorporating interactive technologies into their instructional practice, university degree programs, and faculty development programs.

Information technologies are revolutionizing the ways we communicate and learn in business and industry as well as in education. Whether we embrace these interactive technologies or choose to keep them at bay, we cannot ignore their increasing importance in an increasingly techno-logical society. As Dede (1996) asserts,

> Educators must help all students become adept at dis-tanced interaction, for skills of information gathering from remote sources and of collaboration with dispersed team members are as central to the future American workplace as learning to perform structured tasks quickly was to the industrial revolution. (p. 30)

As the technological revolution unfolds, we must critically assess the characteristics and the quality of instruction. The focus of this collection is upon the qualitative assessment of the teaching and learning with interac-tive technologies already taking place. This introduction will present an analysis of the relevant scholarly literature in the disciplines of communi-cation, education, instructional technology, and distance education as they relate to the concerns of this book.

REVIEW AND ANALYSIS OF THE SCHOLARLY LITERATURE

In reviewing the literature, certain themes immediately emerge. Interac-tive technologies are revolutionizing the way university faculty think and talk about teaching and learning. The invention of these technologies (in particular, the Internet and the World Wide Web) has become the catalyst for a burgeoning body of scholarly literature.

Debates and Discussions

First, according to the research, increasing dialogues (debates and discus-sions) about teaching and learning with technologies are already occur-ring. For example, the Carnegie Academy for the Scholarship of Teaching and Learning (CASTL) was established in 1998

> to foster a scholarship of teaching that aims to improve the quality of student learning and raise the level of con-versation about teaching in colleges and universi-ties ... [and] to help foster communities of scholars who share, critique and build upon each other's accomplish-ments. (Huber, 2000, pp. 20–21)

CASTL invites teachers/scholars to make an important contribution to the scholarship of teaching and learning by examining and publishing their classroom practices as well as the underlying assumption and theories that inform those practices, thus providing "readers with a wider range of references to draw on as they identify and examine issues relevant to work with students and classroom practice" (Huber, 2000, p. 23). The challenge, according to Huber (2000), is "to reconceptualize relationships between the disciplines, so that lessons flow in all directions rather than demanding the diffusion of one privileged way of knowing" (p. 28).

Disciplinary Agreement

Second, an analysis of the literature suggests agreement across the disciplines under review in regard to the following.

Communication is a multidisciplinary concentration and is fundamental to every human activity, for it is the primary thinking and socializing tool; it is the process by which humans come to know, believe, and act. Communication is a complex symbolic process in which meaning is created and negotiated as persons in conversations co-construct their own social realities (Berger & Luckmann, 1966; Carey, 1975; Dance, 1967; Harper, 1979; Mead 1934; Pearce & Cronen, 1980).

Teaching is a complex process that by its very nature is centered in communication. Teaching is a reflective and analytical practice as well as an intellectual transformative act. It works when it engages students in active, co-responsible ways of knowing so that teaching and learning become reciprocal enterprises as teachers and learners coexist in a communal space of shaping and transforming knowledge and understanding (Barker, 1982; Conquergood, 1993; Dewey, 1933; Giroux, 1988; Sprague, 1993; Staton-Spicer & Wulff, 1984; Strine, 1993; Wulff, 1993).

Collaborative learning is similar to cooperative learning and problem-based learning in which knowledge is constructed and negotiated in social/cultural contexts with others in a collaborative process. It emphasizes the interdependence of the learners and the communal nature of the process as knowledge is negotiated and constructed through dialogue, problem solving, and authentic experiences. It is based on constructivist philosophies and learner-centered methodologies in which knowledge is constructed through active engagement (sense making) with ideas and phenomenon (Bruffee, 1993; Dunlap & Grabinger, 1996; Fosnot, 1989; Gergen, 1985; Goodman, 1984; Johnson, Johnson, & Smith, 1991;

Lebow, 1993; Myers & Jones, 1993; Savery & Duffy, 1996; Slavin, 1991; vonGlasersfeld, 1989).

Collaborative (cooperative) learning methodologies are also based on group communication and group theories. To be successful, collaborative learning groups must have an interdependent goal structure as well as a division of labor and resources, equal reward system, individual accountability, and supportive communication patterns. In working and learning together, successful collaboration requires perceiving mutual benefit, building trust relationships, and accommodating differences in values and cultures (Blumenfeld, Marx, Soloway, & Krajcik, 1996; Chrislip & Larson, 1994; Harris & Sherblom, 1999; Moran & Mugridge, 1993; O'Donnell & O'Kelly, 1994; Rothwell, 1998; Smith & MacGregor, 2000; Webb, 1982).

Learner-Centered Philosophies

Third, an analysis of the research literature also shows that collaborative learning and similar learner-centered philosophies and methodologies (i.e., constructivism, problem-based learning) are strongly advocated by scholars as an effective instructional strategy for environments mediated by interactive technologies (Abrami & Bures, 1996; Brandon & Hollingshead, 1999; Brown, 1990; Dede, 1996; Harasim, 1990; Hiltz, 1994, 1998; Jonassen, Davidson, Collins, Campbell, & Haag, 1995; Turoff, 1999).

Advocates claim that computer-supported collaborative learning (CSCL) helps instructors avoid the pitfalls of Internet correspondence courses that rely on information acquisition and rote learning (Dede, 1996; Pea, 1993). As Pea (1993) argues, "combinations of new computer technologies that facilitate collaboration and communication among learners can support and enhance learning, particularly distance learning" (p. 288). Hiltz (1998) concludes from her research that "collaborative learning designs are more effective for online learning than pedagogical approaches that emphasize individuals working alone with materials posted online" (p. 6). Similarly, Turoff (1999) argues for collaborative learning as the methodology in the virtual classroom in which students "may communicate and work together as small project teams. It is the key difference that makes most of the quality improvements possible" (pp. 22–23).

Moreover, in his extensive and historical review of the literature in instructional technology, Koschmann (1996) argues that "we are currently witnessing the emergence of a new paradigm in IT [instructional technology] research; one that is based on different assumptions about the nature of learning and one that incorporates a new set of research practices" (p. 10). As Koschmann explains, this paradigm—CSCL—is based in collaborative learning models and assumptions, which have their foundation in social constructivist practices of instruction. (There are a number of scholars who claim that using interactive technologies in instructional practice calls for a paradigm shift in teaching to a more student-centered, interactive, and collaborative way of learning. For example, see Amundsen, 1993, Dede, 1996, Garrison, 1993, Kolodner & Guzdial, 1996, Koschmann, 1996, and Trentin, 2000). Koschmann adds that

> the central focus for research in CSCL is on *instruction as enacted practice*... [and it]...tends to utilize the research methods of the social sciences...and focus on process rather than outcome. (Koschmann, 1996, pp. 14–15)

This type of research method is centered in grounded theories of observational data (e.g., Glaser & Strauss, 1967) and in the construction of thick descriptions (e.g., Guba & Lincoln, 1981) of the phenomena under study. Finally, Koschmann (1996) explains that the learning process is best understood

> as a distributed, ongoing social process, where evidence that learning is occurring or has occurred must be found in understanding the ways in which people collaboratively *do* [italics added] learning and *do* [italics added] recognize learning as having occurred. (Qtd. in Jordan & Henderson, 1995, p. 42)

What the Scholarly Literature Reveals

What is particularly significant is that these scholars and researchers from a variety of disciplines (using both qualitative and quantitative methods) have independently reached the same conclusion: Learning is a complex collaborative process based on constructivist philosophies and active learning methodologies. Furthermore, this analysis reconfirms that collaborative learning has a strong and valued history in our educational institutions. Therefore, as we design our classrooms of the future, we must continue to be reflective practitioners (Dewey, 1933) and transformative intellectuals (Giroux, 1988).

CONCLUSION

As the interactive technology revolution continues to evolve and impact higher education, our efforts must be centered on a perspective of communication and learning as complex collaborative processes. For what is needed at the cusp of this revolution is critical analysis of the human lessons learned as faculty and administrators plan for the future of teaching and learning in higher education. Interactive technologies have truly made us a global village, but it will be the ability to understand and appreciate the differences in cultures and values, to learn to clarify the roles and expectations of collaborators and learners, to learn to risk and trust, and to value working and learning together for mutual benefit—in essence to learn to communicate effectively with others—that will make these collaborations successful and enduring.

REFERENCES

Abrami, P. C., & Bures, E. M. (1996). Computer-supported collaborative learning and distance education. *The American Journal of Distance Education, 10* (2), 37–42.

Amundsen, C. (1993). The evolution of theory in distance education. In D. Keegan (Ed.), *Theoretical principles of distance education* (pp. 61–79). New York, NY: Routledge.

Barker, L. L. (Ed.). (1982). *Communication in the classroom: Original essays.* Englewood Cliffs, NJ: Prentice-Hall.

Berger, P. L., & Luckmann, T. (1966). *The social construction of reality: A treatise in the sociology of knowledge.* New York, NY: Doubleday.

Blumenfeld, P. C., Marx, R. W., Soloway, E., & Krajcik, J. (1996). Learning with peers: From small group cooperation to collaborative communities. *Educational Researcher, 25* (8), 37–40.

Brandon, D. P., & Hollingshead, A. B. (1999). Collaborative learning and computer-supported groups. *Communication Education, 48* (2), 109–126.

Brown, J. S. (1990). Toward a new epistemology for learning. In C. Frasson & G. Guatheir (Eds.), *Intelligent tutoring systems: At the crossroad of artificial intelligence and education* (pp. 4–35). Norwood, NJ: Ablex.

Bruffee, K. A. (1993). *Collaborative learning: Higher education, interdependence, and the authority of knowledge.* Baltimore, MD: Johns Hopkins University Press.

Carey, J. W. (1975). A cultural approach to communication. *Communication, 2,* 1–22.

Chrislip, D. D., & Larson, C. E. (1994). *Collaborative leadership: How citizens and civic leaders can make a difference.* San Francisco, CA: Jossey-Bass.

Conquergood, D. (1993). Storied worlds and the work of teaching. *Communication Education, 42* (4), 337–348.

Dance, F. E. (Ed.). (1967). *Human communication theory: Original essays.* New York, NY: Holt, Rinehart, and Winston.

Dede, C. (1996). The evolution of distance education: Emerging technologies and distributed learning. *The American Journal of Distance Education, 10* (2), 4–36.

Dewey, J. (1933). *How we think: A restatement of the relation of reflective thinking to the educative process.* New York, NY: D. C. Heath.

Dunlap, J. C., & Grabinger, R. S. (1996). Rich environments for active learning in the higher education classroom. In B. G. Wilson (Ed.), *Constructivist learning environments: Case studies in instructional design* (pp. 65–82). Englewood Cliffs, NJ: Educational Technology Publications.

Eliot, T. S. (1952). *The complete poems and plays: 1909–1950.* New York, NY: Harcourt Brace.

Fosnot, C. (1989). *Enquiring teachers, enquiring learners: A constructivist approach for teaching.* New York, NY: Teachers College Press.

Garrison, D. R. (1993). Quality and access in distance education: Theoretical considerations. In D. Keegan (Ed.), *Theoretical principles of distance education* (pp. 9–21). New York, NY: Routledge.

Gergen, K. J. (1985). The social constructionist movement in modern psychology. *American Psychologist, 40* (3), 266–275.

Giroux, H. A. (1988). *Teachers as intellectuals: Toward a critical pedagogy of learning.* Granby, MA: Bergin & Garvey.

Glaser, B., & Strauss, A. (1967). *The discovery of grounded theory.* Chicago, IL: Aldine-Atherton.

Goodman, N. (1984). *Of mind and other matters.* Cambridge, MA: Harvard University Press.

Guba, E., & Lincoln, Y. (1981). *Effective evaluation.* San Francisco, CA: Jossey-Bass.

Harasim, L. M. (Ed.). (1990). *Online education: Perspective on a new environment.* New York, NY: Praeger.

Harper, N. (1979). *Human communication theory: The history of a paradigm.* Rochelle Park, NJ: Hayden Book Company.

Harris, T. E., & Sherblom, J. C. (1999). *Small group and team communication.* Boston, MA: Allyn and Bacon.

Hiltz, S. R. (1994). *The virtual classroom: Learning without limits via computer networks.* Norwood, NJ: Ablex.

Hiltz, S. R. (1998). Collaborative learning in asynchronous learning networks: Building learning communities. *Proceedings of WebNet '98 World Conference on WWW, Internet and Intranet, 1* (1), 1–7.

Huber, M. T. (2000). Disciplinary styles in the scholarship of teaching: Reflections on the Carnegie Academy for the Scholarship of Teaching and Learning. In C. Rust (Ed.), *Improving student learning through the disciplines* (pp. 20–31). Oxford, England: Oxford-Brookes University, The Centre for Staff and Learning Development.

Johnson, D. W., Johnson, R. T., & Smith, K. A. (1991). *Cooperative learning: Increasing college faculty instructional productivity.* Washington, DC: George Washington University.

Jonassen, D., Davidson, M., Collins, M., Campbell, J., & Haag, B. B. (1995). Constructivism and computer-mediated communication in distance education. *The American Journal of Distance Education, 9* (2), 7–26.

Jordan, B., & Henderson, A. (1995). Interaction analysis: Foundations and practice. *Journal of the Learning Sciences, 4,* 39–103.

Kolodner, J., & Guzdial, M. (1996). Effects *with* and *of* CSCL: Tracking learning in a new paradigm. In T. Koschmann (Ed.), *CSCL: Theory and practice of an emerging paradigm* (pp. 307–320). Mahwah, NJ: Lawrence Erlbaum Associates.

Koschmann, T. (1996). Paradigm shifts and instructional technology: An introduction. In T. Koschmann (Ed.), *CSCL: Theory and practice of an emerging paradigm* (pp. 1–23). Mahwah, NJ: Lawrence Erlbaum Associates.

Lebow, D. (1993). Constructivist values for instructional systems design: Five principles toward a new mindset. *Educational Technology Research and Development, 41* (3), 4–16.

Mead, G. H. (1934). *Mind, self, and society.* Chicago, IL: University of Chicago.

Moran, L., & Mugridge, I. (1993). Policies and trends in inter-institutional collaboration. In L. Moran & I. Mugridge (Eds.), *Collaboration in distance education: International case studies* (pp. 150–164). New York, NY: Routledge.

Myers, C., & Jones, T. B. (1993). *Promoting active learning: Strategies for the college classroom.* San Francisco, CA: Jossey-Bass.

O'Donnell, A. M., & O'Kelly, J. (1994). Learning from peers: Beyond the rhetoric of positive results. *Educational Psychology Review, 6* (4), 321–349.

Pea, R. (1993). Seeing what we build together: Distributed multimedia learning environments for transformative communications. *The Journal of the Learning Sciences, 3* (3), 285–299.

Pearce, W. B., & Cronen V. E. (1980). *Communication, action, and meaning: The creation of social realities.* New York, NY: Praeger.

Rothwell, J. D. (1998). *In mixed company: Small-group communication.* Toronto, Ontario: Harcourt Brace.

Savery, J. R., & Duffy, T. M. (1996). Problem based learning: An instructional model and its constructivist framework. In B. G. Wilson (Ed.), *Constructivist learning environments: Case studies in instructional design* (pp. 135–148). Englewood Cliffs, NJ: Educational Technology Publications.

Slavin, R. E. (1991). Synthesis of research on cooperative learning. *Educational Leadership, 48,* 71–82.

Smith, K. A., & MacGregor, J. (2000). Making small-group learning and learning communities a widespread reality. *New Directions for Teaching and Learning, No. 81* (pp. 77–88). San Francisco, CA: Jossey-Bass.

Sprague, J. (1993). Why teaching works: The transformative power of pedagogical communication. *Communication Education, 42* (4), 349–366.

Staton-Spicer, A. Q., & Wulff, D. H. (1984). Research in communication and instruction: Categorization and synthesis. *Communication Education, 33* (4), 377–391.

Strine, M. S. (1993). Of boundaries, borders, and contact zones: Author(iz)ing pedagogical practices. *Communication Education, 42* (4), 367–376.

Trentin, G. (2000). The quality-interactivity relationship in distance education. *Educational Technology, 40* (1), 17–27.

Turoff, M. (1999). Education, commerce, communications: The era of competition. *WebNet Journal: Internet Technologies, Applications & Issues, 1* (1), 22–31.

vonGlasersfeld, E. (1989). Cognition, construction of knowledge, and teaching. *Synthese, 80,* 121–140.

Webb, N. M. (1982). Student interaction and learning in small groups. *Review of Educational Research, 52* (3), 421–445.

Wulff, D. H. (1993). Tales of transformation: Applying a teaching effectiveness perspective to stories about teaching. *Communication Education, 42* (4), 377–397.

SECTION I

PROGRAM DEVELOPMENT FOR DISTANCE EDUCATION

Developing an MBA Online Degree Program: Expanding Knowledge and Skills via Technology-Mediated Learning Communities

Richard G. Milter

> *It must be considered that there is nothing more difficult to carry out, nor more doubtful of success, nor more dangerous to handle, than to initiate a new order of things. For the reformer has enemies in all those who profit by the old order, and only lukewarm defenders in those who would profit by the new order. . . . This arises partly from the incredulity of mankind who do not truly believe in anything new until they have an actual experience of it.*
>
> —Niccolo Machiavelli

Founded in 1804, Ohio University is the oldest state university in Ohio, with an enrollment of 20,000 on the main campus in Athens. Educating approximately 1,800 undergraduate students is the main mission of the College of Business and its 75 faculty members. The college also provides graduate education with a full-time resident MBA program, an executive MBA program offered at one of its five regional campuses, and an MBA program in Malaysia.

This chapter describes the development phases and continuous improvement cycle of the MBA Without Boundaries program, launched in March 1997 following an 18-month design phase by faculty members and external reviewers. The program's foundation is a learning architecture that merges project-based action learning with electronic collaboration for members in project teams. This chapter explicates the use of constructivist learning methods which help to develop and sustain true learning communities with diverse groupings of professionals. Although this example is of a graduate business degree program, the "without boundaries" learning architecture is currently being applied to undergraduate, graduate, and nondegree offerings in various disciplines.

DEVELOPING A NEED: THE SEEDS OF INNOVATION

This story begins on an urgent note. In 1984, the Executive Advisory Board of the College of Business at Ohio University informed the dean that undergraduates were completing their degree work and leaving the college with a good set of technical skills and a fairly broad knowledge base. This was good news, as the college's primary mission is to deliver quality undergraduate education. The proverbial ax fell, however, when discussion centered on the graduate program, more specifically the full-time graduate program. The residential MBA program had approximately 140 students in 1984, half of whom were international. The program was filling classroom space (strong FTE) and using faculty resources allotted to it. On the books, the program was doing well. The advisors observed that MBA graduates were leaving the program with excellent skills in quantitative analysis and financial accounting, but that their ability to think critically and holistically and take on leadership roles was limited.

All in all, this was not too different a message than that which resounded in the literature of the day. MBA graduates across the board were said to be too tied to numerative rationalist approaches when dealing with business problems (see Peters & Waterman, 1982; Porter & McKibbin, 1988). The general challenge that targeted all business schools was to provide more skills training in the use of the knowledge that MBAs were acquiring.

The dean appointed a faculty committee to look into these charges and make recommendations for improvement if needed. After one year of meetings, the committee recommended that three of the existing 12 courses be redesigned to incorporate more attention to critical thinking and leadership. The dean was not happy with these findings, especially since it had taken a full year to develop such a recommendation, and he called upon the logic of the old adage, if you want a job done right . . . , and personally led a task force of volunteer faculty members who worked evenings and weekends for the next two months (over the summer).

Their charge was to take the full-time MBA program apart and put it back together or recommend it be discontinued. The dean made it clear that he either wanted to offer a valuable MBA program or get out of the business of offering such a degree. The task force efforts culminated in a presentation to the entire college faculty in the fall of the next academic year, where they introduced a plan to develop a unique educational platform. It would involve students in an integrative experience where they would confront business issues in ways similar to business leaders and managers. Students would also participate in development of leadership skills via a series of interactive workshops. It was a grand view. It was exciting and daring. Many faculty members from across the four departments in the college (management systems, finance, accounting, and marketing) were genuinely intrigued by the concept. A few were utterly disgusted and thought that it would never work. The vote was taken and passed. The college would take a stride into the land of educational innovation. The full-time MBA program would be redesigned.

PHASE 1: MOVEMENT FROM TRADITIONAL TEACHING TO INNOVATIVE LEARNING MODELS (1986–1990)

Built into the redesign was a series of training experiences for faculty members, which were initiated during the 1986–1987 academic year. During the next several years, the college faculty, under the leadership of the dean, began to seek counsel from others about innovation in education. Experts in skills development provided workshops to help faculty members better understand how to facilitate student learning. Leaders from other educational institutions experimenting with new designs in learning were invited to provide their views. New faculty members were hired with the understanding that innovation in learning was taking place in the full-time MBA program. A partnership, a type of "sister program" relationship, was formed with the Department of Economics at the University of Limburg (now Maastricht University) in the Netherlands. Faculty members at that new institution were also involved in developing innovative approaches to business education. It was an exciting time.

The curricular structure of the full-time MBA program was built around two academic years of course work. The first year exposed students to the fundamentals in each of the academic disciplines, including basic courses in finance, accounting, marketing, operations, and management. The second year provided courses with more advanced attention to these key areas. In addition to these classes, students in the second year were involved in a course that targeted their work on a specifically focused and carefully designed problem. This problem was developed to draw upon the requisite business skills that the students had been learning and challenge them to integrate these skills in working through the problem.

The students worked on three such problems evenly spaced during the three quarters of their final academic year in the program. Having theoretical foundation in a process called integrated contextual learning (Stinson, 1990), this course was titled Integrated Business Analysis (IBA) and was designed by a team of faculty members representing various disciplines within the college. The IBA experiences were enhanced by a series of skills workshops that were threaded within the demands of the problem contexts. These workshops were part of a program called Management Skills Development (MSD), later changed to Leadership Skills Development (LSD). Each year there was a full weekend scheduled off-site for leadership skills development. It was during this period (1988–1989 academic year) that I joined the faculty team as the coordinator of Leadership Skills Development for the full-time MBA program.

Although faculty members and students involved in these early years had the experience of being pioneers with these new approaches, it soon became apparent that what we were developing was not unlike earlier innovations. Specifically, an educational redesign had become well known in the medical education field called problem-based learning (PBL) (Barrows, 1985). Furthermore, this approach was grounded in the theoretical construct of constructivism, where learners shape their own meaning via interaction with their environment (Savery & Duffy, 1995). This was clearly a reaction to the more traditional curricular structure, which can be viewed as more information dispensing in its approach.

After several years offering the IBA experience, students began to feel the pull between the constructivist and traditional approaches. More than that, they were frustrated and confused by the two very different learning architectures provided within the same program. Responding to this feedback, 13 faculty members drawn from all discipline units within the college, and the associate dean/director of graduate programs, came together as a design team to take the next step in the innovation process.

PHASE 2: DEFINING AN MBA'S KNOWLEDGE AND ABILITIES (1992–1994)

The design team began meeting twice each week (one morning and one evening) during the spring term and continued to meet throughout the summer months of 1992. The first question we addressed was, What should MBAs know and know how to do by the time they graduate? Each of the faculty members represented his or her respective functional area and was armed with a plethora of answers to that question. Some of our early discussions proposed that MBA graduates should know as much about each functional area as an undergraduate major. This would mean, for example, that an MBA would have the same depth and breadth of knowledge in accounting as individuals graduating with a degree in that field—accounting majors. It soon became clear that the purpose of our MBA degree, as a generalist degree, was not to prepare students with functional expertise in any specific field (that was the purpose of our undergraduate programs) but to prepare them with a breadth of knowledge, skills, and abilities; the ability to know when to make use of such directed expertise; and, where appropriate, to integrate such expertise in framing and handling a particular business problem.

On occasion, our discussions would become somewhat heated as faculty members defended their own turf areas. Although we had differences in opinions and convictions, we stood together as we searched for the best way to create an answer to the focal question. Literally, this meant frequent banging of heads eventually leading to compromise as we waded through long lists of knowledge and skills attributed to specific functional areas within the business disciplines. Making use of a "reality check"—inviting business executives to react to our listings and make recommendations—is one of the elements that helped to keep us grounded in the task.

We realized that the purpose of our efforts to help others learn was not to prepare them for the business world of today but to prepare them to address tomorrow's challenges. To help us, we sought the guidance and wisdom of futurists. Adding the thoughts, and sometimes even the physical presence of such individuals as management guru Peter Drucker, helped us remain alert to the practical issues of growing business and life skills for the future.

PHASE 3: DEVELOPMENT OF PROJECT-BASED ACTION LEARNING METHODS (1992–1995)

Out of the design team's work sprang a new concept in full-time MBA programs—a 13-month design based upon complete integration of business functions and a fully constructivist learning platform. All learning was delivered via projects. There were no classes.

This program, launched in August 1992, was built around a specified set of learning outcomes. Much of our early work with learning outcomes was influenced by faculty members at Alverno College (well known for their work with outcome assessment), who agreed to lead a workshop for our college (for more on the Alverno experience, see Mentkowski, 1988). Additionally, the educational research scholars and leaders in problem-based learning development at Maastricht University (then called University of Limburg) in the Netherlands, shared their research findings and developed some key training workshops involving members of our faculty (for more on the Maastricht experience, see Gijselaers, 1995). While focusing on more macro problems and working with larger groups, the action learning process employed by our faculty teams was a derivative of reiterative problem-based learning, developed by Howard Barrows (1985), and follows closely the concepts of cognitive constructivism (Savery & Duffy, 1995) and cognitive apprenticeship (Collins, Brown, & Newman, 1990). This is exactly the direction that most corporate universities are moving based upon a better understanding of how adults and professionals learn. (For a more complete description of our use of the action learning process, see Milter & Stinson, 1995; Stinson, 1990; Stinson & Milter, 1996.)

This project-based action learning approach challenges faculty members to serve as facilitators of learning rather than providers of information. This model is based on the extensive research in problem-based learning that arises from a constructivist philosophical view of how learning occurs within or is constructed by the learner as opposed to being provided by external sources. In the constructivist view of learning, the learner is challenged to make discoveries on his or her own, rather than being fed the information (O'Loughlin, 1992), while the professor acts as a facilitator or mentor, not a "sage on a stage." In a project-based action learning approach, the role of the faculty member shifts from simply preparing lectures and delivering information to designing the learning environment and interacting closely with learners to facilitate learning and evaluate progress. The instructor also maximizes the sharing of knowledge among learners, as opposed to controlling the content and delivery of material (Leidner & Jarvenpaa, 1995).

The learning outcomes became the key targets upon which projects were designed. Consistent with the principles of constructivist approaches, projects were developed which were authentic, current, and engaging.

Projects for an MBA program should incorporate authentic issues faced by business organizations and be grounded in today's business needs, rather than a historical accounting or case from the past. The projects must also offer a level of interest and excitement that will engage the learners and be linked to the key learning outcomes. Some learning outcomes can also be targeted via a series of learning exercises that may be separate from the specific project team deliverables.

Although teamwork accounts for no more than half the grade for an individual involved in one of our PBL experiences, the team deliverables (assignments, reports, presentations) clearly add an important component to the learning process and evaluation. It is important that faculty members understand and are able to fully relate to the teamwork dimension of project work. Teamwork is a fundamental element of business today. Faculty members who must collaborate to design and deliver integrated learning experiences know firsthand the value of teamwork. Such working knowledge of teamwork pays great dividends as faculty members design, implement, and assess the value of learning via team projects. One of the benefits of faculty collaboration is the cross-learning opportunity. As they work to build projects that incorporate many business dimensions, faculty members gain a much fuller appreciation for various functional or discipline perspectives.

PHASE 4: DEVELOPING BLENDED LEARNING: COMBINING ONLINE AND FACE TO FACE METHODS (1992–1996)

During the early 1990s, faculty members at the College of Business were challenged to provide graduate education to managers and professionals in part-time MBA programs offered at various locations in the southwest quadrant of the State of Ohio. Classes convened each Thursday evening and one weekend each month throughout the two-year program. Since many participants lived several hours from the classroom site, a mechanism was needed for the learners to collaborate on the projects. Lotus Notes was chosen to fulfill this need. Using the discussion databases within Notes, participants and faculty members were able to collaborate asynchronously between the face to face sessions. Discussion between teammates, completion of learning exercises, and feedback from faculty members was enabled using the Notes software. Part-time MBA programs were offered in the Ohio cities of Portsmouth, Lancaster, Ironton, and Marietta. As faculty members grew in their abilities to provide better learning facilitation and encourage more collaboration among the learners, genuine learning communities were developed. During the graduation dinner of the last iteration of the part-time programs before the launch of the MBA Without Boundaries program, the participants requested that they be permitted access to the database structure so that they could continue to share and collaborate with each other. Not only was the request granted, but databases are now open to all graduates of the MBA Without Boundaries programs for as long as it is possible.

PHASE 5: LAUNCHING AND IMPROVING THE MBA WITHOUT BOUNDARIES PROGRAM (1997–2001)

In March 1997, the MBA Without Boundaries program was launched as a distance offering using a project-based action learning format. This followed over a year of development work by the core design faculty team and an external review board comprised of key individuals from corporations and learning centers. The MBA Without Boundaries program places the learners into exactly the type of projects and work situations that they will face as leaders of the knowledge-age organizations of the 21st century. Participants learn basic business concepts in the context of their use, maximizing their ability to both recall and apply those concepts as they move back into the work world. Participants also develop the skills (communication, collaboration, teamwork) and the personal characteristics (initiative, creativity, personal responsibility) that have become so necessary for success. Participants develop a high level of comfort with information technology as they regularly access information through the Internet, collaborate electronically over time and space, and develop and make professional-level computer-driven presentations.

The Structure of the MBA Without Boundaries Program

The MBA Without Boundaries program uses a combination of electronic collaboration and intensive residency experiences to expand the potential for personal growth and individual learning. The degree program begins with a week-long experience on campus, where an orientation to the learning architecture is provided. Participants also work through the first of seven team projects (which lasts four days), are introduced to the second project (which lasts three months), receive feedback on a series of behavioral assessments, and engage in training workshops targeting key leadership skills.

The program begins with an intensive one-week residency (Sunday, 1 p.m. through Sunday, noon). After three months of online interaction and collaboration, program participants meet again for an intensive weekend (Thursday, 1 p.m. through Sunday, noon). Each project begins and ends in a residency. Participants progress through the program as a cohort group and work on nine projects over the course of two years. Participants come together every three months during the two-year program: three extended weekends and one full week each year.

The program targets nine major projects that tend to be large macro problems that address business holistically. Within each project are multiple smaller problems that participants must address to manage the total learning problem. Participants construct their knowledge of business practices by working their way through the problems. Their learning is aided by the ability to access appropriate content on a just-in-time basis, and learn content at a time when it will be most useful to them in their management of the learning problems. Some of the problems and exercises are designed to challenge individuals separately, while others challenge collaborative learning teams.

Learning Outcomes, Skills, and Projects

A core team of six faculty members is selected for each class in the program. The faculty team, in regular consultation with the external review board, designs seven of the nine projects. The other two are individual projects of personal interest which are designed by the participants (these projects often benefit their company). Each project is developed to meet specific learning outcomes, and two or three of the team-based projects will typically involve working with a real client company. Prior to launching these projects, much preparation work is performed by faculty and client management to assure the project specifications meet the targeted learning outcomes.

In order to provide a foundation for the total program design, meta outcomes are developed by faculty members in discussion with executives and futurists. Content-to-action outcomes are more specific learning goals that participants need to learn in order to fulfill project expectations. Each project has a set of content-to-action learning outcomes that are specifically linked to actions required during the projects. These outcomes are shared with participants and jointly agreed upon during reiteration of the problem statement on the first day. For the two individual projects, participants develop a set of personal learning outcomes they wish to target. The meta outcomes, a sampling of content-to-action outcomes, and a listing of leadership skills development targets for the MBA Without Boundaries program follow.

Meta Outcomes—Approached Through Total Program Design

- Holistic understanding of business and the environment in which business functions

- Solid grounding in business fundamentals

- Knowledge of current business practices and the ability to apply that knowledge

- The ability of self-directed lifelong learning

- A proactive orientation with the ability and appropriate self-confidence to take initiative, function independently, and act expediently

- The ability to address business contingencies with speed, agility, and flexibility

- The ability to work effectively in an ambiguous environment

- The ability and self-confidence to clarify roles through interaction with others, internal and external to the organization

- The ability to identify problems, develop creative alternative solutions, and apply appropriate analysis to make optimal decisions

- The ability to manage time, resources, priorities, and stress

- The ability to accurately assess one's self

- The ability to function as a change agent and transforming leader

- Communication skills, with particular emphasis on the ability to achieve results through speaking and writing clearly, logically, and concisely to diverse audiences

- The ability to collaborate effectively—to influence others and be influenced in return, to listen and understand, to work out differences so they do not become destructive conflicts, and to use diverse perspectives, cultures, and expertise to maximize effectiveness

Sample Listing of Content-to-Action Outcomes—Approached Through Multiple Projects

- Analyze an industry and develop a reasonable foresight for the industry

- Create, interpret, and use financial statements

- Develop global sourcing strategies and programs

- Incorporate ethical and social issues in the process of making business decisions

- Develop a program to create and bring a new product or service to market

- Select from among alternatives the most appropriate operational improvement techniques or programs and design the implementation strategy

- Develop alternative business models, partnerships, and strategic alliances

Leadership Skills Development Targets—Approached Through Behavioral Workshops

- Personal selling with customer orientation

- Creativity and ideation

- Goal planning and team building

- Negotiation

- Conflict management

- Judgment, decision-making, and problem solving

- Ethical leadership

- Managing in culturally diverse environments

- Assessing performance in real time

- Career development and personal learning

Learning Project Descriptions

Specific project constructions change depending on the learning needs, organizational backgrounds, and current issues facing the world economy. It is important to note that projects are designed to fulfill stated learning outcomes. All projects, except the initial one, which takes place during the week-long residency, span three months and are launched in one residency and completed in the next. Descriptions of learning projects developed for use with the MBA Without Boundaries program are as follows.

Project 1: The business concept. The primary purpose of this project is to introduce participants to the learning methodology that is used in the MBA Without Boundaries program. They also become acquainted with each other and learn to use the information technology to do research and collaborate. It is a macro-level project that looks at the business as a business and helps participants develop an understanding of the business concept and business models, and develop a framework that can be used to incorporate more micro-level learning in future projects. There is an attempt to ensure that the project utilizes a situation that is current in the news.

Project 2: Developing and introducing a new product or service offering. This project helps participants develop a more complete understanding of a business model from all perspectives of the value chain, from customer to suppliers. Further, participants are introduced to the concept of innovation and of making a business case. Participants are asked to actually develop a new product/service/offering concept, develop a plan to introduce and market it, and perform the demand and financial analysis necessary to make the case and sell their concept to management.

Project 3: Financing the firm. This project is designed to develop in-depth understanding and performance ability in financial analysis. It includes developing understanding of financial institutions, capital formation, financing activities, and financial analysis techniques. Participants consider financial analysis from both a micro and a macro level.

Project 4: Improving operations. This is an individual project that requires participants to focus on an operational improvement in their own company. This project helps participants develop an in-depth understanding of operations and operations improvement, including such things as process analysis, reengineering, and quality improvement techniques. While it is an individual project, participants are paired with a colleague mentor and faculty mentor to collaborate on ideas and review work.

Project 5: Developing a new business. This project moves the participants back to a more macro perspective. While they build on their understanding of market, operational, and financial issues, the more important thrust is to develop an in-depth understanding of business models and the holistic nature of business. Participant teams are expected to develop a business plan and presentation package to present to venture capitalists.

Project 6: Going global. In this project, participants develop an understanding of international trade and global business. They learn how to perform a country analysis, how to understand and incorporate consideration of cultural differences, how to deal with international monetary issues, etc. This project also involves an international residency, normally starting in the second weeklong residency.

Project 7: Business in the broader environment. In this unit, participants focus on the interrelationships among business and its environmental context. The social environment, the political environment, the technological environment, and the economic environment are all potential targets. While any particular project may emphasize the interaction of business and a single environmental element, the total environmental system is the major target for learning in this project.

Project 8: Managing in a turbulent environment. This project targets knowledge and skills required to help a company and its management capitalize during a period of discontinuous change and permanent whitewater. Participants perform futures analysis and develop a migration path to help a company create its future. They also assist the target company to develop an implementation plan to introduce continuous change appropriate to the organization and its culture.

Project 9: Focus on self. This individual project targets areas of emphasis important to the individual participants. Each participant is encouraged to engage in a project that is in some way related to current or anticipated work responsibilities. Participants also complete activity on their Individual Learning Plan and their professional portfolio during this project.

THE ROLE OF TECHNOLOGY-MEDIATED LEARNING

Technology has played an important role of support for the collaborative work performed in this program. In early development of the full-time MBA program and the part-time regional MBA programs, Lotus Notes was employed as a collaborative tool. It was selected because of its collaborative power as well as its prominence as an instrument for information processing and sharing in business.

The actual power of electronic collaboration was more fully appreciated within the part-time regional MBA programs. These programs were also transformed to incorporate project-based action learning formats. Although they gathered together in class on a weekly basis, many students lived great distances from one another, making out-of-class meetings difficult. Working on project teams requires collaboration between the face to face sessions. Such collaboration was simply not possible before the advent of electronic support like Lotus Notes.

During the final design phase of the MBA Without Boundaries program, Lotus released the software then called Lotus Notes Domino (later called simply Domino) that provided web-based collaborative performance similar to that of the original Lotus Notes. Because students only needed access to the web to make use of it, this software seemed ideal for meeting the collaborative needs of our learning communities. It allows individuals to work together even though they may be separated by time or space.

During the three-month span between the residencies, online collaboration takes place between participants, faculty, and external experts. Lotus Domino is used to provide a platform for teams to work together and for faculty members to interact with the teams, individuals, and other faculty members. It also enables instructors to provide learning materials in the form of word documents, spreadsheets, graphic presentations, and audio/video presentations.

The intranet home page also contains links to a help document, chat rooms (using Microsoft NetMeeting), earlier project databases, and the college and university home pages. A Question of the Week database is used for some projects. In this database, each week a faculty member poses a relevant question for participants to respond to during a two-week period. The questions must meet the same criteria as project design in that they are authentic, current, and engaging. An example of a previous question follows:

> Are the good times over? It seems that the last year may have brought a significant economic downturn. Let's discuss it from both an economic and a practical point of view. Are we in for a soft landing or a hard landing? What factors created the softening? What role, if any, did the Fed play? How does the Fed impact economic prosperity? What is the difference between monetary and fiscal policy? Who controls what? Do old economy measures, theories, and actions work in the new economy? These questions should get us started.

Responses are evaluated on the basis of their ability to move the discussion forward by adding new insights, additional research findings, and appropriate synthesis reflection. Participant evaluation for each project is typically split 50/50 between team deliverables and individual performance. Individual performance is composed of the learning exercises, concept discussions or questions of the week, reports, and post-project assessments. Team deliverables include preliminary and final reports and presentations.

BUILDING LEARNING COMMUNITIES
VIA ONLINE COLLABORATION

Participants use the various databases to submit information, ask questions of faculty members and outside experts, discuss issues with colleagues and faculty members, socialize, and collaborate on their project teams. After a couple of days, most individuals become adjusted to using the asynchronous mode of interaction provided by the Domino database for these activities. There are, of course, times when synchronous discussion is preferred. When the team members need to reach consensus about a future direction or value of a specific timely piece of information, they meet together at the same time. The database contains links to a chat room (Microsoft NetMeeting) that allows a team to hold a synchronous session. The chat software records these sessions, and the chat log is placed in the team's database for tracking and archival purposes.

The Domino database allows participants to move quickly through various discussion, teamwork, data sources, chat, and other areas of collaboration. It allows participants to sort by topic, date, person, or category. It also allows for searching by key words. Because it is on the web, URLs that are entered into the database immediately become hotlinks to the source sites. This makes it convenient for sharing detailed information on an as-needed basis. This ability is pervasive in the learning approach used by the MBA Without Boundaries program. The use of this web technology enhances the ability to deliver learning modules, information, tutoring, coaching, instruction, and collaborative space when the learner needs them. Given the differences in learning and living needs among a group of learners, it would be difficult to offer such a program without the support of a software tool like Lotus Domino.

To facilitate project work, teams of participants are given their own databases to conduct team business. This gives participants a record of their progress on the project and allows faculty members to track the progress of each team. This enables faculty members to monitor and interact with the participant team, offering advice if needed or requested.

Participant teams use these databases to post and discuss information related to the project and to post draft reports and presentations for discussion. Using discussion databases also allows less aggressive team members to participate more easily than in face to face team meetings where a few members might dominate the discussion.

One of the leadership skills workshops in the initial residency focuses on developing effective team skills and conducting effective meetings. Participants are challenged to recognize the appropriate use of synchronous and asynchronous channels for meeting with others. Sharing information in most cases calls for asynchronous channels. This permits others to digest information before gathering together to make decisions. The use of synchronous meetings to exchange ideas or share information is highly discouraged. Asynchronous collaborative channels like Lotus Domino allow idea and information exchange across time and distance boundaries. When teams at a distance need to make a decision after individuals have accessed information, they can use a synchronous support such as Microsoft NetMeeting.

Collaboration using asynchronous channels levels the playing field for all types of thinking styles. For persons needing to more slowly digest information or others needing to perform repeated analyses, the use of Lotus Domino databases provides an opportunity for individuals to move at their own pace. The software enables programs based upon self-paced learning to do just that—allow learning at the pace of the learner.

FACILITATING LEARNING AND PROVIDING FEEDBACK ONLINE

One element of facilitating learning is the ability to offer critical information as needed by individual learners. During the three-month distance period of each project, faculty members provide learning content material via "streaming video" by placing five- to ten-minute clips onto the Domino database. Participants use RealPlayer to play the video and audio, and PowerPoint slideshows to view these segments. Participants can question any content material online in the project discussion database. They can view the video connect as often as they wish merely by clicking on the icon for the clip. This is an example of the just-in-time content delivery system used in the MBA Without Boundaries program. This is in contrast to the just-in-case-you-need-it-someday content delivery system apparent in most traditional educational models.

Another element of facilitating learning is providing feedback about the process or the content being dealt with by the learners. Faculty members react to entries made by participants in the databases and deliver feedback on a continuous basis. Each project has a faculty member serving as the project leader who tracks individual entries required on the learning exercises, learning modules, and concept discussion databases. Each team is assigned a faculty monitor who tracks the team's deliverables and learning issues during the project. With few exceptions (team preference), the team databases provide open access to all members of the learning community, both participants and faculty members. This enables learners to prosper from all comments, analysis, and feedback that occur in the databases.

CONCLUSION: LESSONS LEARNED FROM THE DEVELOPMENT PROCESS

Many lessons have been learned as our faculty members and learning participants moved through the various phases of developing what has evolved into the MBA Without Boundaries program. In working with the visionary leader of innovative learning at Ohio University, Professor John Stinson, I agreed at the outset of development that if we ever thought we had gotten it right, it would be time to get out of the business. We appreciate the value of continuous improvement. We have also learned to value the contributions of external advisors from the world of business. Our executive review team members provide valuable insights and suggestions as we develop and upgrade our learning outcomes and improve the administration of the program. We have learned that recognition as a best-practice partner in technology-mediated learning by a national study does little to convince faculty skeptics of the value of the program. There will always be closed-minded individuals in the ranks of the academy who feel threatened by educational innovations. It is important to remain focused on the goals and learning outcomes of our development process and not become sidetracked by detractors.

Such learning works in concert with the development of genuine learning communities. Graduation for MBA Without Boundaries participants brings with it the recognition of having earned the degree. Perhaps more important to each participant is the fact that they have become a member of a true learning community. It is a learning community that has been nurtured by both face to face interaction and technology-mediated collaboration. The driver that will remain constant for these learning communities is the technology-mediated support. Each graduate will always have a place to interact with other graduates, new participants, faculty members, and executives. It is a community developed by breaking through traditional boundaries. It is a community of learners that will continue to thrive without boundaries.

REFERENCES

Barrows, H. S. (1985). *How to design a problem-based curriculum for pre-clinical years.* New York, NY: Springer.

Collins, A., Brown, J. S., & Newman, S. E. (1990). Cognitive apprenticeship: Teaching the craft of reading, writing, and mathematics. In L. B. Resnick (Ed.), *Knowing, learning, and instruction: Essays in honor of Robert Glaser* (pp. 453–494). Hillsdale, NJ: Lawrence Erlbaum Associates.

Gijselaers, W. (1995). Perspectives on problem-based learning. In W. H. Gijselaers, D. T. Tempelaar, P. K. Keizer, J. M. Blommaert, E. M. Bernard, & H. Kasper (Eds.), *Educational innovation in economics and business administration: The case of problem-based learning* (pp. 39–52). Norwell, MA: Kluwer Academic Publishers.

Leidner, D. E., & Jarvenpaa, S. L. (1995, September). The use of information technology to enhance management school education: A theoretical view. *Management Information Quarterly, 19* (3), 265–291.

Machiavelli, N. (1981). *The prince* (D. Donno, Trans.). New York, NY: Bantam.

Mentkowski, M. (1988). Paths to integrity: Educating for personal growth and professional performance. In S. Srivastva & Associates (Eds.), *Executive integrity: The search for high human values in organizational life* (pp. 89–121). San Francisco, CA: Jossey-Bass.

Milter, R. G., & Stinson, J. E. (1995). Educating leaders for the new competitive environment. In W. H. Gijselaers, D. T. Tempelaar, P. K. Keizer, J. M. Blommaert, E. M. Bernard, & H. Kasper (Eds.), *Educational innovation in economics and business administration: The case of problem-based learning* (pp. 30–38). Norwell, MA: Kluwer Academic Publishers.

O'Loughlin, M. (1992). Rethinking science education: Beyond Piagetian constructivism toward a sociocultural model of teaching and learning. *Journal of Research in Science Teaching, 29* (8), 791–820.

Peters, T. J., & Waterman, R. H. (1982). *In search of excellence: Lessons from America's best-run companies.* New York, NY: Harper & Row.

Porter, L. W., & McKibbin, L. E. (1988). *Management education and development: Drift or thrust into the 21st century?* New York, NY: McGraw-Hill.

Savery, J. R., & Duffy, T. M. (1995). Problem-based learning: An instructional model and its constructivist framework. *Educational Technology, 35,* 31–38.

Stinson, J. E. (1990). *Integrated contextual learning: Situated learning in the business profession.* (ERIC Document Reproduction Service NO. ED 319 330)

Stinson, J. E., & Milter, R. G. (1996). Problem-based learning in business education: Curriculum design and implementation issues. In W. Gijselaers & L. Wilkerson (Eds.), *New Directions in Teaching and Learning in Higher Education, No. 68.* San Francisco, CA: Jossey-Bass.

COLLABORATIVE INSTRUCTIONAL DESIGN FOR AN INTERNET-BASED GRADUATE DEGREE PROGRAM

Mary Anne Nixon and Beth Rodgers Leftwich

No idea is so antiquated that it was not once modern. No idea is so modern that it will not someday be antiquated.
—Ellen Glasgow (qtd. in Quinn, 1999)

The 1990s saw much change in higher education, and, we suspect, these changes will continue in order to meet societal needs and demands. In 1996, the American Council on Education published *Guiding Principles for Distance Learning in a Learning Society*. In this report the task force stated, "Concepts of lifelong learning, individualized or personalized learning, and time-free, space-free 'just-in-time' learning arrangements are emerging, all of which allow learning away from the traditional campus worksite classroom" (p. 5). How does an institution provide effective and efficient learning opportunities off campus? Although distance learning is an obvious answer to us now, establishing an effective program in a traditional university setting is not as intuitive as one may think. Clearly, however, the need for collaboration and communication among faculty, staff, and administration on the university campus is essential in the process of creating and maintaining successful distance learning environments.

23

During the late 1990s, Western Carolina University (WCU) ventured into distance learning by selecting one traditional, campus-based degree program to redesign for asynchronous online delivery. The program, Master's of Project Management (MPM), was chosen for a variety of reasons. The university had recently hired a new dean of continuing education and summer school whose charge was to identify and move forward with distance learning opportunities for the university. At the same time, the enrollment in the traditional on-campus Master's of Project Management program was declining. The degree itself was in high demand; however, the majority of people seeking it were employed full-time with family obligations and unable/unwilling to relocate to western North Carolina. With the university ready to invest in online distance learning and the MPM program in high demand and in need of distance learning delivery, the planning for the first WCU asynchronous instructional delivery degree program began.

We were highly motivated to be the first online with a Master of Project Management degree, having been the first degree program in the United States certified by the internationally recognized Project Management Institute (PMI) in an International Association of Management Education (AACSB) accredited college of business. In addition, the MPM distance learning program would be the first at WCU and a landmark project not only for the College of Business, but also for the university. Other universities were transforming courses and programs into distance learning environments; however, few were totally asynchronous.

This chapter will demonstrate how collaboration and communication were essential in the success of this transformation from on-campus to online. The two major efforts necessary for redesigning courses and programs are 1) collaborative institutional team development and 2) collaborative redesign of the program curriculum (with faculty in other disciplines, with faculty teaching in the program, with accrediting agencies, and with administration).

COLLABORATIVE INSTITUTIONAL TEAM DEVELOPMENT

Western Carolina University's College of Business had the first Project Management Institute (PMI) accredited Master's of Project Management (MPM) degree program in the United States offered in a fully accredited institution. From the mid-1980s until the late 1990s, this degree was offered only in a traditional classroom setting. Our challenge was to transition this degree program to a successful Internet-based one and to assure the online program would fulfill the reasoning for the transition.

A cross-disciplinary, interdependent team of administrators, faculty, and support staff who volunteered to collaborate in the program's design and implementation accomplished the transition successfully. Each person brought skills and experiences to the challenging and highly motivating problem solving environment that being "the first" provided. The new program gained recognition as an area of strength to the university during the reaffirmation of the College of Business's accreditation by the Accreditation Council of the AACSB, the premier accrediting organization for business programs. As noted in *The Western Carolinian* (2001), "... the [peer review visiting] team's report noted several areas of strength... [including] extensive teamwork in the innovative redesign of an online master's degree program in project management..." (p. 3).

In retrospect, the methods we used to design, implement, launch, and support WCU's online degree program were examples of a well-designed and well-planned project. We used the very team-building principles we teach our students, the most basic of which in project management terminology is called "partnering" with the project stakeholders—those who have either a positive or a negative "stake" in the outcome of the project (Kellogg Corporation News, 1992). In educational settings, these stakeholders are the immediate faculty, staff, administrators, students, and accrediting agencies.

EFFECTIVE COLLABORATION FOR PROGRAM DEVELOPMENT: A 12-STEP PROCESS

In researching the professional project management literature, we discovered approximately 12 generic elements for effective project collaboration (Joki, 1998; Moore, Maes, & Shearer, 1995; Moore, Mosley, & Slagle, 1992; Schmidt, 1994). We found ourselves in the position of practicing what we teach in transitioning to an Internet-based degree program—establishing strategic partnering or collaborative teams based on the following success principles.

Step 1: Thorough Research and Planning

Faculty teaching in the program conducted a survey to determine the educational/training needs of our prospective students, project/program managers working in business and industry. The results indicated that while many industries continue to invest in helping employees successfully complete the nationally recognized certification examination, they would prefer employees complete a graduate degree program and certification. An online MPM degree program that would help students prepare for certification, receive a graduate degree, and continue to meet job responsibilities met this need.

The concept had been explored, the need documented, the administrative go ahead given, and the date of delivery established. A process needed to be instituted and a team formed. The faculty realized they could not do it alone. According to Luck (2001), "To get a course ready for online delivery, a much larger team is needed, including people responsible for marketing, academic advising, registration, materials distribution, and program management" (p. 2). This was more than a course; it was an entire degree program. So, a team was critical.

Step 2: An Administrative Champion

From the very beginning, this project had three executive-level champions: the chancellor of the university, who has earned for our campus the designation of being one of the "most wired" universities in the state, and two deans—one in charge of the financial and administrative (logistical) issues, and the other responsible for curriculum and accreditation issues. While this support was critical to the success of the program, it was not a chief motivating factor for the team.

These three and other administrators cut through red tape and provided funding for development and initial training. External grants were written, and internal (university) funds were earmarked for computer hardware and software, faculty and staff travel to attend distance learning workshops and training sessions, and curriculum design stipends for faculty who were willing to spend a summer redesigning their traditional classroom courses for online delivery. Faculty and staff were given the opportunity to be on the cutting edge of something new and exciting, to interact and work with colleagues in the university community toward a common goal, to travel, to learn, to professionally grow, and to create an innovative degree program.

Step 3: An Effective Kickoff Meeting

Moore, Mosley, and Slagle (1992) state, "Partnering is generally established through a structured, facilitated process, normally consisting of organized workshops to bring the participants together. This process is designed to provide an environment for developing the cooperative attitude and commitment needed to drive the partnership" (p. 18). The traditional on-campus degree program faculty retreated to an off-campus location (a sister institution's retreat facility over three hours from WCU's campus) to dissect the old curriculum and rebuild the new one over a four-day period. This intensive, goal-oriented retreat also served as a well-known team-building device—putting everyone together in the same place (Schmidt, 1994).

By being away from the general distracters on our own campus, the retreat provided the MPM team with uninterrupted time to reflect and create. Participants of this retreat included a faculty representative from each of the discipline areas within the MPM curriculum—project management, management, finance, law, economics, and accounting. In addition, the associate dean of the College of Business, the MPM program director, the MPM lead faculty member, the distance learning librarian, and the curriculum designer actively participated. The MPM program director, the lead faculty member, and the instructional designer organized the retreat. There were many others who worked at arranging rooms, food, snacks, equipment, meeting facilities, and transportation. The success of the retreat can be attributed to multiple sources: a well-prepared faculty, an excellent retreat environment, a belief in our goals, administrative support, and a focused agenda with a group-designated leader responsible for keeping the team on task (Nixon & Leftwich, 1998).

Step 4: Common Prioritized Goals/Objectives Established

We created a strategic partnership in which the team owned the project and was given the opportunity to assist in decision-making. Also, as a result of participating in decision-making from the beginning, stakeholders began the well-known process of buying into the project. According to Schmidt (1998), one of the basic tenets of team building is that "Everyone should know, and be committed to a single set of project goals and objectives" (p. 29). From the start, we as a team had the opportunity to assist in making important decisions regarding the types of program support, computer equipment, and software needed, as well as deciding on in-house server support as opposed to outsourced support.

Step 5: Preplanned, Effective, and Consistent Communication

The multidiscipline faculty and staff retreat team, numbering 15, made the conscious decision to resolve conflict using problem solving methods and to communicate openly, often, and effectively. This preplanned communication parallels the project management principle of creating a plan to manage communication much like costs or schedules are managed. This is not an obvious part of the collaborative efforts of a team, but very necessary. Luck (2001) states that,

> While many factors contribute to the success (or failure) of a project, a team development process requires excellent communication among team members to ensure that things run smoothly. How that communication takes place will vary from team to team, based on the preferences of the group. The key is not *how* communication takes place, but rather that it *does* take place. (p. 4)

We found it important to try to personalize the otherwise fairly stark email communication among team members. This meant adding a personal note at the beginning of an email to set the tone of the communication. For effective communication, it is important to be very clear in the wording of the message—concise and brief, but not to the extent of being cold and demanding. Any informal small talk introducing an email message would set a friendly tone rather than beginning with a brusque down-to-business communication. In an attempt to be concise and businesslike (and without first giving a friendly salutation), a faculty member sent an email enumerating a prioritized list of things that needed to be accomplished. The recipient's supervisor took exception and responded, via email, to the faculty member, criticizing her tone as being that of "a lady of the manor talking to the yard boy" which was not conducive to a cooperative team spirit. The two met face to face to clarify the misunderstanding and noted the very valuable lesson learned from the experience.

Step 6: Prior Identification of Roles and Responsibilities

By virtue of their positions and responsibilities within the university, team members naturally fell into specific categories. Faculty members were able to concentrate on course content and the design of learning activities and assessment, while the other members of the development team provided input in their areas of expertise. The entire team, as listed below, was too large for weekly interaction, so a steering committee representing each major area volunteered to meet weekly. Minutes of these meetings were circulated via email. Team members from each area included:

- College of Business: associate dean and director of the Master's of Project Management degree program

- Continuing Education and Summer School: dean, administrative assistant, and computer technician/webmaster

- Faculty Center for Excellence in Teaching and Learning: media specialist

- Library: distance education librarian

Step 7: Commitment, Discipline, Constant Monitoring, and Follow-up

As Luck (2001) suggests, it is important to describe each individual's roles and responsibilities and to establish timelines for each task in the process. Were it not for a high level of commitment from various divisions of the university, the many separate pieces of this big puzzle would have never been assembled.

Weekly meetings were established for progress updates and to provide an avenue for discussion on upcoming tasks to be accomplished. Commitments to team members to produce results—a lesson plan, research and reports on types of technology available, identification of ways to access more materials electronically—were critical to the success of the project.

Throughout the planning process, other routine university activities began to take priority. Several faculty and staff team members resisted committing to a timeline and responsibility matrix for submitting their deliverables (products and services). As deadlines approached, the spirit of cooperation transformed into one of mistrust in which individuals began documenting futile attempts to complete tasks. Instead of developing the degree curriculum as a whole unit, as we had originally planned, the program deliverables (the courses/modules) were created just in time to test and revise prior to online posting. Substantial revisions and enhancements continue to take place as modules are modified for ensuing cohorts of students (continuous improvement). The quality of the individual lessons within each course has been maintained as a result of the overall planning process described above.

Step 8: Trust Among All Participants

Trust is not always easily maintained; however, where there is continuing commitment and support for the project, consistent communication (emails, telephone conversations, nonadversarial meetings/brainstorming sessions), and team member follow-through, trust can be established and nurtured. As in any team, participation in the planning of the work to be accomplished followed by consistent, high-quality performance on a weekly basis resulted in team bonding. When emergencies or personal situations arose, other team members stepped in and shared responsibility.

Trust does not always run completely throughout a team. To varying degrees, personality conflicts and mistrust exists in almost every large team effort. The key for us was to proceed with the work, knowing that we had deadlines to meet and that the work had to be done—regardless of who did it. As the momentum of being first began to wane, the first day of class deadline began to loom largely on the horizon; we had students waiting. Something had to be done. The magic solution or formula for how this occurred for our project is simple: We had empowered enough project champions to carry the project to completion. Champions can be individuals or a small group committed to the project whose skills and dedication manage to lead the larger team through the difficult times.

Step 9: Shared Risks and Rewards

The main risk in this project can be compared to making extensive plans for a big party only to have no one attend. This, thankfully, has not been the case. Careful attention was given to marketing and advertising the new program in traditional as well as online arenas. The program has grown quickly, and a new faculty member has been hired to meet the need. Another perceived risk was the transparency of each lesson plan that could reveal the professor's competence (or possible lack thereof). There was also the fear that the university or others could use this permanent documentation of the professor's expertise without the need for the professor. Institutional policies are presently evolving. Both faculty and administrators have input into this question of who owns what and what kind of price tag should be attached to intellectual property rights in materials developed for online courses.

The reward system contained both intrinsic and extrinsic rewards. The obvious intrinsic rewards were working with colleagues and being on the cutting edge of technology. Another surprising intrinsic reward was the flexibility telecommuting allows—teaching from anywhere, at any time. This can also be a distinct disadvantage—nowhere to run and nowhere to hide. Internet connections are widely available, and professors are constantly on call. Extrinsic rewards included the opportunity to travel and participate in workshops, receiving a creative and innovative teaching award from colleagues, additional merit pay, and promotion considerations for the extra preparation online teaching requires. All of these work well for faculty; however, institutional regulations concerning staff rewards prohibited merit pay. Position upgrade procedures at this university are too time-consuming and often frustrating for both the staff member and their supervisors to use as rewards for participation in this development process.

On the other hand, much like many other teams launching an online program or course have discovered, there is an obvious increased workload which jeopardizes faculty and staff rewards if the institution maintains a traditional institutional reward system that undervalues online teaching and stresses alternate priorities. As Luck (2001) points out,

> the collaborative/shared authority work environment in which course development takes place was identified by some respondents as an incentive and by others as a problem . . . the process of developing a course with a team of individuals in a collaborative/shared authority work environment may be a new experience for these faculty members. (p. 5)

This emphasizes the need for conscious planning, support, and rewards for the collaborative efforts of everyone on the online team who is willing to undertake the multiple challenges such activity presents on a daily basis. Staff members, for example, had a more difficult time realizing extrinsic benefits. Many staff were going above and beyond their formal work plans and spending countless hours (sometimes without recognition). There are probably few administrators or faculty who understand the under-representation and lack of rewards for staff efforts.

Step 10: Effective Leadership Skills

With all the research done on leadership styles and debates on what makes an effective leader, we dare not tread too far down that path in this chapter. In our case, some position leaders (administrators) were effective while others were not. We observed that leadership really had very little to do with formal positions individuals held in the university. Based on the time sensitivity of an approaching deadline, the task to be completed, and personalities of those involved, leaders would emerge and the work was accomplished. At times, official position leaders had very little or no control over (and sometimes no knowledge of) the things that were being completed by the faculty and staff developing the program. Some players drifted in and out based on the perceived success of the project. When things looked good, they were in—when things were in a slump or other activities took precedence—some individuals were out. In retrospect, it was a successful combination of both formal and informal leadership that brought the project together. The biggest success factor was that four or five individuals—faculty, staff, and administrators—championed the project and persevered.

Step 11: In-depth Interviews with Positive and Negative Stakeholders for Input and Feedback

A major key to this success has been the open and consistent communication and requests for feedback followed by sincere attempts to address the issues raised. We still have the feeling that we are all in this together, learning something new each day. The most obvious stakeholders in this collaborative learning process have been the students.

In the design process, the faculty and curriculum specialist consciously took the role of the student. "If I were a student reading these instructions, how would I respond; is the work too complex or too easy?" But of course, the real feedback process had to be established with our ultimate clients/stakeholders—the real students—after the first course was in progress (see Comeaux & Nixon, 2000). The importance of continuous improvement of each lesson as it progresses is critical for the success of that lesson and for the program as a whole.

Faculty and students actively communicate (sometimes multiple times a day) for input and clarification of assignments and submissions. Each week, individuals and teams receive specific comments on their posted assignments. The natural evolution of this process came to include the faculty soliciting and receiving student input on course content, on course applicability to their real-world projects, or just "how's it going?" on course participation. Formal, open-ended evaluations are requested from each student at the end of each semester for each professor who has taught during that semester. These online evaluations are submitted anonymously.

Step 12: Effective Close-out and Team Celebration

The first cohort of ten individuals graduated in August 2000. With the exception of one student (whose boss would not give her release time to attend her own graduation!) all students came to campus for a special reception (paid for by the online center's funds) and the formal graduation ceremony sponsored by the university. The campus support team and faculty met the students and their families face to face after working with them for two calendar years! The excitement of this grand finale and the continuing contact with our alumni provides additional motivation as we work toward the next graduation celebration for the next class of students.

This is a great way to celebrate success—with your students. One word of advice, do not (intentionally or unintentionally) forget to include anyone, no matter how small or large the contribution, on team events and celebrations. All contributors need to be recognized to maintain team spirit.

COLLABORATIVE COURSE CONTENT DESIGN

Course-by-Course Redesign

The redesign of the total curriculum took time, money, and group/team work. Individual course redesign was much more labor-intensive and difficult. The faculty members teaching in the program agreed that a lead professor, Mary Anne Nixon, should work with the curriculum specialist/ instructional designer, Beth Rodgers Leftwich, to develop a model process for distance learning course development.

We met to plan the process and decided to begin by designing one lesson based on current on-campus teaching methods. A template was first developed that required the following faculty input: learning objectives, on-campus classroom activities used to meet these objectives, and evaluation methods. Then two new columns, distance learning activities (to support the same learning objectives) and methods of evaluation to be used for these activities, were added to the template. This method worked well because it required the faculty member to closely examine current practice (on-campus/traditional classroom) before going into an unknown practice (distance learning).

Once the objectives were established and the faculty member was able to match on-campus activities/assignments used to accomplish objectives, taking the mental leap to distance learning meant learning new communication tools. For example, an on-campus activity might be to have students divide into small groups, discuss a particular topic, and report results back to the class. In the virtual classroom, the activity might have the student teams go online to discussion groups (chat rooms or bulletin boards), discuss (either asynchronously or synchronously), and post reports to a class-wide bulletin board.

Since distance learning was new to Nixon, her knowledge base of available computer tools was somewhat limited to email and web sites. We worked through the mental transformation of on-campus to off-campus activities and the process of translating an on-campus place to a distance learning place. Then we diagrammed the appearance of the online classroom. Nixon described the purposes of each of these resources as follows: The library is a place where the professor can ask students to visit in order to gather research, check out books, and reserve materials, among other things; the professor's office is a place where students come for help; and the classroom is a place where the professor and their students share knowledge and information and work on activities to further understanding.

For both of us, place was a common theme throughout these processes. Even though this new place was virtual, everyone wanted to see what it looked like. This place needed to be concrete. Nixon drew rectangles, squares, and circles representing the various places. When this process was complete, a formal diagram emerged. Figure 2.1 is a computer sketch of some of the ideas for the new distance learning environment.

The important part of this design was our discovery process. The mental transformation from on-campus to distance learning had begun. The concrete representation of the diagram helped guide further development.

The technology team agreed on a "canned" software package called WebCT. This software provided the tools and places that Nixon had envisioned (with additional resources she did not know existed). This package was only one of several available in 1996 when this decision was made. These course development software packages have now grown to include

FIGURE 2.1

Distance Learning Environment

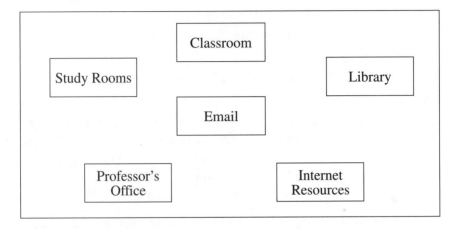

some highly evolved functions. For example, Campus Pipeline software connects WebCT course development software to student records systems, testing systems, grade books, and audio/video integration. Software such as this is defined as portal software and provides users with one entry to a multitude of services.

The project's original virtual classroom design grew by leaps and bounds to include such places as a technical assistance area, bookstore, and registrar's office. The virtual university evolved in response to the needs of the students and faculty involved. The need for places/assistance with textbook purchases, online registration, grades, and advising are as real (if not more so) for distance learning students as they are for on-campus students.

Collaboration between the technology team, the curriculum designer/instructional technologist, the administration, and the faculty members had been instrumental in getting the project to this point; however, the collaboration between the two of us was paramount. We set the momentum and were able to translate the lessons learned—what worked and what did not—as the first lessons were posted and then completed by the students. For example, the use of the formalized template encountered some resistance due to the work involved, but the resulting lesson format and organization increased the quality and consistency of individual lessons and the entire curriculum. This process also greatly reduced the number of student questions via email and telephone when lessons were vague or incomplete. As we continue to revise and expand the first lessons, new techniques, new technology, and new subject matter have made this consistency even more important. The harsh realities were that some faculty just did not buy in to the entire course development process and have subsequently returned to the traditional classroom.

REFLECTIONS AND LESSONS LEARNED

The processes our team used to accomplish this "first" on our campus were neither perfect nor complete; however, as with all good processes, we built in room for error and mechanisms for improvement. After having several years to reflect on the collaborative efforts used in designing the MPM Internet-based graduate degree program, we firmly believe the following to be the most important lessons we learned:

- Synergy works: The development team provided support when needed with brainstorming, contributions, and follow-through activities.

- Collaboration produces a superior product. Without the collaborative design of a collaborative learning environment, the program could not have risen above a standard correspondence course.

- Collaboration between faculty in the design of the total program curriculum added cross-disciplinary depth and perspective.

- Collaboration between faculty and a curriculum design expert verified and enhanced the educational soundness of online classroom activities.

- The design of an androgogically sound course template with learning objectives should parallel student activities.

- Evaluation methods and the design of collaborative student learning activities enhanced student-to-student interaction and sharing of lessons learned.

- The application of real-world and cross-industry applications to lessons increased the educational soundness of online classroom activities.

In sum, collaboration between faculty and technology experts eliminated a trial and error process on the part of a nontechnology-oriented faculty by initially screening available classroom software, investigating the feasibility of using specific technology in the class possibilities, and fielding ongoing student and faculty technical problems and questions as the courses continue. Collaboration in the development and delivery of interactive technology continues to improve as technology improves, as experience reveals newer and better ways to improve the initial product.

Most important, writing this chapter and two previous articles about designing the MPM Internet-based graduate degree program has placed us in the unique position to discuss all aspects of the project and reflect on issues and resolutions. These discussions have led us to believe that the greatest lesson we learned was that we need to collaborate as a team and take time to reflect both individually and with others in the team. For without these two components, projects such as this one are destined to be single agendas without benefit of shared minds and spirits.

CONCLUSION

As much as the faculty, staff, and administration of the university had worked well in the collaborative effort of designing, supporting, launching, and now maintaining the degree program, the day-to-day activities that take place inside the virtual classroom are also designed for a student collaborative learning experience. These adult learners come from all industries—communications, information technology, banking, construction, pharmaceutical research, aviation, energy, and others. In their day-to-day business activities, they conduct projects for their corporations. Their projects have many similarities: They all work in project teams, they all track costs, have schedules, and require careful planning. However, these different industries have, over time, developed independent yet similar approaches to surviving and thriving in the real world of projects.

Probably our most important goal in designing the collaborative learning activities within this degree program was to facilitate a sharing of these common experiences and lessons learned in an educationally sound way. Karl N. Schul, a member of the MPM class of 2000 and Regional Project Executive for Integrated Technology Services IBM Global Services in the Americas, sums this up nicely: "The Master's Program in Project Management has been a wonderful experience for me. The students, or cohorts, as we are called, interact, communicate, and work together without face-contact, as project teams. What a great way of learning!" (http://cess.wcu.edu/cobmpm/alumni/comments.html).

REFERENCES

American Council on Education. (1996). *Guiding principles for distance learning in a learning society* [Online]. Available: http://www.acenet.edu/calec/publications.cfm

(2001, January 17). College of business receives full reaccredidation. *The Western Carolinian,* p. 3.

Comeaux, P., & Nixon, M. A. (2000). Collaborative learning in an Internet graduate course: A case study analysis. *WebNet Journal: Internet Technologies, Applications & Issues, 2* (4), 34–43.

Joki, E. (1998). Partnering for success—Maximizing project management value through a strategic partner. *Proceedings of the 29th Annual Project Management Institute 1998 Seminars & Symposium, 1,* 114.

Kellogg Corporation News. (1992). *The show on Broadway: A model for the partnering continuum process,* parts I & II. Littleton, CO: Author. (Note: Kellogg Corporation is now Petersen Consulting, LLP.)

Luck, A. (2001, January/February). Developing courses for online delivery: One Strategy. *The Technology Source* [Online]. Available: http://horizon.unc.edu/TS/beta.asp

Moore, C., Mosley, D., & Slagle, M. (1992). Partnering: Guidelines for win-win project management. *Project Management Journal, 23* (1), 18–21.

Moore, C. C., Maes, J. D., & Shearer, R. A. (1995). Recognizing and responding to vulnerabilities of partnering. *Project Management Network, 9* (9), 20–23.

Nixon, M. A., & Leftwich, B. R. (1998). Leading the transition from the traditional classroom to a distance learning environment. *Technical Horizons in Education, 26* (1), 54–57.

Quinn, T. (Ed.). (1999). *Quotable women of the twentieth century.* New York, NY: William Morrow.

Schmidt, J. (1994). Partnering with your client. *Project Management Network, 8* (9), 27–30.

Degrees and Programs by Distance Education: Defining Need and Finding Support Through Collaboration

Frank Fuller, Ronald McBride, and Robert Gillan

> *Back then . . . we were all so excited—full of energy: it was as if a new continent was being explored, and we were the explorers, and we now had a chance to change things—to come back from that continent . . . with what we had learned and offer it to the world, to people who hadn't been there. What could be the result? Well, we certainly didn't know exactly, but we certainly hoped there would be some changes.*
>
> —Anna Freud (qtd. in Coles, 1991)

Teaching in distance education can feel like an adventure; the instructors like explorers. On almost every campus it is possible to identify the first person to teach with compressed video; the first one to move a course to the Internet; the first to recruit a student to take a full load with nothing but an Internet connection. Teaching in distance education can bring the explorers together into bands of instructional adventurers: people from disparate disciplines who share an interest in how to teach—

physics or education or music or literature—with the new technologies, and to learn what the technology changes about pedagogy, assessment, or the students in those classes.

Success can change everything, even for those who have benefited from it. With distance education success comes distance education institutionalization, and the explorer can become part of the new distance learning establishment. The old innovation becomes the new norm.

This chapter traces the College of Education, with a large collection of distance courses, through the process of designing and implementing a degree program for the Internet. Northwestern State University of Louisiana (NSU), the state's historic normal school, enrolls about 9,000 students and has traditionally used technology of many kinds to help meet a state mandate to serve the isolated, rural, and undereducated population of northern Louisiana. Technology solutions have been employed for specific instruction, often because one teacher was interested or one special project funded the technology. Moving from course to degree meant moving from individual interest to institutional commitment. The process required collaboration between faculty and university. Often, it became a model for other departments and colleges to follow as they developed distance education courses and programs.

From the point of view of experienced distance education teachers, collaboration brings on both a recognition and change in their practice. As pioneers, the earliest Internet teachers discovered new students, new technologies, and new ways of fostering student learning. The persistent lesson of the collaborative degree planning is that teaching individual classes, no matter how well, is not sufficient. The university really has to offer a degree, rather than individual courses. Hence, it is in offering degrees that the real power of distance education, to capture institutional imagination and change institutional practice, can be realized.

Distance education degrees attract the interest of many universities in Louisiana; therefore, it was natural that NSU should become the center of an effort among three institutions to develop a consortium graduate degree in educational technology to be delivered at a distance. Nicholls State University, with about 6,000 students, serving rural southwestern Louisiana, and the University of Louisiana at Lafayette, serving about 12,000 students in more urban Lafayette, formed the three-university partnership.

Though the focus is on the supporting elements of a degree—resources, registration, student services, and approval measures—this chapter retains the perspective of the individual instructor. The literature is replete with descriptions of how institutions can plan for distance education programs; nonetheless, our observation has been that the individual instructors—those early pioneers—remain central to moving, leading, and sometimes cajoling the institution into supporting students and degrees that are not on campus. The result? Planning and developing courses and degrees to be delivered at a distance must be a collaborative effort to increase the likelihood of success.

Therefore, the purpose of this chapter is to detail the planning and implementation of a shared online Master's of Education degree to meet the requirements for certification in the areas of educational technology facilitation and educational technology leadership. The chapter focuses on phase one of the planned project: collaboration and development stages. As this chapter illustrates, technology is the medium of collaboration, the means of instruction, and the reason for participation. Nonetheless, the project's focus and the success of the program development is not technology alone, but remains on the ways that professional educators at every level honor institutional needs, identify paths to collaboration, and transcend geographic and cultural boundaries.

DISTANCE EDUCATION PROGRAM DESIGN: THE VALUE OF COLLABORATION

Without question, the modern university grows and prospers by sharing resources within the institution. Market forces and the changing needs of the information-age work force necessitate a commitment to collaboration (Stout & Mills, 1998). The stream of newly defined needs requires that educators identify the expectations of their graduates, design solutions to meet those expectations, and prepare to abandon those solutions as new expectations—and new solutions—appear. A growing public anticipation of sharing resources among institutions, such as faculty, student support services, technology, and access to the library, makes distance education and collaborative degrees favored solutions (Gatliff & Wendel, 1998; Stout & Mills, 1998). Many of the elements in distance degrees are novel, of course. Nonetheless, in some ways, the planning process for a distance education degree is no different from any other plan. It begins with realizing a need, defining stakeholders, soliciting opinion, and designing a plan. In this case, the need and many of the stakeholders were apparent.

Institutional Stakeholders

Offering a degree at a distance requires identifying the scope of university services that distance students need and finding ways to make them available. Need for the degree is defined, internal agencies that support the process are identified, individuals within the affected offices are enlisted in the project, and support of—or at least acquiescence to—the project is secured. "Changes, particularly changes involving technology, require us to break with our old way of thinking and consider possibilities for new ways of working" (Geer, 1996, p. 3). Of course, asking for such a commitment to change from professionals whose practice is developed and rewarding within the old arena is not easy. The stakeholders were asked to think outside the box because student services have traditionally been offered to those who take classes on campus. The process of identifying and enlisting institutional stakeholders includes considering virtually every major division of the university. These stakeholders and their roles are identified as part of the planning process for the program design.

Student recruiting and enrollment, because of the distance education planning process, reached students they never saw. Distant access to registration, financial aid, and the business office means that every service could—must—be approached without standing in line. One result of the student services offered to students at a distance is that students close by found the new forms of service more convenient. Many students who never left campus prefer web sites to waiting in line; email to busy signals. Hence, many distance education solutions become resources for everyone.

The admissions office defines a process for applying to the university. Since, by definition, applicants for admission are new to the university, this process needs to be supportive, intuitive, and quick. In some ways, having an electronic form for application causes more problems than it solves, at least initially. Data need to be moved smoothly through the central university system—a collection of eight universities—to the individual campus, from the campus admissions office to the college and, ultimately, to the professor in charge of a program area. Program planners have felt from the first that quick, initial contact with distance education students by the persons whom they would be working with academically is important. Gillis (1999) demonstrated the importance of early, personal communication—face to face or telephone—in keeping students in asynchronous classes. Personal contact with program beginners is even more important.

Fiscal affairs at NSU manages student source revenues, among many other things. The processes of collecting money from students and monitoring a timely system of payment has always been, primarily, an activity accomplished face to face. The fiscal affairs officers have mediated between students who wanted a means to pay from a distance, and policies and auditors that require timeliness and certainty in accounting for revenue collection. Moreover, as with e-commerce, accounting policies established by the state have been adjusted to accommodate the distance learner. As a result of pressure from the Board of Regents, collection of fees and auditing procedures have been modified to support distance education rather than provide obstacles to it.

Student financial aid offices needed to make the scholarship, loan, and tuition support options available to these students. The function is complex, for it involves making information available, advising and guiding students through selection and application processes, and ensuring compliance with program requirements. Serving students does not obviate financial aid obligations of keeping auditable records and following often cryptic reporting conventions. They must ensure a record of commitment on the part of students who are, after all, applying for loans or attesting to their worthiness for scholarship gifts. Face to face explanation of obligations, privacy of individual records, and the need to secure certain I.D. and collect signatures, all militate against the financial aid office's making an easy transition to distance education.

Contract services faced broadened competition as well. Ancillary services like the bookstore met new competitors in the form of services that had not won contracts—and did not pay—for space on campus. Traditional support services become either changed or unnecessary, and new services, like a contract grade distribution service, have affected the way student service and registrar offices deal with contractors.

The computing center plays a pivotal role in the planning process for distance education programs. Distance education demands convenient, consistent interface for campus services, uniform instructional management, and robust support of resource pages. In so many ways, the university computing center constitutes the entire university presence in the minds and experience of distance students; after all, they do not visit faculty members, see the buildings, or walk on the commons. Since the reality of the university is constructed by means of its computer-generated presence to these students, the role of university computing can hardly be overstated. From maintaining the university web page to distance education platforms, this affects student perception of the support system. In the end, this may be the only contact students have with the university.

Information services in the university are not limited to computers, of course. Library services needed to be reconsidered as well. The libraries involved have provided electronic catalogs, index subscriptions, and some periodicals. Yet a substantial collection of other academic services still has to be available in a way that preserves copyright protection and provides access from remote sites. In Louisiana, online services are available to students through LOUIS (Louisiana Library Network) which connects libraries electronically. Students can browse holdings at 38 public and private universities, community and technical colleges, including, of course, holdings of the three universities in the project.

The chief academic officer plays an incalculably important role. The process of moving from distance courses to distant degrees involves anticipating accreditation issues and asking permission from many layers of agencies. For Northwestern, the permission labyrinth includes the university supervisors, the state coordinating board, the Southern Regional Educational Board, and the Southern Association of Colleges and Schools (SACS). Though other states and regions have different boards, the ordeal is similar.

The faculty remain at the center of any set of stakeholders, for they design and teach the classes, advise students, and direct their progress through the program. Since participants approach all classes via the Internet, planners felt strongly that faculty members should have a particular kind of assistance: an instructional designer who would manage technical tasks related to material presentation, bring course content into a format suitable for Internet presentation, and ensure a consistent interface for students moving among several classes. In addition, workshops and training sessions are available to faculty for Internet platforms and other delivery systems such as VC (video compression) and DVC (desktop video compression). Faculty receive certification documents that validate their participation in training sessions and license them to teach courses at a distance.

While faculty have the option to choose to teach at a distance, it does not mean they will. Faculty participation is enhanced by including the scope of distance education as part of the mission of the institution, establishing policy regarding teaching at a distance that applies toward promotion and tenure, establishing models for faculty training and compensation, and developing a research agenda for each discipline using distance learning technologies (Olcott & Wright, 1995).

A SYSTEM FOR PROGRAM DEVELOPMENT: EVOLUTION OF A DEGREE PROGRAM

Of course, identifying and enlisting stakeholders is not sufficient in itself. Beginning a new degree, particularly one that must appear substantially the same among three institutions, requires an extraordinary amount of preparation. A team of instructional designers and technical support personnel must be available to help faculty prepare course materials and interact with the technology. Knowing the subject and the instructional design principles does not necessarily mean that the faculty member knows the delivery platform. Models for delivery, unit and lesson plans, tests, handouts, instructional packages, and electronic presentations or technical services are all affected by the delivery medium—in this case, the Blackboard course management program (Gatliff & Wendel, 1998).

Many distance educators believe the practice of distance education necessitates policy change to accommodate collaboration within the institution (Thach & Murphy, 1994). Moore (1993) suggests, "a distance education system should be thought of as a network of knowledge sources, processors, managers, communication media and learners" (p. 4). A cooperative design for the degree program helps the university attain its goals while maintaining instructional integrity (Foster, 1997). By examining the process systematically, educators can design an infrastructure that accommodates the needs of the distance learner (Thach & Murphy, 1994).

Planning to attract students from a distance quickly becomes a high stakes activity. When a single course is offered that way, the student is too often inconvenienced because the course does not attract enough enrollees, or the interface breaks, or the means of learning do not match an individual's learning style. So long as distance education is an alternative, the primary means of instructional delivery are present as a kind of safety net. An entire program, however, attracts different participants.

They commit to a program that will be provided to them by an institution that is not, necessarily, near to hand. Hence, the first step in offering the program requires every phase along the way be planned and ensured.

None of the institutions were completely unsophisticated in using the Internet to deliver individual courses. Initially, traditional courses were moved online over a period of semesters. The first documents to be distributed this way included syllabus, course calendar, assignments, lecture notes, sample work, templates, resource links, and papers. The next additions were generally discussion forums, posting areas for student projects and text-related activities, graphics, audio, and some experimentation with video. Each phase of the process provided feedback to the instructor for improvement in the next semester. This slow but functional approach allowed the early innovators to enter the distance education market with budget or formal institutional commitment.

The first evidence of institutionalization commitment was the adoption of a campus-wide instructional platform. This involved the university computing center, continuing education, and the participating colleges. This move created the nucleus of an electronic learning organization, for the need to support the platform required both decision-making and resource allocation at a central level. At this point, instructors were no longer on their own to create web sites to support instruction, but became part of a university-wide initiative.

The additional features and standardization provided by the early distance platforms like Web Board, Top Class, Blackboard, and WebCT fostered widened acceptance by student populations and resulted in a rapid demand for courses. Students became accustomed to the look and feel of an Internet course at the institution and were eager to take more.

More courses and a broadening student population moved Northwestern to decisions about degree programs. Should whole degrees be offered online? Should students be served entirely at a distance? What would be the nature of that service? How much of the student service program was the university obligated to provide to students who never set foot on campus?

These were challenges. They were also problems, as new interest and new technology demanded more and more of teachers who believe themselves already overworked by their commitment to innovation. At this juncture, the State of Louisiana adopted new certification requirements for building-level and district technology specialists. This new seven-course requirement prompted the College of Education faculty to reexamine a master's degree option and our entire process for online course and program development. This could be seen as crisis-driven development, and it resulted in competing institutions (Northwestern State University, Nicholls State University, and University of Louisiana) talking with each other and asking, with a single voice, for help from the state-level university coordinating board for higher education. This resulted in a request to the Louisiana Regents for a distance education initiative grant to define and provide additional support and development funds for a collaboration to develop the seven required courses, a common degree format to contain them, and a structure of student services to support the program.

Grant-funded programs provided resources to plan services and design courses. Nonetheless, the most important result of participating in the funded project may have been that agreeing to receive the funds meant that the institutions agreed to design a structure for implementation and a set of shared objectives for a distance degree. The resources were, in most ways, less important than the cooperation and commitment that they incited. The funds—only $100,000—provided travel between campuses, an instructional designer, three graduate assistants, and some release time and incentive pay for collaborating faculty members. Though not essential to the development model, the granted funding became an incentive to breaking down barriers between the institutions.

Beginning as a conversation among faculty members of the three institutions, the initial objective was a series of key leader meetings to lay out a general agreement on the organization and content of the courses to be developed. These conversations led to the identification on each campus of a faculty member with educational technology or distance learning experience who demonstrated an interest either leading or co-developing one of the seven courses. This resulted in the establishment of seven three-person teams. Subsequent meetings resulted in the adoption of an instructional design model for planning courses and a development template. Development environments for the seven courses were created on Blackboard using the developmental template. Each Blackboard course had documents posted, providing samples of similar courses currently offered by all the universities. Papers related to the course topics and the ISTE (International Society for Technology in Education) standards that guided the program. A local survey of educational technology coordinators, identifying topics and skills they considered essential to building-level and district coordinators, supplemented planning material. The course planning structure was designed to allow the three universities to create courses that fit within the culture of the individual campus and still serve goals common to all the participants. With a common design strategy, ISTE objectives, a client needs assessment, and a structure of regular conversation among designers from all three institutions, the courses offer a familiar environment to distance students, yet retain the flavor of the individual offering institution.

Following the opening of the forum, the instructional designer met with individuals or small groups to review the design process and the use of Blackboard tools in teaching the courses. Desktop conferencing, compressed video, email, and telephone meetings supplemented Blackboard and provided synchronous conversation for the team leaders and members.

The instructional designer, supported by graduate assistants on each campus, provided additional assistance to faculty members where needed. The designer kept the teams together, providing help where necessary to keep the development process on schedule. This assistance, coupled with the initiative taken by several of the designers, tended to set standards, support the development process, and maintain timelines. In all, the development process took less than six months.

A New Structure for
Student Support at Northwestern

As program development progressed, each of the stakeholders played an important part in implementation. In every case, helping design the infrastructure for the degree required the university office to change procedure, allocate resources, or rethink customs. During the planning phases of course development, parallel administrative initiatives occurred as all three campuses reviewed student support issues and shared the status of current methods of addressing distant student needs on each campus. While the outgrowth of this was not a common model, all three institutions made significant advances in addressing online student needs. We will discuss the result of this process as it applied to Northwestern. In the case of the other two institutions, the results were similar, though the details were necessarily a little different.

The first evidence of this service was a uniform web presence that provided students with links for admissions, service, forms, grades, and fee payment (www.nsula.edu/ensu). Additionally, a state initiative that allowed uniform, online application to all public college graduate programs (www2.nsula.edu) sped the implementation of admissions services.

Each administrative unit was challenged to define electronic links for all student services, providing the online student a resource set equal to that of the traditional student. The challenges to the university were, in large part, demands from students that had been made to early distance education instructors:

- How do I pay fees from New York?

- Where do I get admissions, graduate assistant, or graduation forms?

- What is being offered next semester?

- How do I check grades, buy a textbook, check out a library book, apply for financial aid?

Student services identifies and serves many student needs that are only tangentially related to matriculation. A significant element of this process—and one that is not completely resolved—lies in answering questions concerning the actual needs of distance education students. They clearly are not entirely the same as the needs of students who live on campus, but do not constitute a subset of those traditional student needs, either. Some needs are unique to distance students, just as there are some that are unique to students on campus.

The web site, eNSU, continues to evolve as a service system for electronic learning. It acts as a key to coordinate computer center services with every element of the campus. In some ways, the comprehensive web service is defining the way the campus reviews and renews all services. Several university offices have been required by this process to make substantial changes in their programming practices and resource allocation.

The registrar and business affairs offices have designed and implemented online application, registration, degree audit, and grade reporting. The seemingly obvious strategy of offering application fee by credit card has solved many initial problems for new students unaccustomed to dealing with the university through web pages.

The computing center, having to deal with connectivity and software compatibility, has become much more directly involved with students, student computing accounts, and problems related to computers away from campus. Connection and use tutorials and readiness quizzes have been useful for helping students—and helping the computing center—anticipate some problems and automate some solutions. Web-based contact to services creates a vehicle that is convenient to all students and satisfies most.

The ways university libraries have addressed both distance resources and distance students is a field of study in itself. Two kinds of decisions from the university library had particular impact on distance education. The first was a shift in purchase policy from paper to electronic journal subscriptions, making resources available to many students. The second, a significant investment in indexes and databases for research, had to include ways for off-campus students to gain access to resources that are often sequestered within the library itself. Students need a way to secure password-protected access to library resources, regardless of their location.

Another library initiative was the online course pack. Staff members scanned and assembled published documents, selected by instructors, to make them available in portable document format (PDF) files that conformed to copyright fair use policy. In many ways, the actual work of assembling the packs was less important than the librarian's skilled assurance that copyright protection had not been violated.

Several campus support services, including services for students with disabilities, counseling, and other kinds of traditional service have not been defined; call it online emotional support. The persistent task of needing to know about the new population that distance education brings to the university is focused in this area. Each of the universities collaborating in this project recognizes an insufficient picture of the distance education student as a client for student services, and perceives, as well, that distance education students do not realize or expect that the university where they have matriculated has such services available.

In some ways, the provost—the chief academic officer of the university—has had the most central role. Faculty members work differently in distance education classes; they work very differently in distance education programs. The faculty rewards and support structure, from conference travel to evaluation of instruction, is affected by distance teaching, and the induction process for teachers into the company of distance educators often falls on the shoulders of those experienced in this kind of teaching. Successful faculty members must spend time mentoring those who are just beginning to relearn their teaching practice. Redefining the way faculty members are recruited, evaluated, supported, and rewarded for these efforts lies at the heart of the success of the program.

EVALUATING PROGRAM SUCCESS: ADDRESSING ACCREDITATION

Beginning with a state mandate and an interinstitutional model, the distance education degree program overtly examines a number of assumptions that other kinds of planning can easily overlook. At the same time, the new plan of study—technology coordinator—and the remote population has prevented participants from being seen as—or from seeing themselves as—part of the regular student body that has simply elected a plan of study that is available over the Internet. Making comparisons between the effectiveness of distance programs and traditional ones is extremely difficult. Evaluation, nonetheless, presupposes some basis of comparison between traditional and distant program completers. For example, the Southern Association of Schools and Colleges (2000) requires that distant programs meet broad standards that are normed to traditional programs:

- The institution assesses student capability to succeed in distance education programs and applies this information to admission and recruitment policies and decisions.

- The institution evaluates the educational effectiveness of its distance education programs (including assessments of student learning outcomes, student retention, and student satisfaction) to ensure comparability to campus-based programs.

- The institution ensures the integrity of student work and the credibility of the degrees and credits it awards.

Distance education generates an enormous pressure to view courses and programs from a normative perspective. Responsive evaluation requires one to be aware of different media, a new student body, changed perspectives about teaching and learning, and the altered institutional base for program support. Formative evaluation—the reflection of each instructor and that person's instructional support environment within the college or department—comes more or less easily as instructors and departments try to define good teaching, adequate support, and appropriate compensation in this setting. Evaluation of instruction comprises three elements: a student evaluation of instruction, common to all courses, though administered on line as part of the access procedure to the Blackboard course management software; an administrative "visit" to classes, again through the Blackboard program; and a brief, journal-based, reflective portfolio, kept by each instructor.

Summative and audit evaluation—systematic data to document resource expenditure and inform decision-making—has been less successful. The *sui generis* degree, involving a participant cohort and a unique interinstitutional collaboration, has not provided a persuasive basis for planning other programs at the universities.

REFLECTIONS AND LESSONS LEARNED

Centralized impetus for certification and a centrally created market that each of three universities perceived a need to share created a need. The need-driven program attracted the attention of many offices on the campus that had never, previously, seen distance students as part of their responsibility. Indeed, the program attracted the attention of officers who had never seen distant students at all and who were not particularly eager to see them now.

The project described here was instigated by people that have been teaching through distance means for many years. The participants—the stakeholders—were not uniformly experienced. Indeed, they were not even uniformly interested in offering a degree by distance means. Beginning with a state mandate and an interinstitutional model, the distance education degree program caused all the stakeholders to examine a number of assumptions that other kinds of planning can easily overlook. At the same time, the new plan of study—technology coordinator—and the remote population kept participants from being seen as—or from seeing themselves as—part of the regular student body that had simply elected a plan of study that is available over the Internet.

As distance education continues to propagate and colleges and universities join the ranks of distance education providers, the need to collaborate, to build and maintain programs, will become more important. Program offerings continue to grow; budgets do not. Institutional collaboration is the best method to bring the players together, extend resources to those who need them, and build support infrastructure more attuned with higher education in the electronic age. But while collaboration is good, it may not always be necessary. However, the particular set of circumstances described here helped define a process that can be useful for institutional planners, regardless of the program mandate. Northwestern State University was focused on the process of planning the degree because of the commitments that arose from obligations to the granting agency and to the other, cooperating, institutions.

If teaching in distance education feels like an adventure, then the instructors share the special bond of having invented new ways to teach with the new technologies. The distance education innovators share the sense of life on an instructional frontier. They invent strategies and methods, learn from each other, explore alone and together, and return with tales of remarkable success or glorious failure. Moving an entire institution to a posture of service to distance students requires additional efforts and long-range commitment. If teaching a class can be likened to going west in a Conestoga, then offering a program resembles building the railroad. For every professional interested in the welfare and future of higher education, examining the entire relationship between every element of the university and every constituent, near and far, is an expansion of immense proportions and implication. In this project, technology is the medium of collaboration, the means of instruction, and the reason for participation. Nonetheless, the project's focus is not technology alone, but remains on the ways that professional educators at every level honor institutional needs, identify paths to collaboration, and transcend geographic and cultural boundaries.

REFERENCES

Coles, R. (1991). *Anna Freud: The dream of psychoanalysis.* Reading MA: Addison-Wesley.

Foster, L. (1997). *A degree of distinction: A collaborative model for degree delivery via distance education.* Paper presented at the 49th Annual Conference of the American Association of Colleges of Teacher Education, Phoenix, AZ.

Gatliff, B., & Wendel, G. (1998). Inter-institutional collaboration and team teaching. *The American Journal of Distance Education, 12* (1), 26–37.

Geer, C. (1996). *Interactive distance learning: An impetus for collaboration.* Cincinnati, OH: Clermont County Educational Service Center. (ERIC Document Reproduction Service No. ED 401 874)

Gillis, L. B. (1999). *A model for training asynchronous distance education instructors: The virtual College of Texas.* Unpublished master's thesis, Northwestern State University.

Moore, M. (1993). Is teaching like flying? A total systems view of distance education. *The American Journal of Distance Education, 7* (1), 1–10.

Olcott, D., & Wright, S. (1995). An institutional support framework for increasing faculty participation in post-secondary distance education. *The American Journal of Distance Education, 9* (3), 5–17.

Southern Association for Colleges and Schools, The Commission on Colleges. (2000). *Distance education: Definition and principles* [Online]. Available: www.sacs.org

Stout, N., & Mills, L. (1998). *Ft. Hood and the Texas A & M University System: Collaboration and distance learning.* Paper presented at the Annual Distance Education Conference, Austin, TX.

Thach, L., & Murphy, L. (1994). Collaboration in distance education: From local to international perspectives. *The American Journal of Distance Education, 8* (3), 5–21.

Beyond Demographics, Content, and Technology: The Impact of Culture on the Design and Implementation of a Distance Education Program

Richard Olsen and Robert Schihl

"Distance? You want us to offer our accredited doctoral degree program by distance?"

It was the fall semester of 1994 when the dean of the Regent University (Virginia) School of Divinity began probing the possibility of offering a joint distance learning degree with the College of Communication and the Arts. Divinity and communication (rhetoric) have historically had a synergistic relationship and many of the courses taught in our college, such as organizational communication, interpersonal communication, and textual analysis, would complement their offerings in theology and preaching. The dean argued that there were many potential applicants who cannot leave settled families and career positions to pursue their degrees, yet they need these degrees to carry out their work and advance in their careers. Images of mail order degrees and a host of other questions made the project seem risky at best. Would our emerging reputation suffer and our degree be treated as less credible if it were gained by distance learning? Would such perceptions taint all Regent degrees? However, the opportunity to reach the students he described—a student profile we, too, were familiar with—made it imperative to at least explore the possibility.

Many colleges and universities have similar tales of the initial discussions about distance education. It is now considered rather normative, and arguments would likely be made only by those trying not to adopt some form of distance education. The decision-making process regarding distance education is certainly a complex one. Motives for the initiative need to be identified, technology platforms need to be determined, instructors need to be identified, and training needs to be developed. The list goes on. Ideally, such decisions would be made with an almost singular focus on what Smith and Tillman (1999) define as instructional design: "the systematic and reflective process of translating principles of learning and instruction into plans for instruction materials, activities, information resources and evaluation" (p. 2). Yet we know that there are many other factors that subtly and significantly affect decision-making. Some administrators and some grant criteria, for instance, might encourage an institution to value technology rather than people. Consequently, one is encouraged to go high tech and scramble for a reasonable rationale for doing so.

This chapter steps back a bit from the technological and pedagogical decisions to examine how the larger organizational culture often influences this decision-making process in positive and negative ways. In a sense, we are responding to slightly modified versions of the questions that guided Tommerup's (2001) analysis of his institution's culture:

- What are the animating characteristics of the nontraditional academic culture(s) which we have evolved at our institution? How do these affect the formal and informal teaching and learning that transpires there? (p. 368)

- As we attempt to inquire nonjudgmentally into the ways our institution's culture(s) affects teaching and learning, how can we understand and manage the biases and blindspots that we inevitably bring to our assessment research by virtue of the fact that we have been socialized into this academic culture ourselves? (pp. 368–369)

Several features in his questioning are worth noting. First, while Tommerup focuses on traditional, on-site teaching, we are assessing the decision-making regarding the implementation of a distance education program. Second, his emphasis on a nonjudgmental posture and management of culture features is important. We are not looking to exalt or deconstruct the culture or decision-making practices at Regent. It is neither ideal nor suspect. However, analysis guided by Tommerup's questions and those we have raised above does offer useful lessons for those making similar decisions.

We argue through this analysis that it is important to be explicitly aware of the larger cultural factors that might positively and negatively influence the distance education design process. To make this argument, we offer a case study of the development of an international graduate-level distance education program in the College of Communication and the Arts at Regent University. Certainly, creating this distance education program required significant collaboration between faculty, administrators, vendors, and students. The journey has not been without its breakdowns, detours, and setbacks. Yet the collaboration and the quest for the appropriate interactive technologies have been worthwhile and ultimately beneficial for both faculty, by coordinating a tool box of communication technologies and pedagogical strategies that maintain their identity and mission as educators, and students, by being able to take courses while continuing their current careers and maintaining some stability in their family life.

REGENT UNIVERSITY

Regent University began as CBN University (Christian Broadcasting Network) in 1977. It was one of several high-profile projects of Pat Robertson, most known for his hosting of the *700 Club* television program. The all-graduate university has grown to include programs in law, government, business, leadership studies, education, divinity, and counseling, in addition to the founding program of communication and the arts. The university has become completely independent of CBN in order to seek accreditation from various bodies and maintain its credibility as an institution of higher learning. The PhD program in the College of Communication and the Arts was fully accredited by the Southern Association of Colleges and Schools (SACS) in 1991. Fall 2000 enrollment was at 2,385 across the seven programs. Of that enrollment, there are 863 distance education students. Student-to-faculty ratio is 15–20 to 1. Fifty-nine percent of students are 30 years of age or older. Diversity of the student population is manifest, with African Americans comprising 14% of the student body and Asians, 8%.

Regent's status as a Christian graduate-only institution is almost singularly unique. It is this special status that led to the consideration of distance education fairly early in the history of the institution.

DISTANCE EDUCATION AT REGENT UNIVERSITY

The School of Business was the first to make significant use of distance education at Regent University in the fall semester of 1991. The school chose to use an audiocassette-based model along with a workbook and voice telephone support. Advertisements on billboards stressed that the reader "could be studying for your MBA right now." The program targeted traveling sales staff, trainers, members of the military, and those with significant commutes, and it worked. Currently, the Internet, email, and attached documents play a significant role in that program as well.

In the College of Communication and the Arts (CCA), we ultimately chose a different platform for offering distance education, but it was not a simple process. While the business school offered one model, a local state university was offering an undergraduate program of studies making significant use of bulletin board services to some 400 students. Another larger university was gaining a global reputation delivering instruction via videotape to satellite video sites, including military bases worldwide. Each model had merits, and the proximity to CBN's satellite resources made even the rather expensive option of video classes a possibility. One of the ways to begin exploring options was with a course in the college that served a unique purpose for master's students.

The master's degree within the CCA at Regent University often attracts students with an undergraduate degree unrelated to communication. Because of the obvious disadvantage these students would have in a graduate setting, the administration and faculty decided to establish a prerequisite/premedial (addressing deficiencies ahead of time) course that introduced students to the discipline. Initially, students were not allowed to take other courses until they had completed Introduction to Communication Studies. Many students requested a way to take the course before they matriculated to campus. During the time that the PhD distance program was being discussed, it was decided that distance education also provided a solution for those wishing to take the introductory course.

The success of the business school's audiocassette-based courses led to the adoption of that format, and students were told that the class was being moved to the classroom equipped with microphones. The instructor of this introductory course had planned for it to be an interactive discussion for those taking the class on-campus and had little time to adjust his pedagogical approach to meet the constraints of audiocassette. In truth, it was unclear at that time what those constraints might be. The result of this ill-fated venture, begun in the fall of 1995, was a 17-cassette course that was dominated by group discussion. A workbook and reading packet accompanied the cassettes. It was a frustrating process for the instructor and the on-campus students to only listen and not participate in a group discussion.

A second version of the cassette-based course was constructed using a talk show model with one primary instructor along with Regent faculty as guest experts on fundamental topics necessary for orienting the students. This was much more efficient (eight cassettes) and introduced incoming students to many of the communication faculty at Regent. Student satisfaction for the second version was significantly higher, but it was decided that the course be overhauled again.

Each option was discussed and ultimately eliminated: Video production was too costly to make it the primary means of instruction even if the satellites were already available, the bulletin board service seemed too limited given the global and, therefore, very asynchronous nature of our student body, and the audiocassette also seemed an ill fit for our curriculum since it is rarely lecture based. A third version of the course, begun in 1998, brought it in line with a more interactive model. What emerged as the ideal platform for delivery was computer-based mediated education. It is in this iteration of the curriculum that we make explicit connections with the topic of this volume. The department ultimately adopted a set of interactive technologies that emerged through efforts of collaboration with students, faculty, technology experts, and the other technologies identified above. Even though we rejected many media options, the process of finding the choice that was right for us involved a significant amount of collaboration about what kinds of things were valued in teacher-student interactions, what kinds of products and outcomes the program should stress, and what kinds of tasks would be seen as valuable by faculty and students. How can the interactive technology choices we make duplicate and/or enhance the collaborative nature of graduate education? The search itself required collaboration among the communication faculty.

While synchronous chat rooms were initially appealing, we realized that we were attempting to make the new seem like the old and familiar. What eventually emerged was a system that utilized the World Wide Web and a browser to store permanent documents including application forms, catalog copy, and course materials such as syllabi. A requirement of standardized software configurations for each student allows for significant use of email and attached documents for student projects, student-teacher and student-student interaction. That computers and the web are at the core of Regent's system is reflected by the fact that one can only apply for the distance program online. There is no hard copy or postal mail-based application option. If a student lacks the hardware and computer knowledge to negotiate the application process, they surely are not ready to succeed in the educational environment utilized by the university.

Instructional Adaptation to an Interactive Technology Environment

Training in what was, then, fairly new technology, and assisting faculty with necessary changes to course material and the pedagogical approaches that were needed to teach distance students was the next challenge to meet as a group. Our students would remain in various time zones around the world and references to due dates needed to reflect that dynamic. In addition, language in syllabi that referred to "class" or "lecture" or even "presentations" needed to be changed to terms such as "course," "notes," and "shared documents." The concept of interaction had to be rigorously defined. An interaction might be seen as any event that takes place between a learner and the learner's environment (Moore, 1989). We attempted to operationalize this through such concepts as "comment email" and "questions email." There was also a policy that such emails be copied to each classmate and the instructor. One of the useful strategies that emerged while training faculty was a handout that listed pedagogical options and challenges typically encountered in a graduate class: the first day, guest speakers, student presentations, and the like. The second column addressed how such events translated into instructor and student behaviors within the traditional classroom setting. A third column then suggested ways such interactions might translate to the distance learning environment.

Early in the process, Regent staff assisted with mailing out hard copies of certain documents, course readings, and textbooks. Eventually, those tasks were outsourced to services such as Specialty Books (www.specialty-books.com) and Follett Express (www.fes.follett.com), who not only provide new and used books (and often repurchase them) but obtain copyright clearance and bind and distribute finished packets of published periodical articles and other learning resources (cassette tapes and computer software).

As the Internet has grown, more and more resources are being found that replace the need to use hard copy texts. The audiotaping of guest lectures can be easily digitized and uploaded on the course web site for students anywhere in the world. In addition, online versions of significant works by almost every philosopher in the history of the field serve as valuable resources for distance education courses. Identification of such resources has been a critical step for the program since getting hard copy resources to remote locations could end up taking a bulk of a semester. In addition, while we require that students have some proximity to a graduate level university, quality and access vary greatly.

Evaluation strategies were also a pressing issue in adapting to the technology and the development of the program for two reasons. First, there was internal concern for the rigor and integrity of the program, and second, such rigor and integrity had to be demonstrated to outside evaluators. Fortunately, at the doctoral level, the typical form of evaluation, even for on-campus students, is the independent research paper. Additional strategies have also proven useful. Some faculty require a certain number of email exchanges to the entire class and/or to the instructor. Papers—both in draft form and as final products—are shared with classmates and these students are required to respond to and critique the papers within a defined protocol. Open book exams are also used and, when necessary, a procedure for proctored exams has been developed. Software has made it possible to use the Internet for long distance phone calls. Providing specific software configuration guidelines has been critical for taking advantage of such features.

When offering feedback to student papers, faculty had to resist the impulse to print hard copy and respond via handwritten comments. Instead, several strategies have proven useful. First, one may elect to bracket [ ] comments. Microsoft Word offers an edit feature that allows faculty commentary to appear in color. Both of these features actually insert text into the body of the paper. Another Microsoft Word feature allows extensive feedback without changing the body of the paper. It is called " insert comment" and creates what amounts to a floating footnote that is identified by a highlighted word. When the cursor is placed on the highlighted area, the comment appears in a text box. A right click allows the student to delete the comment.

Keeping the Technology Current and the Program Accredited

Regent University needed to make it as easy as possible for faculty to carry out their distance education obligations. Consequently, faculty teaching distance education courses were provided with faster computers on campus and at home, as well as appropriate software upgrades. Serial line Internet protocol (SLIP) telephone lines were provided for faculty so that access to the campus resources and the Internet was as smooth and fast as possible. Computer support personnel visited faculty homes to install and configure software necessary for the tasks associated with distance education. This institutional commitment has been vital in overcoming initial resistance from faculty.

Changes continue as advances in hardware and software occur. Cold-Fusion now provides html templates that make web page creation far easier than when we began. However, the mainstay of the distance education program remained a freeware browser (Netscape or Microsoft Explorer) and freeware email (Eudora or Outlook) that have proven rather cost effective for both the institution and the students.

Accreditation has been a central concern throughout the development of the program. Upon launching the distance education program in the fall of 1995, the College of Communication and the Arts needed to apply for a "substantive change" application from its accreditation agency, the Southern Association of Colleges and Schools. This required a site visit. Because distance education was still relatively new, there was not a single member of the first accreditation team from SACS that was actually doing computer-mediated distance education. Their primary concern centered on "how do we know the student who gets the grade or the degree is the student who did the work?" Our response was threefold. First, such a question is as germane for a residency-based graduate program as it is for a distance program given the independent nature of most graduate assignments. Second, there is ongoing dialogue with classmates and instructors that would make such deception very labor-intensive and difficult on the part of the student. Third, the program does have some residency requirements that provide face to face interaction. The team was satisfied with the responses and left the site visit stating that Regent offers a model for accreditation for programs of this nature. The parting challenge offered by the visitation committee was to seek ways to increase interaction among the students in ways analogous to those opportunities that a college campus provides.

To meet this challenge, Regent has begun creation of a virtual campus built around the functions a campus provides for students: informal interaction, administrative tasks, campus media, and special events. We created everything a distance student might use if he or she were on campus, including a virtual file cabinet with electronic forms and a full directory (with photos and clickable email addresses) for all faculty and staff. Distance students can access a virtual chapel, view music videos, films (from the cinema and TV programs), and photo exhibits (from the journalism program), as well as videotaped theater presentations (from the theater program).

It became apparent that the browser/email approach to distance learning was primitive and not as interactive as it could be, so we sought out course support software that would make a greater impact on learners. To do so, a university-wide committee reviewed over 30 delivery systems and vendors and chose Blackboard, an e-learning software platform program administered by Blackboard, Inc. (www.blackboard.com). Blackboard is a total online course environment facilitating everything from a discussion board and a virtual classroom with a white board for synchronous multi-logs to a course calendar and grade book for faculty. It creates and corrects online examinations (and timed delivery of them) and also provides grading statistics to faculty.

A general listserv has also been established for alumni and current students that provides significant alumni news and the all-important job posting/networking opportunities. This is especially important given the competitive nature of the media industry and the specialized nature of employment of those with advanced degrees.

CULTURAL FACTORS
IN THE DISTANCE EDUCATION PROCESS

Stanton (1990) discussed the act of teaching by invoking an ecological/cultural metaphor. As such, we engage in teaching within sub-systems that are within larger systems. She highlights the classroom context, the institutional context, and the societal context. Of particular importance to this analysis is the institutional context that "refers to the particular type of organization or school (including the physical facilities as well as structural properties) and the social atmosphere or culture" (Stanton, 1990, p. 42). She also reminds us that the department may have its own unique culture that may be influenced by its disciplinary affiliation, among other factors. Several institutional factors have both fostered and hindered the successful development of distance education at Regent.

Christian Institution

Regent's unique status as a graduate-only Christian school affected us in real ways when conceiving of the distance education program. While there were initial feelings of hesitancy, there was almost immediate recognition of the need to launch such an effort. A historic marker of Christianity has been its global perspective. Consequently, it was consistent with our existing logic to think globally and to realize that we have potential students around the world.

A second way that our worldview affected the design of the PhD program was in the configuration of the residency requirement. The residency requirement involved an initial four-week seminar and at least one week on campus each year after that. A major aspect of that two-week annual visitation is the breaking of bread together. The sharing of a meal, while not central to the faith, is still an important dimension.

In more obvious ways, Christianity is reflected in course content, discussion prompts, and the like. A careful balance is drawn as the CCA faculty seeks to model and foster the integration of faith and learning. Two guiding questions provide this balance: How does our faith inform our understanding of X and how does our understanding of X inform our faith? This was rather easy to model in a synchronous class discussion. The challenge has been in making static course materials and asynchronous exchanges also reflect such critical engagement.

Lesson: Examine your institution's perceived relationship with the outside world. The administrator calling for distance education may be the only one who is not an isolationist on campus. Similarly, many initiators of distance education argue for it in terms of monetary gain. That may not be the cultural mandate to capitalize on. Reaching the unreached is a cultural mandate that is firmly established at Regent. Seeing a relationship between that existing cultural mandate and the call to distance education made the commitment an easy one.

Disciplinary Roots

Teaching is an act of communication. Cicero identified the three purposes of speech: to delight, to persuade, and to teach. As a consequence, those with little background in formal pedagogy do not feel they need additional training in how to teach. That was a potential hindrance to faculty development. Fortunately, the relative lack of computer mastery with regard to Internet and web potential adequately humbled all of us as we developed the initial web-based offerings.

Our disciplinary heritage also had an upside. Most of the faculty members were familiar with the idea that media affects the message and there is an ingrained logic of adapting one's communication to new constraints. We did not yet have the best strategies of adaptation in place, but the logic of adaptation and the awareness of the need to do so were deeply ingrained by our disciplinary training.

Lesson: Identify ways in which your specific discipline offers potential obstacles and opportunities in the adoption and implementation of distance education with interactive technologies. What disciplinary concepts can serve as metaphors or design touchstones? Ever since Aristotle first systematized the discipline of rhetoric, the concept of audience adaptation has been central. This made it easy for faculty to see the value and necessity of the hard work needed to create appropriate pedagogy, not simply translate the new in terms of the old.

Recency/Credibility

A big source of concern surrounding the decision to go distance was the potential to lose hard-won credibility. Many of the faculty remembered the foundational years of CBN University that began in empty and abandoned corporate facilities and classroom trailers. They now enjoyed a beautiful campus, brick buildings, and full accreditation. It was not an easy thing to risk. Current students and recent alumni were also concerned about the perceptions of their degrees, and in fact called for a distinction to be made between those earned on campus and those earned via distance. These concerns seem ill founded now, since the quality of the program has actually enhanced the reputation. For instance, the SACS accreditation review established the program as a model program, and while the on-campus program has received full accreditation, it has never received that level of recognition. By the fall of 1997, SACS invited one of this chapter's authors, Robert Schihl, and two other Regent administrators to present a panel to SACS members at their annual convention on our academic and research background to the development of our distance program. The same author found that his presence in other national distance gatherings (e.g., Syllabus Conference) promoted a takeover from scheduled presenters to demonstrate how Regent accomplished distance education, much to the delight of attendees. The Regent College of Communication and the Arts distance education web page was bookmarked by presenter and attendees alike as some of the best examples of doing distance education. All this led to major consulting for Schihl in distance education development (e.g., Texas A&M, Hampton University, etc.). After that, papers proposed to national conventions (Syllabus Conference, National Communication Association, etc.) won and continue to win ready approval for presentation.

Lesson: We live in a world of meanings, not things. Deal honestly and openly with the subjective meanings and the emotions that surround issues of technology, computer-mediated communication (CMC), and changes in pedagogy. One strategy that worked for us was to enlist our detractors to help address the very concerns they raised. The other author of this chapter, Richard Olsen, was one of those vocal teaching fellows concerned about the credibility of his degree. His concern was for the lack of engagement and the quality of life for the faculty. Rather than ignoring or debating these concerns, he was asked to help address them by assisting another faculty member in designing the sessions and planning the meals for the first four-week residency program. His apprehensions about a dehumanizing educational experience fueled his efforts to make the residency portion satisfy his concerns. In the process, he became a supporter of the program.

Egalitarian Culture

The size of the on-campus program and its graduate-only nature helps to create a strong sense of collegiality between students and faculty. The upside to this is that teaching fellows are given substantive assignments. However, in the case of the audiocassette-based course, this became a weakness rather than strength. The teaching fellow who was asked to teach the course had no real position from which to resist the request. In addition, while being delegated the task, he was not fully empowered to carry it out. He was put in the roles of content expert and curriculum designer with no real authority to say "you will guest lecture on this topic on this day" or to purchase other enhancements for the course. While considered an excellent teacher by his students and peers, he did not have a formal background in curriculum design, distance education, or even media production. But then, no one did in those fledgling days of distance education. The learning curve was steep and the rough draft became the final copy. The errors were errors of enthusiasm: For all the right reasons, the teaching fellow was asked to do too much and it resulted in a substandard product despite good faith efforts by all parties.

Lesson: There are actually two lessons here. First, count costs. There is a biblical parable about the man who started to build a tower without counting the costs. He is shown to be a fool. Fortunately, the audiocassette course was a small tower and we were not fools for very long. Initial design and implementation is resource intensive. Creating enhancements such as brief taped interviews, course media, or course activities, and identifying web-based resources is very time-consuming. Build that lead-time into your timetable. Second, if you are going to delegate, empower. Realize that those asked to design and teach courses using CMC need authority and collaboration. They need to meet with technology experts and other distance course teachers. Give them time and resources to do that and, in the true spirit of collaboration, ask how the project is coming and what needs to be done to make it happen. While web sites and courses are always changeable, the initial investment of resources is important and should not be taken lightly. Some institutions will treat such a class as a publication, as a way of justifying and rewarding the time needed. That is one strategy of empowerment.

Dealing with the Joneses

Regent had the advantage and disadvantage of having three successful but completely different models of distance education occurring within 20 miles of the campus. The success of the business school's audiocassette efforts was a contributing factor in the decision to offer the ill-fated Introduction to Communication Studies. The convincing presentations by each of the other "proud parents" both clarified and clouded our decision-making process. There are two basic reactions we can have to a successful neighbor: to compete with them or to imitate them. Neither reaction is healthy.

The fundamental flaw in either of those reactions is that we design the program in response to their program, not our situation. To compete with Old Dominion's video-based distance efforts, for instance, might have manifested with "hey, we've got CBN's satellite farm, we can do it better than they do and really serve our students and show them how it's done." Imitation takes the form of "we need to do it their way if we want their results." To a limited extent, imitation was a factor in the decision to create our own cassette-based course.

Lesson: Identify your mentors and models but ultimately emerge with your own unique institutional response to the call for distance education with interactive technologies. Realize that what may be working well for another institution may be unrelated to the superficial features of the program. For instance, it may not be the specific technology that makes it work, but the institutional commitment to training and rewarding course development. That commitment might make any platform a success. If you adopt video because it works for the institution up the road, but fail to see the real reason for their success, a disaster is on the horizon.

The Robertson Factor

Pat Robertson's idea of a medical relief plan is a wide-bodied Lockheed L1011 he dubbed the flying hospital. His efforts in most everything he has done are big. He defines himself as a Christian businessman, not a televangelist. He willingly adopts the label of entrepreneur. He did not support the policy of tenure when founding Regent University because, among other reasons, one should continue to demonstrate they are worth keeping on the payroll. The director of an opera once said, "Do it big, or stay in bed." Such a saying might have been uttered by Pat Robertson, Regent's chancellor. Media blitzes and "Operation Blessing" are just two examples of the language he uses to describe his various efforts that reveal the scale with which he expects to operate.

His business acumen has provided many millions of dollars for the university. It has also presented obstacles. The timetables of an entrepreneur do not translate well to the timetables of academics. In addition, the scale at which he attempts, and often succeeds, encourages others in the university to initiate or launch programs they do not yet have the infrastructure or critical mass to maintain. When a journal is launched and then folds, it is a minor embarrassment to the university. However, if a distance education effort is launched, secures students, and then fails, real damage to real people is done. It was very important when launching our program to critically evaluate the sustainability of the program. A video-based model might have offered a far more spectacular christening, but it quickly would have exhausted the technical and personnel resources of the College of Communication and the Arts.

Lesson: Understand your leadership. While the program should reflect the nature and values of the institution, it should not be unduly influenced by the personality of the leadership. In this case, we have the unique situation of a highly visible and controversial Christian leader/celebrity who has single-handedly created the university and provided millions of dollars for its endowment. However, his interests shift. While Regent may be high on the priority list for a time period, the programs must be sustainable when other projects, such as flying hospitals, take attention and finances away from the university. In other institutions, such leadership might be diversified through a board. However, the principle is still the same. Is this a sustainable program that reflects the strengths of the institution and not the personality of the board or individual leaders?

REFLECTIONS

Having identified some of the specific lessons learned along the way we come full circle to the more global reflection guided by the questions Tommerup offered earlier in this chapter. The second question that focuses on biases and blindspots that may emerge because we are socialized into the academic culture is particularly relevant.

Regent University is a graduate-only institution and is consequently characterized by small classes of generally motivated students. What is typical of the pedagogy in graduate settings is a rather nondirective approach to teaching, often answering the question, What did you think of the reading?, or hearing student presentations. This strategy certainly has merits, but was often the default strategy for lack of training in teaching and time constraints due to research, grading, and administrative obligations. This situation is not unique to Regent. In 1993, the American Association of Colleges and Universities along with the Council of Graduate Schools launched the Preparing Future Faculty (PFF) initiative designed to "enhance doctoral students' preparation for faculty life" (Morreale, 2001, p. 12). Institutions participating in the PFF program recognize that while doctoral programs emphasize research, many academic positions do not, and future faculty need to be prepared to work with populations, technologies, and pedagogies.

The adoption of interactive technologies provided a catalyst for collaborating and talking about teaching. The specific challenges of distance education required much more specific assignment descriptions, much more intentional discussion questions, writing prompts, and the like. In addition, lectures needed to be converted to handouts and PowerPoint slides. Assignments needed to be constructed that fostered specific application of the material. In sum, one of the important global impacts of using CMC in the distance program has been a general elevation of the pedagogy on campus.

Because of the learning curve and constant changes in technology, there has been an ongoing dialogue about pedagogy. Distance faculty have a need to collaborate among other distance faculty, and this discussion of teaching and technology and that type of dialogue was not present before the explicit integration of CMC. This informal dialogue has also been supplemented by formal workshops on PowerPoint, video and audio streaming, and net conferencing to increase expertise and collaboration.

The challenges associated with even basic mastery of CMC and keeping up with changes in such technologies seems to require collaboration among all but the most technically gifted. Not only does the technology foster collaboration when used correctly, the act of learning to use it correctly is also best conceived of as a collaborative act.

CONCLUSION

It is hoped that the case study presented in this chapter is useful on at least two levels. First, the discussion of "how we did it at our place" may offer some useful guidelines for others who are in the process of identifying which approach is appropriate for their situation. Second, an explicit analysis of some of the cultural features that influenced that decision-making process were also offered so that others might identify how such factors operate in their own institution. Has distance education been beneficial for Regent University? Yes. Has it had some unanticipated costs? Yes. Course load, student-teacher ratios, task variety, issues concerning the possibility of distance faculty, all are issues still being addressed. And when these are done, more will surface. But the victories are ongoing too. Recently, the college conveyed a doctoral degree to a student from Thailand who will use her advanced degree to address intercultural communication in her native country. That is the ultimate fruit of distance education.

REFERENCES

Moore, M. (1989). Three types of interaction. *The American Journal of Distance Education, 3* (2), 16.

Morreale, S. (2001, April). The preparing future faculty program . . . What's in it for communication studies? *Spectra, 37* (4), 13.

Smith, P. L., & Tillman, J. R. (1999). *Instructional design* (2nd ed.). Upper Saddle River, NJ: Prentice-Hall.

Stanton, A. L. (1990). An ecological perspective on college/university teaching. In J. A. Daly, G. W. Friedrich, & A. L. Vangelisti (Eds.), *Teaching communication: Theory, research and methods* (pp. 39–52). Hillsdale, NJ: Lawrence Erlbaum Associates.

Tommerup, P. (2001). Learning to see academic culture through the eyes of the participants: An ethnographic/folkloristic approach to analyzing and assessing the cultures of alternative institutions. In B. L. Smith & J. McCann (Eds.), *Reinventing ourselves: Interdisciplinary education, collaborative learning, and experimentation in higher education* (pp. 368–390). Bolton, MA: Anker.

SECTION II

PROFESSIONAL COLLABORATIVE ENDEAVORS: TEACHING ACROSS THE DISTANCE

Virtual Visiting Professors: Communicative, Pedagogical, and Technological Collaboration

Scott A. Chadwick and Tracy Callaway Russo

This chapter describes how a virtual visiting professor (VVP)—a subject matter expert who shares that expertise with a class via synchronous or asynchronous information technology without coming to campus—provides content enrichment, sparks interaction, illustrates and enacts use of communication technologies, and engages students' curiosity and imagination. The challenges of effectively using a VVP within the collaborative teaching and learning environment occur on three fronts: communicative, pedagogical, and technological. In this chapter, we draw upon our collective experiences of incorporating VVPs in courses and serving as VVPs, describing how we applied this approach to the classroom.

Throughout the Internet's short history, its dominant promise has been that this communication medium will bridge distances among people, build communities where none existed, and bring the power of expertise to bear on problems, all without the traditional limits of time and location (Negroponte, 1995; Rheingold, 1993). In addition, expectations of communication technologies have included serving as a means of opening markets for goods and services and bringing education and training to students who are constrained by work, families, or physical circumstances (Brown & Duguid, 2000). Web-delivered classes are proposed to meet the needs of nontraditional students who require greater flexibility to accommodate work or families, to teach technical and information gathering skills as well as content, to support outreach beyond their institutions' geographic area, and to help institutions remain competitive. Online classes are especially significant for learners who cannot come to campus, who are physically disabled, who are reticent or have trouble articulating ideas, or who use English as a second language (Russo, Campbell, Henry, & Kosinar, 1999). These promises have been realized in many cases. New business models exist for producing (see www.dell.com), brokering (see www.amazon.com), or making markets for products and services (see www.priceline.com) (Jutla, Bodorik, Hanjal, & Davis, 1999). Usenet, bulletin board, and other discussion sites have provided information, interaction, social support, and community (Baym, 1998; Constant, Sproull, & Kiesler, 1997; Walther & Boyd, 1997).

Education is one area significantly affected by the potential for connection, information, and communication available through the Internet. New models of enacting the educational experience in mediated environments abound. Classes can be delivered wholly or in part using communication technologies. Some of the available channels include radio broadcasts or audiotapes, videotapes, video transmission, or video streaming on the Internet, in addition to text online. Research shows that the outcomes of the traditional face to face (FtF) educational experience (the classroom method) can be equally achieved virtually, and improved upon by combining classroom and virtual learning (Chadwick, 1999).

Although individual classrooms may be constrained from using some of the high-end technologies by limits in readily available technology, technical support, or funds, instructors are not necessarily constrained from receiving the benefit of the connection, information, and communication available through the Internet. Several approaches can connect classrooms with a wealth of external resources. First, many institutions support software that allows instructors to post materials online for student use in traditional classroom contexts. Instructors can combine classroom and virtual learning by integrating web-delivered material and connecting with students through regularly held FtF lecture and discussion sections. Yet another powerful method takes advantage of components of both classroom and virtual teaching and learning by conducting a class supplemented with information via the web, using communication technology to provide access to subject matter experts in real time at no extra costs to the students or the university. The virtual visiting professor model is such a method.

VIRTUAL VISITING PROFESSOR

It is natural for the virtual visiting professor to be a faculty member from another institution, but a practitioner or a professional from outside the academy may provide the most value to students, depending on the needs of the class. A VVP supplements course content and interactions provided by the classroom teacher, sharing new information, methods, and experiences with students. The information technologies connecting the VVP with the students allow for robust mediated presence in the virtual classroom.

Connection of a subject matter expert and a class may be synchronous or asynchronous. In the synchronous, or real-time, approach, conferencing technology allows an expert to make a presentation to a class in the role of guest speaker. A variety of software programs such as NetMeeting or PlaceWare also support combined presentation of visual materials, including PowerPoint presentations, audio or video files, photographs, and the like, with the speaker's voice and/or image. The second scenario is asynchronous; here the expert posts lecture text or other resources and is available through a threaded text-based online discussion or a bulletin board program for interaction with students either during or outside class.

While we have both served as a VVP, neither has received compensation for doing so. We accrue institutional prestige for teaching innovations, but the institutional value of that is uncertain at our Research I universities. Colleagues ask us, "Why do you take the time and effort to serve as a VVP?" Our answer is that we find incorporating a VVP rewarding because it allows us to:

- Diversify the voices present in the classroom.

- Incorporate material that we, as the classroom teachers, may not be familiar or comfortable with, especially in areas that are changing rapidly.

- Verify or reinforce claims, in this case about effects of communication technologies in organizations.

- Enact, illustrate, or illuminate material or processes that would otherwise remain abstract.

- Stimulate students with a novel context that encourages them to think and participate at a different level and to different situational components than normal.

- Address differences in student learning styles.

- Receive feedback from a participant observer about course material and student responses.

APPLYING THE VVP MODEL TO ENRICH A CLASS

We have served as virtual visiting professors for other instructors' classes, have invited VVPs into our own FtF classrooms, and designed and facilitated asynchronous web-delivered classes that incorporated VVPs to supplement and support online interaction. Our experiences and the distance education literature indicate the importance of eight key components in helping a virtual visiting professor connection meet its considerable potential.

In the following section, we will describe our own experiences as visiting virtual professors and as the classroom instructor in a VVP context. Examples from a class taught in the fall of 1999 by Tracy in which Scott was a VVP illustrate how integrating electronic guest lecturers into either an FtF or online classroom achieves pedagogical and communication objectives and how practical issues of these connections can be handled. The exemplar class, Communication Technology and the Workplace, integrated undergraduate and graduate students and examined effects of communication technology in organizational life. For the VVP session, Scott was connected to the class via a telephone conference call and speakerphone in the classroom, and the students were connected to the web to see both his photographs and material he had loaded onto his web site for access by the class.

Identifying Objectives for a VVP and Applying the Resource

The pedagogical inspiration for the exemplar VVP presentation was Tracy's concern that students not just talk in the classroom about the challenges and potential of mediated or electronic communication but that they also experience some of the effects. In addition, she was eager for students to consider some of the important issues emerging around electronic commerce and organizational responses to them. Scott had been doing research in one such area, trust in electronic commerce, and this, plus his experience with teaching technology and communication, made him an ideal choice.

In a VVP context, there are more decisions than whether an individual has subject matter expertise, however. Adding remote delivery complicates the familiar challenges of articulating one's knowledge, grasping how to integrate it into the ongoing stream of the class, and connecting with the students. In general, we have found in an audio-supported remote presentation that asking the speaker to be more than usually verbally animated is helpful; the objective is to heighten use of the available communication channels. We also have found that visuals contribute significantly to VVP presentations. Among the most useful have been photographs of the speaker made available on the web. In the exemplar situation, two photographs were supplied, one the traditional university portrait, the other a casual shot of Scott seated on his motorcycle. These photographs were accompanied by the captions "Corporate Scott" and "Playtime Scott," leading to a discussion with the students of which picture evoked more feelings of trust and why.

Arranging for Technology

Although both our universities have facilities to make connections by television, there are relatively few studios, and these frequently are booked. In addition, there were no funds to pay for the line connections required to support video. Therefore, we chose other means of connection that met the pedagogical objectives and the practical ones. Even this straightforward approach was not without challenges, however. We discovered early in the planning process that although it had a telephone line, Tracy's regular classroom had no telephone jack and would not support the needed telephone line. One of the graduate students in the class offered to help set up a room in another building with a speakerphone and an Internet line.

In the end, he made all the connections and assured that the technology worked effectively.

Most institutions have support personnel who can help coordinate the technological requirements. Instructors can build connections between those support people on each side to help ensure that systems are compatible. Some technology is downloadable or available at low cost; others require institutional license. The more expensive option is not necessarily better; we have found that it is the connection among participants, especially the connection between students and the VVP, which is critical. In another of our experiences, the telephone was the only available technology, but it served well. In her role as VVP for a colleague's class in another state, Tracy emailed some simple PowerPoint slides to the classroom instructor, who also captured her photograph from a web site. The connection between classes was a telephone call, but coordination between the instructors enhanced it further, and students reported that the experience was a positive one.

The key to ensuring a quality connection between the students and the VVP is to coordinate the VVP's material and presentation to maximize his or her presence mediated by the available technology. In our experience, however, the more that immediacy is facilitated by the technology through multiple channels of communication (e.g., voice, text, images, audio), the more students act as though the VVP is actually present with them (see Gunawardena & Zittle, 1997).

Preparing the VVP

Intellectually, the most challenging part of being a VVP is building a seamless link with the classroom teacher's course content. Scott noted that he would be coming into the class midstream and would need to segue from points already covered to his own content, then set the stage for a segue back for Tracy to pick up. Rather than learning the entire body of course content, and knowing he would be talking with the students about online trust in e-commerce, he sought to learn from Tracy everything that would be covered related to that topic. One lingering concern was how well the students would know it by the time he came on the scene.

Reading the students' threaded discussions posted on the class web site and asking Tracy how well the students were grasping the course content allowed Scott to fine tune his approach. He also sought background information on the students, their majors, their levels in school, and their industry background. He was looking for all those incidental pieces of information we use in our own FtF classes that are ordinarily unavailable to a VVP. Acquiring that information built a sense of who the audience would be, furthering Scott's ability to tailor his message to them.

Coordinating the Players

Several types of coordination are key. One form relies on prior discussion between the instructors about the material to be covered and how the VVP's contribution fits into the ongoing class pace and content. The classroom instructor's role is to coordinate and choreograph both sides by providing signals. Noting during the class period how what the VVP has just said supports ideas previously covered in the classroom helps both students and the VVP connect the two components.

Additionally, the classroom instructor can provide information about nonverbal student responses. Although nonverbal signals (other than paralanguage cues) are absent from VVP interactions except where video conferencing is used, it is easy to ask for feedback about the interaction process during the class itself. In the exemplar context, we had agreed that Tracy would cue Scott about how students reacted to the material he was presenting. At one point in this class, Scott made a powerful point and then was silent, awaiting response. Many students nodded, but Scott could not see them, so Tracy provided context, "I see lots of head nodding." This cued Scott to ask a specific question, to which he received responses from several students. If a comment confused the students, Tracy would paraphrase, using codes familiar to her students. Informing the VVP and the class in advance that the classroom instructor will verbally transmit the nonverbal signals helps the VVP stay within the flow of discussion, not appearing surprised or flustered when the classroom instructor provides that feedback.

Because one of the richest contributions available through these technologies is the communication between teachers and students that it affords, where synchronous interaction is possible, it should be given priority. Therefore, the classroom instructor also must be sensitive to time, both supporting wait time while students process responses and allowing sufficient time for questions and answers.

Preparing Students

As we have noted, we found that providing pictures of the VVP helps students prepare to "meet" the virtual guest speaker. Supplementing the pictures with an online biographical sketch and a verbal introduction also helps set the initial interaction stage. Briefing both students and the VVP on the uses, capabilities, and limitations of the technology to be used helps minimize technology-based interruptions (or ameliorates situations where technology does not perform exactly as well as we would hope). Designing the interaction to stay focused on predetermined learning goals helps students learn course content regardless of the technology used.

In addition to those with synchronous connections, some of our VVP experiences have been entirely text-based, with an asynchronous time frame. In these situations, the visiting virtual professor contributes as a guest expert to a class' online threaded discussion. For example, Scott contributed to particular threads in several entirely asynchronous classes Tracy taught. This context is more challenging than synchronous situations, since these classes rely on "pull" technology in large measure. That is, students must take the initiative to go to a particular web site and pull up the information there; no information appears in their email or otherwise comes to prompt their action. Although the instructor can send messages to students that a VVP will be available in a particular module or related to particular content or tasks, it becomes the responsibility of the student to go to that site, and the responsibility of the VVP to be there. Another challenge is that interaction in asynchronous contexts is less immediate because of time lags between postings, so the VVP must be especially active and vigilant during the agreed-upon period in order to support student expectations and content needs.

Assessment

Incorporating a VVP into a class presents special opportunities for assessment of student understanding, as well as evaluation of class objectives and procedures. Making the classroom processes more public by adding an outside participant observer, one who is familiar with the teacher's objectives and at least some of the course content, provides powerful assessment opportunities.

Although reflection about the VVP experience and the material the guest contributes can become part of summative or end of semester evaluations, our experience is that VVPs can easily integrate formative assessment feedback as the class progresses (see Cross & Steadman, 1996; Huba & Freed, 2000). For example, the VVP can query the students about material previously covered in the course, alerting the classroom instructor to changes that may need to be made going forward. We have found that quick "reality checks" during a VVP presentation can help all parties adjust direction, confirm understanding, and provide clarification or elaboration. As a means of building a relationship with the students, it is natural for the VVP to ask how students would most like to move through material, instead of assuming that the VVP's preferred method of teaching matches the students' preferred method of learning. The VVP may ask students to write and send emails summarizing the interaction, noting the concept they believe is most important, or describing the content covered that does not make sense to them. Collecting that information, stripping personal identifiers from it, then posting it back to all students with the VVP's comments allows everyone to benefit.

Debriefing Students

Students need to be debriefed on the material covered in a VVP presentation so they can reflect on it and how it integrates with the courses as a whole, but as important is debriefing on the conferencing process itself. Debriefing the conferencing process allows opportunities to discuss the technology behind the interaction, the nature of mediated interactions and mediated presence, and the applicability of this type of communication in other contexts (e.g., virtual group work in geographically distributed organizations).

During debriefing, the instructor may elicit feedback from the students regarding the interaction dynamics between them and the VVP. This provides students the opportunity to think about how to improve the mediated process, both from their perspective and the VVP's point of view. Perhaps the biggest benefit to the students in this situation is that they will think and talk about the interdependency of the teaching and learning processes, as well as about the interdependency of group members as they interact in a variety of learning and professional contexts.

Providing Instructor Feedback

Once the virtual interaction is over, the instructors can talk about what went well and what could be improved in the next interaction, from both perspectives. Lacking nonverbal feedback from students, the VVP may have an imperfect sense of his or her own performance. In that case, the classroom instructor should be specific in reporting both short-term and long-term student reactions. The classroom instructor can describe the reactions students had to different communication techniques used by the VVP. The VVP can ask for suggestions about how better to include all students in discussions. The VVP will benefit greatly when the classroom instructor shares his or her knowledge of the students and their interaction patterns. Further, the VVP can provide an outsider perspective about the classroom dynamic and suggestions for other useful approaches.

PREPARING TO TEACH WITH OR AS A VVP

There are two types of advantages to incorporating VVPs into the classroom. One focuses on content, the other on process. Content must be carefully selected, just as with any live visitor to the classroom. Students also learn from the process of electronic presentation and from the heightened opportunities for communication. The information technologies connecting the VVP with the students can provide immediacy and presence, opening the path for engaged discussion, question and answer sessions, and feedback on the learning process.

Within any individual class, a variety of decisions must be made affecting the course content and the process through which students engage that content, each other, and the teacher(s). Designing a course to take advantage of a VVP should not adversely affect the course content, but can significantly expand the process components. By its interactive nature, the VVP portion of a course will strongly emphasize process. Seeking to transition smoothly from the classroom teacher to the VVP and back calls for the entire course to be interactive and process driven. In our VVP courses, most components affect both process and content, or just process alone (Table 5.1).

Students in our VVP classes routinely express concerns about what will be expected of them in this unfamiliar context, whether material presented by an invisible instructor will be intellectually accessible to them, and how they will be assessed. We help the students prepare for this new learning experience in three ways. First, we preview both the course content and the processes students will use during class. Students' primary

Table 5.1

Course Components as Content or Process Driven

Course Component	Content Driven	Process Driven
Student preparation		X
VVP preparation	X	X
Learning styles		X
Course content	X	X
VVP social presence		X
Assessment	X	X
Debriefing students	X	X
Technology used	X	X

concerns are technological in nature, but they need also be taught mechanisms through which to engage in meaningful discussion when their teacher is only virtually present, mediated through the web and a telephone, for example. These conversations about communication processes are appropriate regardless of course content and long-range application to other classes, as well as to students' professional and personal lives. Second, as described earlier, we introduce students to the VVP through descriptions, pictures, and stories. Finally, Scott has found some success in having students conduct a root metaphor analysis (Smith & Eisenberg, 1987) on their traditional classes, describing the culture and practices of those classes metaphorically, then considering their concerns with the VVP class. Metaphors used by students in our VVP courses are similar to those used by first-year college students: feelings of newness and concerns about status, control, engagement, and satisfaction (Jorgensen-Earp & Staton, 1993). As time and events pass in the VVP course, Scott returns the students to their metaphors, asking them to construct metaphors for their experiences in the VVP course, reflecting on the differences in the course and their resulting behaviors.

Just as students need be prepared, so, too, do VVPs. The VVP must know where his or her content fits within the general scheme of the course, who the students are, and, optimally, how those students learn best. Through our own collaborative teaching experiences, we have found our teaching styles are similarly student focused. We are significantly more concerned with the process through which students learn than with covering any one specific piece of content. We contend that focusing on the learning process results in students who can learn content far beyond the reaches of our particular courses. We think of this process orientation as being learner-centered, knowing that students in learner-centered classes ask significantly more questions, share more information, and generate more ideas than do students in teacher-centered classes (Greeson, 1988). Further, teaching from a learner-centered paradigm frees us to use any useful teaching method, something more difficult to achieve when constrained by focusing primarily on delivering content to students (Engelkemeyer & Brown, 1998).

We design our VVP classes strategically, taking advantage of our own and our VVP's teaching styles. Electronic communication and information access often provide data using a variety of channels and in a variety of forms. We incorporate web sites associated with an electronic visitor as one tool for students who learn via different learning styles, whether by handling and experimenting with information (e.g., playing games, investigating a site) or through reflection and abstract conceptualization of information (e.g., through audio or video recordings) (Kolb, 1976; 1981). These approaches, with the novelty they introduce, also stimulate students who learn best through various styles. Whether in FtF or VVP classes, the more learning styles accommodated within the class, the better all students learn (Stice, 1987). But in our VVP classes, we have two teachers who play off one another in an attempt to accommodate as many learning styles as possible. In this case, two is better than one.

In traditional FtF courses, it is fairly easy to separate content—items to be learned—from process. For example, there might be a textbook (the content) which the students read and study (process). But, in Tracy's online courses, all content is on the web. Students engage journal articles (content) via the technology that is the intellectual focus of the class. In that case, it is not possible to clearly distinguish a separation between content and process. The technology used makes certain content possible, and both prescribes and limits how students can interact with that content. For example, talking to Tracy's students via the telephone and PlaceWare constrained what Scott could show and how he could show it. With the technology available to him now in his office, he could engage in synchronous desktop video conferencing, constructing and sharing text, images, and graphics while talking with Tracy's students.

Social or mediated presence refers to the extent to which people interacting in a virtual environment or through electronic means perceive others there as real or salient (Russo & Campbell, 2001). Perceiving others in these environments as immediate or real appears to be critical to establishing a context in which individuals attend to others and feel comfortable sharing ideas, raising questions, trusting one another, and collaborating. Students who perceive others in mediated environments as real often report higher satisfaction with their learning experience (Gunawardena & Zittle, 1997).

As Garton and Wellman (1995) and Sproull and Kiesler (1991) have described in reviews of the literature, some scholars have argued that an asynchronous online environment allows fewer communication channels through which to send and receive messages, reducing a communicator's ability to establish his or her own presence or to perceive others as being present. Others, however, have argued that computer-mediated communication (CMC) is rich enough to sustain immediacy and an elaborated sense of others in the environment (Walther, 1992). The higher the social presence of others, the more communicators—in this case, students—are likely to pay attention to them and be influenced by them. The degree to which we as VVPs have presence in the classroom is dependent on two factors: the capacities of the technology used and our ability to maximally use that capacity. For example, Scott's ability to present his complete self, and the students ability to see and feel Scott as a real teacher and as part of their learning process, was quite different when he interacted with students via a threaded text-based online discussion than when he utilized web-based images and a telephone.

In our FtF classes, we use feedback from students as formative assessment. But in most cases, we separate the process of teaching from that of assessing. In contrast, in our online classes the act of generating formative assessment is embedded in the teaching process. Again, technology is both the content and the process through which the content is engaged. Thus, the act of assessing the learning process is simultaneously process and content driven.

As described earlier in this chapter, students are debriefed both about the process of learning with the VVP and the content provided by the VVP. As we have listened to our students' comments during debriefing, we find they describe what Dirr (1999) refers to as the "dialogic nature of learning" (p. 27). Students find they learn through four types of dialogues, or conversations:

- Conversations a learner has with an instructor

- Conversations among groups of learners

- Conversations a learner has with instructional resources

- Reflective conversations a learner has with himself or herself

With this knowledge gained from debriefing, we design our VVP classes to use information technologies to facilitate and support each of those conversations in a virtual environment. For instructor-learner conversations, email, threaded web-based discussions, voice and audio streaming from the instructor to the learner offer online feedback, opportunities to answer questions, encourage, correct, and challenge students, and a connection through which to establish personal relationships. Groups of learners can converse using email and threaded web-based text discussions. Learners may contact other learners through a class listserv or an email distribution list. These conversations may represent, replace, or supplement other types of class discussion. In addition, specific assignments require students to reflect on and document what and how they are learning.

Summary

Engaging students with a VVP expands their learning opportunities in several dimensions. First, they are directly exposed to new ideas and patterns of interaction from the VVP. This is in addition to their educational experience with their classroom teacher. Second, the VVP course is designed around the student's educational needs. The resources made available to the students, and the ways in which they are made available, are learner focused. The mediated communication within the class becomes a way to engage the learning process, but also can become a focus of investigation for the students. Third, integrating the VVP into a course mirrors the modern reality of technological convergence. Information technologies used in the class are not mere tools, but are as much a part of the structure and process of the educational experience as are reading texts, writing papers, and turn-taking in discussions. The technology, the course content, the teachers, and the students are interdependent on each other, collaborating to construct and benefit from the learning process.

REFLECTIONS AND CONCLUSION

When we started on our path of using and serving as VVPs, neither of us knew how this pedagogical experiment would turn out. Our experiences provide us one overwhelming lesson: It works. We find students are engaged in course content and the experience of using the technology they are studying. Students refer to the VVP experience throughout the semester and in subsequent classes with us. Students comment, and we find in their work, that using technology, rather than just talking about it, brings home the realities of the theories we discuss and helps students understand what they may expect in professional contexts. We believe using a VVP enhances course content by drawing on expertise not otherwise present or difficult to develop quickly. This style of teaching naturally supports uses of activities, assignments, discussion, and technology that address differences in student learning styles. It also allows valuable feedback among instructors as they respond from their own perspectives to a shared learning environment.

Making the VVP learning environment work depends most heavily on coordination, not just between instructors, but also with students and technology support personnel and systems on both ends. That coordination must include prior consultation among the teachers, choreography of the VVP visit, and diagnostic discussions after the interaction. Such coordination is not impossibly difficult, and the benefits to all parties outweigh the additional effort required to organize the experience. We both continue to learn and grow professionally from VVP endeavors.

REFERENCES

Baym, N. (1998). The emergence of online community. In S. Jones (Ed.), *Cybersociety 2.0: Revisiting computer mediated communication and community* (pp. 35–68). Thousand Oaks, CA: Sage.

Brown, J. S., & Duguid, P. (2000). *The social life of information.* Cambridge, MA: Harvard Business School Press.

Chadwick, S. A. (1999). Teaching virtually via the web: Comparing student performance and attitudes about communication in lecture, virtual web-based, and web-supplemented courses. *The Electronic Journal of Communication, 9* (1) [Online]. Available: http://www.cios.org/getfile/Chadwick_v9n199

Constant, D., Sproull, L., & Kiesler, S. (1997). The kindness of strangers: On the usefulness of electronic weak ties for technical advice. In S. Kiesler (Ed.), *Cultures of the Internet* (pp. 303–322). Hillsdale, NJ: Lawrence Erlbaum Associates.

Cross, K. P., & Steadman, M. H. (1996). *Classroom research: Implementing the scholarship of teaching.* San Francisco, CA: Jossey-Bass.

Dirr, P. J. (1999). Distance and virtual learning in the United States. In G. M. Farrell (Ed.), *The development of virtual education: A global perspective* (pp. 23–48). Vancouver, British Columbia: The Commonwealth of Learning. Available: http://www.col.org/virtualed/index.htm

Engelkemeyer, S. W., & Brown, S. C. (1998, October). Powerful partnerships: A shared responsibility for learning. *AAHE Bulletin,* 10–12.

Garton, L., & Wellman, B. (1995). Social impacts of electronic mail in organizations: A review of the research literature. *Communication Yearbook, 18,* 434–453.

Greeson, L. E. (1988). College classroom interaction as a function of teacher- and student-centered instruction. *Teaching & Teacher Education, 4* (4), 305–315.

Gunawardena, C. N., & Zittle, F. J. (1997). Social presence as a predictor of satisfaction within a computer-mediated conference environment. *The American Journal of Distance Education, 11* (3), 8–25.

Huba, M. E., & Freed, J. E. (2000). *Learner-centered assessment on college campuses: Shifting the focus from teaching to learning.* Boston, MA: Allyn and Bacon.

Jorgensen-Earp, C. R., & Staton, A. Q. (1993). Student metaphors for the college freshman experience. *Communication Education, 42,* 123–141.

Jutla, D., Bodorik, P., Hanjal, C., & Davis, C. (1999, March). Making business sense of electronic commerce. *Computer, 32* (3), 67–75.

Kolb, D. A. (1976). *The learning style inventory: Technical manual.* Boston, MA: McBer.

Kolb, D. A. (1981). Learning styles and disciplinary differences. In A. W. Chickering & Associates, *The modern American college: Responding to the new realities of diverse students and a changing society* (pp. 232–255). San Francisco, CA: Jossey-Bass.

Negroponte, N. (1995). *Being digital.* New York, NY: Vintage.

Rheingold, H. (1993). *The virtual community: Homesteading on the electronic frontier.* New York, NY: Harper Collins.

Russo, T., & Campbell, S. W. (2001). *Perceptions of mediated presence in an asynchronous online course: Interplay of communication behaviors and medium.* Paper presented at the annual meeting of the National Communication Association, Washington, DC.

Russo, T., & Chadwick, S. A. (2001). Making connections: Enhancing classroom learning with a virtual visiting professor. *Communication Teacher, 15* (3), 7–9.

Russo, T. C., Campbell, S., Henry, M. P., & Kosinar, P. (1999). An online graduate class in communication technology: Outcomes and lessons learned. *The Electronic Journal of Communication, 9* (1) [Online]. Available: http://www.cios.org/getfile\Russo_v9n199

Smith, R. C., & Eisenberg, E. M. (1987). Conflict at Disneyland: A root metaphor analysis. *Communication Monographs, 54,* 367–380.

Sproull, L., & Kiesler, S. (1991). *Connections: New ways of working in the networked organization.* Cambridge, MA: MIT Press.

Stice, J. E. (1987). Using Kolb's learning cycle to improve student learning. *Engineering Education, 77,* 291–296.

Walther, J. B. (1992). Interpersonal effects in computer-mediated interaction: A relational perspective. *Communication Research, 19* (1), 52–90.

Walther, J. B., & Boyd, S. (1997, May). *Attraction to computer-mediated social support.* Paper presented at the annual meeting of the International Communication Association, Montreal, Canada.

Intrapersonal Communication, Interpersonal Communication, and Computer-Mediated Communication: A Synergetic Collaboration

Leonard J. Shedletsky and Joan E. Aitken

Collaborating put our communication skills to the test. When we mentioned to other faculty members that we were writing about collaboration, many had horror stories to tell us. For instance, a psychology professor told us that one of his collaborators stopped talking to him and made decisions unilaterally. This occurred without warning toward the end of their collaborative book writing. He had no idea why. Speaking of the importance of communication between collaborators, Eaves (1997) wrote about the gritty street-level realities of communication among collaborators. He acknowledged that collaborating raised his appreciation for cooperation and compromise. It was a relief for us to find out that we are not alone. Collaboration plays a very important role in the life of an academic, and yet we enter into it with little understanding of the process.

We collaborated on teaching the course Intrapersonal Communication, and it taught us something about working out differences. It provided us with the impetus to rethink the relationships among intrapersonal communication, interpersonal communication, and computer-mediated communication (CMC). At first glance, these concepts may seem far apart from one another, but after much introspection, we found a close relationship among them. Intrapersonal communication is the process of assigning meaning to stimuli and producing meaningful stimuli. The model of intrapersonal communication proposed by Roberts, Edwards, and Barker (1987) suggests that it is not a level of communication distinct from interpersonal communication or computer-mediated communication. Instead, it is a set of processes involved in assigning meaning to stimuli and encoding stimuli at all levels of communication. CMC refers to human communication mediated by computers. For instance, the World Wide Web is that part of the Internet that most college students and faculty are clicking their way through these days. Intrapersonal communication points to the mind and the individual; computer-mediated communication prompts images of the globe, networked computers, and connections between millions of people.

The purpose of this chapter is to explain how online collaboration worked for us and for our students in an intrapersonal communication course, and how intrapersonal communication, interpersonal communication, and computer-mediated communication work together cognitively and collaboratively.

THE BEGINNING

Prior to collaborating on the course, Shedletsky had been exploring this juxtaposition by offering a course on intrapersonal communication with a home page approach. That is, the class met with the teacher in the traditional classroom, but the course was supplemented with a home page containing a syllabus, learning activities, links, and a discussion area. This intrapersonal class was taught for three semesters, fall 1996, 1997, 1998, at the University of Southern Maine (see http://www.usm.maine.edu /com/intrap.htm). During this phase, we were piloting the idea of using a home page in connection with the intrapersonal course by observing computer-mediated communication, discussing intrapersonal processing, and using questionnaires to gain knowledge from the students about their reaction to the online elements of the course. From 1996–1998, students used the home page for completing assignments, readings, posting responses, self-evaluation testing, research, and displaying some of their papers for the course. We found that students strongly liked the home page approach, especially where they could self-assess intrapersonal behaviors and collaborate via electronic discussion.

Encouraged by the results of this approach, we collaborated on the course and taught it with a common home page. Thus, in the spring of 1999, we team-taught the course on two campuses, the University of Southern Maine and the University of Missouri, Kansas City.[1] Shedletsky taught undergraduates in the classroom with the home page supporting the course, and Aitken taught graduate students totally online. Students located in Maine and Missouri were able to meet in electronic groups.

An important part of the team-taught class was discussion between students at the two sites. We envisioned graduate students being able to offer undergraduates the benefits of their more advanced stage of study. And we also thought that being able to discuss intrapersonal experiences with interested peers at a distance would heighten interest and involvement.

THE ROLE OF CMC

In part, we were and are motivated to use this new medium because we believe that the networked computer is an intensifier of the intrapersonal aspects of communication (Shedletsky, 1993). That is, the computer enhances or helps to bring to awareness the information processing aspects of communication, the assignment of meaning, and the use of implication and inference. The computer encourages the mind to work even harder than in other modes with regard to thinking about the message, the metamessage, and the social action intended. The computer brings to consciousness fundamental aspects of communication that are more often transparent in other modes, aspects such as turn-taking, sequencing of utterances, adjacent placement in discourse analysis terms (Nofsinger, 1999), context, and ambiguity. The computer promotes cognitive reorganization as well as reflection on the process of assigning meaning, and, at the same time, it promotes active learning and the ability to work cooperatively in teams with people who think differently from oneself.

A cornerstone of the course is the student's self-assessment of her or his own intrapersonal processing. Online instruction in intrapersonal communication makes available access to measuring intrapersonal processes that would otherwise be very difficult to access. For instance, our students were able to measure their visual memory, communication apprehension, and depth of processing. Moreover, students were required to write to the discussion board, to describe their self-assessments, to respond to specific questions on the readings, and to post summaries of group discussion.

The study of intrapersonal communication is metacognition. And the CMC component reinforces the social nature of our cognitive selves (Martin, 1997). As Harnad (1996) writes,

> Human cognition is not an island unto itself. As a species, we are not Leibnizian Monads independently engaging in clear, Cartesian thinking. *Our minds interact* [emphasis added]. That's surely why our species has language. And that interactivity probably constrains both what and how we think. (p. 397)

Combining CMC with intrapersonal communication creates a space in which we can observe our minds interacting. By "space" we mean a presence in our minds as well as before us on the computer monitor, but it is the psychological space that we are concerned with here. The combination of CMC and intrapersonal communication facilitates our consciously looking both inward and outward, observing our own cognitive behavior, and describing that behavior in words for others. We can compare others' description of their internal behavior with our own. CMC as a medium facilitates our reflection because it disrupts our habitual modes of assigning meaning, and it operates as a tool of interpersonal communication that facilitates awareness of our intrapersonal behaviors in relation to others. Writing about the relationship between intrapersonal and interpersonal communication patterns, Lippard-Justice (1989) observed, "Humans structure the reality of their experience; they do not receive it. When one reclaims the capacity to create self and encounter in the moment, she or he is truly competent both intrapersonally and interpersonally" (p. 453).

Teaching intrapersonal communication is challenging and elusive, a content calling for unique pedagogical approaches. The processes of intrapersonal communication are not easily observable because they are internal and cognitive. They operate at high speed. Intrapersonal communication examines ideas in the mind, emotions, memory, perceptions, intentions, meanings, and other intangibles. So we used CMC to create a sense of hands-on introspective experience for the student. Being able to discuss these introspections with others adds the power of intersubjectivity, a power not to be underestimated. CMC required that students verbalize their internal behaviors. Experienced teachers know that students value discussion with other students. Students learn a great deal from discussion, not only the content of the other person's experience and interpretations, but also the skills of discussion itself. Online discussion provides the added dynamics of diversity, directness, and focus on subject areas. Direct focus is especially important when dealing with highly subjective variables, such as emotion, attitude, and perception. At the same time, online discussion is a rich medium for noting how our minds interact. It helps to turn our attention to aspects of communication that are transparent in more familiar media. We must think about the connections between utterances and the intentions behind them.

How Collaboration Benefits Faculty

It comes as no surprise that faculty have found that collaborative instruction is a valid way of teaching via computer, perhaps because of the array of skills needed for computer-mediated instruction (Wepner, 1998; Whittington & Campbell, 1999). Given standard patterns of faculty anxiety, student frustrations, and the lack of institutional support staff for faculty who use technology in higher education (Saba, 1999), a team teaching approach gives each faculty member someone with whom to talk, learn, complain, and solve problems. Eaves (1997) put it this way: "Collaboration is about lots of things besides the division of labor, like reassurance in the face of technical panic" (p. 3). In addition, because distance education has always been on the fringe of acceptability in higher education, new media methods which effectively provide distance education are bound to be viewed as suspect (Lesh & Rampp, 2000). Thus, perhaps one of the strongest arguments in favor of collaborative instruction is credibility: Faculty and administrators see that a check and balance system exists under the name of team teaching. Finally, the rewards for teaching with technology have been minimal, the work generated primarily by faculty interest and curiosity, while their colleagues voice concerns about the quality of teaching (Husmann & Miller, 1999). With no financial or promotion rewards for the extra work, collaborative teaching can provide a reward in and of itself, acting as a motivational stimulus that helps the faculty member learn. When you combine the dynamics of teaching with computer technology and the broad and complex terrain of intrapersonal communication, you can begin to see why collaboration is useful.

HOW COLLABORATION AND CMC
BENEFITS STUDENT LEARNING

In the Intrapersonal Communication course, we consider computer-mediated communication advantageous for several reasons. CMC is inseparable from intrapersonal and interpersonal communication, in the same way that meaning and social action are inseparable from communication at all levels, whether face to face or mediated. In addition, CMC instruction has been used in improving interpersonal skills. The interpersonal links of computers make this type of instruction appropriate for topics related to interpersonal communication (Neal, 1994; Walther, 1996; Walther, Anderson, & Park, 1994).

Research suggests that CMC offers a unique environment for developing interpersonal relationships (Lea & Spears, 1995; McCormick & McCormick, 1992; Parks & Floyd, 1996; Scharlott & Christ, 1995). Many users are comfortable meeting people via computer, so they are able to meet more diverse people than they would in their home and work environment. While online, some people feel less inhibited in their communication, so they behave in more experimental ways. Others feel safer because they are not face to face with another person, so they talk more freely and self-disclose more easily. Relationships may develop more rapidly because of the emphasis on self-disclosure. CMC's heavy text-dependence requires people to talk; there are no options for just being there or engaging in activities in relative silence as people do when typically developing face to face relationships.

The specific advantages in CMC lend themselves well to difficult content. For example, students can search material privately and can explore what interests them at whatever level they choose. Thus, students can avoid material they already know or consider inappropriate. In addition, students can read and discuss material they want to study, including information that may seem too uncomfortable to read in a more public setting (e.g., college library or traditional classroom). There are many specific web sites and chat rooms available through computerized instruction, in which many people exhibit a willingness and ability to discuss challenging topics (e.g., Finn & Lavitt, 1994; Matheson & Zanna, 1988).

Intrapersonal communication, interpersonal communication, and computer-mediated communication work together in this course, reinforcing one another and reminding students of their close ties and interrelations. Our students experienced this synergism in the activities of the course and the computer-mediated communication format. Repeatedly, students were engaged in testing and measuring their intrapersonal behavior, in reading about intrapersonal communication, and in expressing their views and their intrapersonal experiences in online discussions. Students had to look both to themselves and others, reflect upon their own intrapersonal behavior, and discuss their findings with classmates. Whether students were writing in their journals; writing a response to a course reading; or exploring their own visual memory, depth of processing, or analyzing their listening behavior, they ultimately shared their ideas with others by giving and receiving feedback. Writing position papers in response to readings was a major way in which this combination engaged students in the course. Students were instructed as follows:

> Ideally, each day as you read the text, discuss your views in class, and read outside of the required reading, as you have experiences, or reflect on your intrapersonal experiences, you will have ideas that you can elaborate on for the group discussions. The position paper is an opportunity to think out loud about issues that interest you and that are connected to the course. Use the position paper to get on paper ideas that benefit you. You may wish to use the position paper to ponder what confuses you in the reading (or discussion), to be creative about your views on intrapersonal communication, etc., to show where the reading is not consistent or accurate, to defend an idea represented in our book, to offer an alternative view, or to elaborate on something said in the group discussion. Also, there may be times when I will pose a question for you to respond to in your position paper. Position papers are intended to keep us all engaged with the material and to generate discussion in the group meetings. Position papers will be collected at the end of each meeting at which they are due. Position papers may build ideas for you that culminate in your final essay.

For the position paper exercise, students were instructed to:

- Write at least a one-page position paper for five of our meetings. You will be expected to read the assigned reading for each meeting—before that meeting—to review carefully the main points in the reading, and to arrive at the meeting prepared to comment on the reading.

- At each of the five meetings, you will work in a small group for the purpose of discussing your position paper.

- Present your position paper in the group meetings or online and give one another feedback on the ideas presented.

- Please date each position paper and be prepared to hand it in at the end of each meeting at which it is due; position papers are graded.

Position papers were written and graded individually and students were individually accountable for their papers. The posted papers also served to generate face to face and online discussion. Some of the best position papers were used as exemplars (see http://www.usm.maine.edu/com/position.htm).

Similarly, students engaged in online exercises, such as the visual memory test, and then offered their experiences online and gave one another feedback, sharing their individual intrapersonal experiences. For instance, here is a typical student exchange in the discussion board.

> Student A: I was pleased with how well I did on this test [visual memory]. I marked 29 items that I remembered and got them all correct. I missed two items but had no incorrect answers. I scored a 93%.

> Student B: I got the same score, too, and no incorrect answers. I would have liked to see the test tell us which ones that we did not choose—the two images that we could not remember. I would be curious to know what the pictures were and if a higher percent of people taking the test missed the exact same images—now that would be neat to analyze, huh??!!

Experiential learning activities in intrapersonal communication are key to the learning experience (Shedletsky, 1989). We required students to take part in numerous activities that allowed them to explore their own intrapersonal behavior. The exercises served to motivate students to observe themselves and to increase awareness of and control over intrapersonal communication. Furthermore, the exercises allowed students an unstructured arena in which to explore a wide range of intrapersonal behaviors, some of which are mostly private (e.g., emotions, attitudes, physiological reactions, confusions). For instance, students kept an intrapersonal journal for the course in which they reported responses to assignments, analyzed their listening behaviors, wrote freely, discussed their willingness to communicate, reported the results of cognitive style testing, and considered ways of reconstructing events from memory (see http://www.usm.maine.edu/com/intradoc.htm). Having to discuss these measures and learning activities required each student to encode and analyze internal communication.

It became clear that students enjoyed doing the online exercises, writing the position papers, taking part in the groups, and the online discussion. These features helped to enact the theoretical principles of communication that connected intrapersonal communication, interpersonal communication, and computer-mediated communication (Roberts, Edwards, & Barker, 1987).

LESSONS LEARNED FROM ONLINE COLLABORATION

Support? More varied points of view? Technical help? We experienced multiple advantages to team teaching online. As concerned faculty, we helped each other understand and deal with the politics of online work: Suspicion surrounds faculty who teach online (Shedletsky & Aitken, 2001):

- We helped each other in dealing with technical difficulties.

- We enumerated our weekly frustrations about teaching online to someone who understood, then brainstormed possible solutions. Those challenges are easier to face with the support of a colleague. Support is a most important value when it comes to teaching collaboratively online.

- We offered differing perspectives from which students could learn. Sometimes a student responded differently to a teacher without direct authority over the student. Plus, we often contributed a point of view or reference to specific literature that deepened and focused our online discussion.

- The other faculty member would contribute to the discussion, it seemed, just when it was needed or the other felt overwhelmed by the relentless daily demands of online discussion, adding much needed flexibility for each of us.

- With two instructors, we offered a wider range of instructional materials for our students (Appendix 6.1). In designing the web site, we combined our instructional materials for students, and have made some of these materials available (http://www.usm.maine.edu/com /intradoc.htm).

In teaching the intrapersonal course, one of the biggest hurdles turned out to be the specific online application that we would use for our electronic discussion. One of the authors was familiar with a private email discussion group method and the other was familiar with a university Webboard. We adopted Webboard, but when students at a distance had problems accessing it, the pressures of keeping the courses going caused a divergence to set in. Both instructors reverted to the familiar. We decided, then, to use both applications. Student reaction seemed to be, "I am sticking with the one I know," and discussion suffered. Only a few students bothered to keep up with both systems, and given the enormous amount of posted materials on two systems, the quantity of material began to feel overwhelming. In a rare instance, where students met with an online encounter that they found unpleasant, there seemed to be little motivation to work it out. We plan to limit these problems in the future by using more lead time to work out joint strategies and by using only one posting system.

The key lesson learned was that open communication between collaborators is necessary to optimize the quality of the work. Some conflict is inevitable and must be engaged. As in all contexts, the trick is to resolve conflict in a productive way. Retreating to two separate discussion areas reduced the opportunity for discussion and preempted a joint solution. When one perceives a disadvantage in having to deal with someone else's ideas, then the antidote is open communication.

The collaboration was a plus for our students, in spite of the problems. The course provided students with an opportunity to experiment with collaboration themselves, between the two classes as well as within each class. The course offered students an online text, resources of many kinds provided by the additional instructor, such as discussion with students quite different from those in their conventional classroom, and materials developed for the home page.

AN INTERPERSONAL PERSPECTIVE ON COLLABORATION

There is a subtle piece to collaboration that we have experienced but which is difficult to notice and even more difficult to verbalize. It is the interpersonal side of collaboration, the give and take, the energy generated or sapped by collaborating. The disadvantages are largely embedded in the interpersonal dynamics. Like any partnership, compromise is in order. Team teaching may mean neither faculty will always be able to do what she or he wants, or, at the very least, the instructor may need to argue for her or his position. Typically, faculty tend to be extremely independent and self-reliant individuals who seldom need consensus from anyone about how they teach or conduct their research. We have collaborated with people before, and it is often not a pretty picture. There have been times when others thought collaboration was 10% of the work for 90% of the recognition. Our experiences have suggested that creating an effective partnership is having two hardworking people willing to give 100% of the effort, with alternating recognition.

Judging from our experience, a successful collaboration leads to additional projects. Our first collaborative venture was coediting the textbook on intrapersonal communication, *Intrapersonal Communication Processes* (Aitken & Shedletsky, 1995). (See the endnote for online course and textbook information.) Interestingly, we collaborated on the book before we ever met in person. We had a shared interest in intrapersonal communication and knew of one another as professionals in communication, but we never actually met in person until after the book was published. While we spoke a few times on the telephone, most of the actual collaboration was accomplished online, sending manuscripts back and forth and using email for discussion. We met for the first time at a National Communication Association (NCA) conference and began a productive sequence of coauthored presentations. Eventually, we coedited an online publication for NCA, *Communication Teacher Resources Online.* So, by the time we offered our intrapersonal course as a collaborative effort, we had negotiated a work relationship, learned how to work together online, and worked together on numerous projects.

We have seen our students collaborate in small group assignments and that, too, is often fraught with discontent. Collaboration is a delicate matter. Perhaps a close analogy would be parenting. Faculty like their autonomy, and collaboration requires faculty to show patience, compromise, and accountability to a colleague. We each bring our own beliefs and values to the task; we try to nurture a creation and give our sincerest concern. We want the project to be the best possible, and we feel a strong investment of our own identity during the process. In collaboration, faculty may feel that their "name" is at stake, that their reputation is up for review, that their chances of moving forward under tenure and promotion guidelines is on the line. The locus of control shifts away from the individual during collaboration. What one produces collaboratively will influence one's self-perception and the perception of colleagues. Given such powerful forces, it is no wonder that collaboration is a delicate matter.

When we consider our collaboration, the following are some of the dynamics that are critical to our success:

- A belief in the ability of your collaborator.

- A belief in your collaborator's belief in your ability.

- A belief in the other's good intentions (i.e., that she or he will give a timely, unselfish, and fair effort).

- An ability to speak your mind, give honest feedback, and receive honest feedback. The success of the project needs to rank above faculty sensitivities.

- An eagerness to please your collaborator (i.e., to want to work hard for the reward of recognition from your collaborator).

CLOSING PERSPECTIVES

Our students responded positively and learned well in the course, which was, of course, the main objective of our collaboration. We also believe our students learned more by observing our collaboration—including watching us model how we handled disagreement.

As colleagues, we are still friends. We are still collaborating on projects. In fact, we are collaborating more than ever. So, collaboration has been good to us. We are productive, in that we energize one another. We each offer a slant that is a bit different than the other would have alone, so we enlarge our canvas. Does the work benefit from the combined effort? We think so. We see ourselves as competent, mature scholars, and we have mutual respect for the other's abilities. We care about what work bears our names. Hence, we are proud to collaborate because we believe the quality of our work together achieves something significantly more than what we do alone.

As stated earlier, so much of the collaborative experience is dependent upon the communication between the collaborators. Our experiences in collaborating with faculty run the gamut of nightmare to dream come true. So, we cannot make a blanket statement about collaborating as good or bad, advisable or not. But carefully laid out expectations, workaholic tendencies, a blend of personalities, and a balancing of skills seem to be the essence of a viable partnership.

In the fall of 2001, we repeated our course collaboration with our home page approach, online textbook, online learning activities and tests, and readings and discussion. Our online skills have increased and our partnership has strengthened. The main change was to clarify more expectations and pilot in advance. We learned that we need to talk openly about decisions relevant to the project. Ducking the talk hurts the quality of the work, so there is no point to taking differences personally. In a sense, we created our own faculty development program because we found it informative to try each other's ideas as a way to expand our instruction. A little discomfort was a thought-provoking and growth-producing experience.

Finally, according to our cost and benefit analysis of collaboration, we plan on many more projects. As a potential collaborator, you will need to do your own calculations.

References

Aitken, J., & Shedletsky, L. (Eds.). (1995). *Intrapersonal communication processes.* Annandale, VA: Speech Communication Association and Hayden-McNeil.

Eaves, M. (1997). Collaboration takes more than e-mail. *The Journal of Electronic Publishing,* 3 (2)[Online]. Available: http://www.press.umich.edu/jep/03-02/blake.html

Finn, J., & Lavitt, M. (1994). Computer-based self-help groups for sexual abuse survivors. *Social Work with Groups, 17* (1–2), 21–46.

Harnad, S. (1996). Interactive cognition: Exploring the potential of electronic quote/commenting. In B. Gorayska & J. L. Mey (Eds.), *Cognitive technology: In search of a humane interface* (pp. 397–414). The Netherlands: Elsevier Science.

Husmann, D. E., & Miller, M. T. (1999, Fall). Faculty incentives to participate in distance education. *Michigan Community College Journal: Research & Practice, 5* (2), 35–42.

Lea, M., & Spears, R. (1995). Love at first byte? Building personal relationships over computer networks. Under-studied relationships: Off the beaten track. In J. T. Wood & S. Duck (Eds.), *Understanding relationship processes, series 6* (pp. 197–233). Thousand Oaks, CA: Sage.

Lesh, S. G., & Rampp, L. C. (2000, October). *Effectiveness of computer-based educational technology in distance learning: A review of the literature.* (ERIC Document Reproduction Service No. ED 440 628)

Lippard-Justice, P. (1989). The relationship between intrapersonal and interpersonal communication patterns. In C. Roberts & K. Watson (Eds.), *Intrapersonal communication processes: Original essays* (pp. 444–455). Scottsdale, AZ: Gorsuch Scarisbrick.

Martin, G. I. (1997). Getting personal through impersonal means: Using electronic mail to gain insight into student teachers' perceptions. *Research and Reflection: A Journal of Educational Praxis, 3* (1) [Online]. Available: http://www.gonzaga.edu/rr/v3n1/martin.html

Matheson, K., & Zanna, M. P. (1988). The impact of computer-mediated communication on self-awareness. *Computers in Human Behavior, 4* (3), 221–233.

McCormick, N. B., & McCormick, J. W. (1992, Winter). Computer friends and foes: Content of undergraduates' electronic mail. *Computers in Human Behavior, 8* (4), 379–405.

Neal, J. S. (1994, January). The interpersonal computer. *Science Scope, 17* (4), 24–27.

Nofsinger, R. E. (1999). *Everyday conversation.* Prospect Heights, IL: Waveland.

Parks, M. R., & Floyd, K. (1996, Winter). Making friends in cyberspace. *Journal of Communication, 46* (1), 80–97.

Roberts, C., Edwards, R., & Barker, L. (1987). *Intrapersonal communication processes.* Scottsdale, AZ: Gorsuch Scarisbrick.

Saba, F. E. (1999, November 1). New academic year starts with controversy over the use of technology. *Distance Education Report, 3* (21), 1–2.

Scharlott, B. W., & Christ, W. G. (1995, Summer). Overcoming relationship-initiation barriers: The impact of a computer-dating system on sex role, shyness, and appearance inhibitions. *Computers in Human Behavior, 11* (2), 191–204.

Shedletsky, L. (1993). Minding computer-mediated communication: CMC as experiential learning. *Educational Technology, 33* (12), 5–10.

Shedletsky, L. J. (1989). *Meaning and mind: An intrapersonal approach to human communication.* Annandale, VA: Speech Communication Association and ERIC Clearinghouse on Reading and Communication Skills.

Shedletsky, L. J., & Aitken, J. E. (2001, July). The paradoxes of online academic work. *Communication Education, 50* (3), 206–217.

Walther, J. B. (1996, February). Computer-mediated communication: Impersonal, interpersonal, and hyperpersonal interaction. *Communication Research, 23* (1), 3–43.

Walther, J. B., Anderson, J. F., & Park, D. W. (1994, August). Interpersonal effects in computer-mediated interaction: A meta-analysis of social and antisocial communication. *Communication Research, 21* (4), 460–487.

Wepner, S. B. (1998, Spring). Your place or mine? Navigating a technology collaborative. *Journal of Computing in Teacher Education, 14* (3), 5–11.

Whittington, C. D., & Campbell, L. M. (1999, February). Task-oriented learning on the web. *Innovations in Education & Training International, 36* (1), 26–33.

Appendix 6.1
Array of Instructional Materials

Available at: http://www.usm.maine.edu/com/intradoc.htm

The plan is to locate particularly interesting, provocative, and informative documents, tests, and exercises here in this space. You ought to check here every so often to see what is available. The documents will be listed here and, wherever possible, a clickable link provided. What follows is a list of the documents to be read.

> An Intrapersonal Communication Model
> Communication Models
> Intrapersonal Intelligence
> The Journal
> Reentry to School
> Journal Writing
> Listening Others/Self
> SIER MODEL
> SIER STAGES
> Metamemory
> Willingness to Communicate Scoring
> Willingness to Communicate
> Cognitive Style
> A Sample Intrapersonal Journal
> Journal Guide
> Depth of Processing
> Mind Tools
> Personality
> A Reflection on the Mind at Work
> Teaching as Experiential Learning
> Computer Anxiety
> Computer Anxiety Rating Scale (CARS)
> APA/MLA Style Guides
> Cognition & Hypermedia
> Conscious vs. Nonconscious
> Reconstruction from Memory
> COGWEB

Ogden & Richards Triangle
Conversational Indirectness Scale
Implicit Association Test
GAMES, ETC.
CARD TRICK

ENDNOTE

[1] The team-taught intrapersonal course development—which includes a full textbook online—is at http://www.courses.maine.edu/. [P7262_P_002; Use guest for user name and guest for password; outside of Blackboard, see: http://www.usm.maine.edu/com/intrap.htm]

Collaborating on the Instructional Design and Implementation of an Environmental Education Course: The Real Challenges of Collaboration

Richard Huber

Collaborating and teaching with colleagues face to face is a challenge; however, collaborating over distance in an environment surrounded by multiple cameras, microphones, and television monitors will stress the most colloquial of relationships. I began my experiment with a collaborative distance learning environmental education course in the fall of 1997. The idea was for four instructors at different universities in North Carolina to bring their classes together using the state's distance learning network and team-teach their classes. Three science educators and an environmental education specialist from four separate universities agreed to have their classes meet jointly over the state's distance learning system for the first two hours of a weekly three-hour evening class. This collaborative would allow us to invite the very top scientists from each institution to address and interact with our students.

We wanted the course to be more than simply talking heads from the four institutions. Classes meet in distance learning rooms, which have multiple cameras and television monitors, as well as voice-activated microphones to facilitate interaction. We knew, for this course to succeed, students had to be actively engaged in the course topics and issues. But how do we accomplish that with roughly 60 students at four different sites, cameras and television monitors throughout the rooms, and microphones recording students' and instructors' every comment? Could these challenges to classroom interaction and involvement be used to actually enhance student learning?

After teaching this course four times in four years, I have to classify the experiment as less than successful—at least from my goals and perspectives as both an environmentalist and a science educator. We often learn as much or more from our failures as our successes. Thus, the purpose of this chapter is to describe and analyze the instructional design and the implementation of this course and then to articulate what worked, what did not, and why. It is this kind of reflection and analysis that is at the heart of educational research. Good teachers are characteristically reflective about their craft and see themselves as learners throughout their lives. As this chapter will illustrate, what seems solid in theory (instructional design) does not always work in practice. This analysis should prove instructive for all who venture to work collaboratively with others.

Although I worked with three other instructors in the design and implementation of the course and often discussed what was working and not working with the other instructors, this reflection and analysis is solely from my perspective.

WHY I JOINED THE COLLABORATIVE

An environmental educator with Sea Grant at North Carolina State University (NCS) received a small grant to develop a joint environmental education class with three other institutions. The idea was that none of these other schools had the resources or personnel to offer such a course by themselves. One science educator from each of the three institutions was invited to join the project: East Carolina University (ECU), University of North Carolina, Charlotte (UNCC), and University of North Carolina, Wilmington (UNCW). The grant provided a modest amount of money for travel to a planning session and funds to develop a web page for the course.

In the fall of 2000, a fifth site, Johnston County, was added as an extension site for North Carolina State. The first year, the four classes met over the interactive distance learning network for three hours every Wednesday evening for the entire semester. The second year, the four campuses met over the network for the reduced time of two hours per night. Students were asked to continue collaborative dialogue and to post additional unanswered questions on the web during the week. The third hour of class was allocated as time for individual instructors to meet face to face with their students to address their particular needs and goals. In addition, the number of weeks for meeting over the network was reduced from 15 to 12, thus providing additional individual time for face to face classroom meetings.

I thought it would be an enjoyable experience for me and a great learning experience for my students. Frankly, I thought this would be an easy teaching assignment since I would be sharing the teaching responsibilities with three other instructors. Furthermore, it seemed like a perfect way to accomplish what has been a long-time professional and personal goal of mine: to increase environmental awareness through my teaching, and thereby have a positive impact on improving the environment. I hold strong environmental views and believe the key to solving environmental problems is to have a well-educated and thoughtful citizenry with a deep understanding of science and environmental issues. Science teachers are vital in imparting the wisdom and skills necessary to address these difficult and complex issues. It seemed that a course aimed at discussing the critical environmental issues associated with our air, water, and soil from four different perspectives and four different geographic regions in North Carolina would contribute to accomplishing such a goal.

Helping students meet scientists and understand the nature of science was also an important goal of mine for the course. Although science educators may not agree on specific content or approaches for science education programs, "there is agreement that science instruction should facilitate the development of an adequate understanding of the nature of science" (Hammrich, 1997, p. 142). Understanding the nature of science comes, in part, from interacting with other like-minded and knowledgeable individuals in an effort to make sense of data while constructing individual and communal understandings. Driver, Asoko, Leach, Mortimer, and Scott (1994) describe learning science as a process involving social construction of knowledge. In their words, "From this perspective knowledge and understanding, including scientific understandings, are constructed when individuals engage socially in talk and activity about shared problems or tasks. Making meaning is thus a dialogic process involving persons-in-conversation" (p. 7).

INSTRUCTIONAL COURSE DESIGN

The disciplines represented by the four instructors included biological science, marine science, science education, elementary and middle grade education, and curriculum development. It was our hope that the collaborative effort would contribute to a greater breadth of scope than could any one instructor.

Our goals for the course were to provide students with:

- Science content background knowledge needed to teach about local environmental issues

- Detailed knowledge about selected local environmental issues

- Knowledge of resources and techniques for teaching about local environmental issues

- A desire and commitment by the students to make environmentally sound decisions in their professional and personal lives

The course was designed to be crosslisted as a graduate or undergraduate course with each campus having its own course number and title for the class. The course focused on four topic areas: air, water, soil, and critical environmental issues. Three class sessions (two hours over the distance learning network) were allocated to each topic area as follows:

- Session 1: Science content about the area, chemistry, health impact, etc.

- Session 2: An in-depth study of a local issue within the general topic area. For example, while studying air, ozone pollution in the larger cities was examined.

- Session 3: Resources and methods for teaching the topic area.

The plan was for each of the instructors to take responsibility for the planning and execution of the three class sessions for one of the four main topic areas. The selection of speakers for each of the topic areas was done during an online meeting approximately two months before the beginning of the course. Each professor was responsible for the assessment of his or her own students.

Advantages of Instructional Design:
Diversity in Students and Geographic Regions

The multicampus aspect of the course allowed the instructors to invite the very best lecturers and scientists from all four campuses to lecture and interact with students. Environmental education professionals from parks and nature centers provided additional information, resources, and insightful discussions for course topics. Thus, students were able to listen to and interact with talented individuals from all four campuses.

Class participants were diverse and included in-service teachers (Johnston County and UNCC), environmental educators and graduate students in education (NCS), environmental studies majors (UNCW), and elementary education majors (ECU).

For the course to succeed, we knew we had to challenge the students to communicate across the distance with the guest scientists, other professionals, and with each other. Therefore, we designed the teaching methodology to actively engage the students in the topics and issues. The course design encourages an intellectual dialogue of diverse scientists, science educators, and students from four different geographic regions in North Carolina as they discuss critical environmental issues associated with our air, water, and soil. For example, students were able to compare the impact of urban development on water quality issues of a large city in the Piedmont with those of a smaller city in the Coastal Plain of North Carolina.

Despite the distance and the disparity of student backgrounds, we hoped to take advantage of those differences. This was easiest to achieve when we challenged the students to respond to a particularly provocative essay or quote. For example, after reading an essay outlining Paul Ehrlich's 1968 comments in *The Population Bomb*—on how to solve the world population problem—each site was assigned a country and was required to respond to several of Ehrlich's comments as they think that country would have responded. Involvement became intense as students reported on India's, China's, and the United States' response to comments from Paul Ehrlich (1968):

- "Fetal abortions [are a] highly effective weapon in the armory of population control" (p. 88).

- "People in positions of power [i.e., in the Roman Catholic Church] have either ignored the problem or have recommended solutions that are inadequate in scope or proven failures" (p. 82).

- "Give your kids an IUD to take to 'show and tell'..." (p. 182).

During such discussions, the problem for the instructors became not one of how to get students to talk but how to get them to take turns and listen to another country's views.

Challenges of the Interactive Audio/Video Environment

As others have discovered and written about, the interactive audio/video distance learning network has its limitations and challenges. Participants in this project and in other research studies which examine the impact of distance learning environments on classroom communication reported the difficulty of transcending the distance in order to feel comfortable enough to pose questions, and described the experience from the distant site as watching television and being "'intruders in the classroom'" (Comeaux, 1995, p. 360; McHenry & Bosik, 1995).

Although the network allows for simultaneous audio and video interaction, thus providing participants opportunities to ask questions of the presenters and communicate with participants at the other sites, students talked about the difficulty of doing so. The classroom environment with its cameras and microphones makes classroom communication challenging. To pose a question from a distant site (any site other than where the presenter is located) requires initiative, communication confidence and, sometimes, persistence. Despite its limitations, the distance learning network provided an avenue for sharing of university expertise and resources across the state. Students noted in their evaluations that commercial television watching is very passive, so it takes some adjustment to actively engage with a television monitor. As one student noted, "It is somewhat awkward, because you treat it like a TV instead of a two-way device, and it is hard to get comfortable talking to a TV." Another pointed out, "It is also a little socially uncomfortable, in that it is hard to know whose turn it is [to talk] or how to know when you can break in."

The greatest bonding and communication occurred in the rooms that had a boardroom arrangement. These roundtable formats enabled students and faculty to see each other equally and enhanced interaction. The traditional classroom styles (all chairs facing forward) had built-in boundaries—students looked at the backs of heads of those in front, making eye contact with each other difficult. This was especially problematic when a student responded to another student in the same room. In such situations, the individual would have to face forward and, in effect, address the camera rather than follow the more natural inclination to establish eye contact with the individual. This was necessary so that the camera could focus on the student speaking and the microphone could pick up his or her voice.

It was helpful when the site technicians paid attention and maintained tight close-ups of presenters; however, this did not always occur. The closer the camera can focus on the presenter, the greater the perceived eye contact between speaker and audience. This seemed to help increase presenter-participant interaction. When the camera backed off for a full body view, it seemed that students lost interest. Expert technicians can help facilitate the verbal interactions between students and presenters by following the interaction with the cameras. This process works best when the individual who wants to speak or ask a question identifies his or her site so the technician can quickly focus the camera. Frequently during the two-hour session, instructors would ask the technicians to create the split, or four-way screen, so all the sites could see themselves and feel part of the program.

THE COMPLEXITY OF COLLABORATION: WHAT DID NOT WORK IN PRACTICE AND WHY

Not really realizing how complex it might be to coordinate teaching goals, schedules, priorities, teaching methodologies, and values, I plunged headlong into this collaborative, confident in my teaching but concerned about my ability to operate the equipment and how I would come across on television.

During the first year of the course, it became clear that it was going to be very difficult coordinating activities and agreeing on course goals and assignments. I began to wonder if other collaborative distance learning efforts experienced similar challenges. Much to my personal and professional relief, I discovered that others had. In an extensive study of collaboration in distance education, Moran and Mugridge (1993a) articulate findings similar to what our collaborative experienced. In their research, they present an analysis of seven international distance learning collaborative case studies and observe that

> inter-institutional collaboration is an extremely difficult and complicated undertaking... [that is sometimes characterized by] common mistrust of teaching methods and academic standards elsewhere... lack of clarity in specifying the terms of an agreement [or in setting educational goals]; or the absence of real commitment on the part of one or more of the partners. (p. 4–5)

After reading these findings, I felt somewhat relieved to know that the struggles I had experienced had been encountered by others. That it was, indeed, a complex and difficult task to develop a coherent, pedagogically sound, and viable course among four educators. I knew that the four of us would not only have to enjoy working together but to work equally and have similar values and goals toward teaching. What I did not realize was how difficult that would be. I can now identify four major problems with our collaborative: 1) too many partners, 2) unequal commitment of partners, 3) lack of common course goals and objectives, and 4) challenge of the video/audio technology.

Too Many Partners

As observed by Moran and Mugridge (1993b) in their concluding chapter,

> Several contributors to this collection caution against bringing too many partners into the collaboration, at least in the early stages before it has established its own subculture and operational norms.... [the] level of comprehension of others' institutional culture is necessarily superficial when many partners are involved. (p. 154)

Too many people were involved in our collaborative. With four sites and four personalities, it was difficult to find a time to meet, and when we did, often one or more individuals would have something come up that prevented them from joining the group.

Adding a fifth site and facilitator at the last moment really complicated the collaborative. When an administrator at North Carolina State heard about this course, he insisted that a fifth distant site be added at the last minute (a free course). The facilitator at this site never became part of the instructional team. She saw her role as simply turning on the machines and taking attendance. Consequently, the participants at this site were frequently late returning from breaks, did not feel compelled to complete assignments, and were often reluctant to participate in class discussions. Increasing the number of instructors and site facilitators to five created serious difficulties. With this number involved, some of the technicians did not stay as active in the course as they would have if there had only been two or three sites.

Unequal Commitment of Partners

Everyone wants to teach well and be recognized for his or her teaching. In fact, teaching has been described as one of the most private things we do in public. When you add the pressure of three or four distant sites and three or four other instructors, this very personal thing becomes very public indeed. Thus, upon entering this team teaching collaborative, I was confident that my colleagues would feel the same pressure I was feeling and, in turn, commit the time and energy necessary to demonstrate their very best. I trusted the other instructors to be prompt, prepared, and above all, professional in their presentations. Furthermore, it was important that I trust the other three instructors to have a strong commitment to the course. However, as Moran and Mugridge (1993a) so aptly put it,

> Above all, successful cooperation depends on trust—
> between institutional partners, and among the individu-
> als involved.... It is easy neither to develop nor to sustain.
> The technical and human problems involved in the kind
> of collaboration discussed by contributors to this collec-
> tion are considerable; and they can easily lead to the
> breakdown of inter-institutional agreements. (p. 5)

A second problem was the lack of passion and zeal for environmental issues exhibited by two of the instructors. Although this was an environmental education course, only two of the instructors would classify themselves as environmentalists. As such, it is understandable that they would approach education about the environment with a passion and zeal not demonstrated by the other two instructors. The two environmentalists belonged to environmental organizations, read and published in environmental education journals, and, therefore, were able to bring current information to each class and to ask thoughtful and contemporary questions of guest speakers. Although being an environmental educator was not a necessary condition of the collaborative, a strong feeling about the issues raised during the course should have been.

An indication of the lack of priority one instructor placed on this course was evident by the fact that she seldom had speakers lined up in advance and consistently faxed needed information for the class sessions at the very last minute. This did not give instructors at the other sites time to review the material or even make multiple copies for their students. Perhaps the strongest evidence was when she announced one semester that she had inadvertently scheduled another class at the same time as this class and that she would start this class, go teach her other class, and return to our class at the end.

Lack of Common Course Goals and Objectives

Although it seems obvious that individuals working together should establish common goals and objectives, the obvious sometimes eludes us. We certainly had coordinated topics and knew who would teach what. However, as instructors, we did not really wrestle with or clarify the course goals and objectives. There was no common course syllabus and therefore no common assignments. Often assignments (reading and written reports) were made at the last minute and a surprise to instructors at distant sites.

Again, it is instructive to examine the results of other case studies. As Moran and Mugridge (1993b) report in their findings, it is essential to clarify roles and expectations. In their words,

> [the collaborative relationship] has a hard pragmatic edge
> ... and is based on a mutual set of understandings about
> the expected behavior of each partner.... The relation-
> ship[s] must constantly be reinforced by communication
> and compromise.... There needs to be clarity about ...
> the nature of the goal and means of reaching it, and about
> the respective roles of the partners. (pp. 155–156)

The Challenge of the Video/Audio Technology

The interactive video/audio medium did not fit my style of teaching. Although I consider myself a very good teacher, I am not a dynamic lecturer. I teach in a Socratic interactive manner, which was very difficult because, often, I had trouble hearing and seeing the participants. For me to feel comfortable with my students, I needed to be able to see and hear clearly their reactions to a degree not available with the technology. Again, the research literature proves instructive in this respect. In a national survey of 157 interactive television instructors, Mottet (2000) provides several implications as a result of his analysis. The first is that

> [instructors] need to be aware that the lack of student nonverbal responsiveness may not accurately reflect the quality of their instruction, but rather be a partial filtering-out effect of electronic mediation. Instructors need to understand that it may be impossible for them to replicate or control the responsiveness found in the traditional face to face classroom in the interactive television context . . . [and it should not affect] how they perceive their teaching effectiveness as distance teachers. (p. 162)

Working with others reduced some of the pressure of being on camera. I found that the collaborative provided an advantage for me in this area. Although I still struggled to hear and see over the distance learning network, I became comfortable using the system. Developing this comfort level would have taken much longer had this not been a collaborative effort. I suspect I would have viewed teaching on the distance learning system as highly intimidating had it not been for the security of sharing the stage with three other instructors that were also new to the system. Knowing the camera was not only on me but the other instructors as well certainly relieved some of the pressure of teaching on television.

The collaborative also allowed us to receive positive reinforcement from the other instructors and to ask questions about the quality of our presentations. While students can provide valuable input, colleagues can add a perspective that students cannot. For me, the fear of a lecture running short and having empty air time to fill was very real. However, knowing that if a lesson ran short the other instructors would quickly sense the need to fill the void and help out lessened that concern. Having other instructors on the team allowed us to model for students the importance of asking questions and establishing a dialogue among sites—another plus that would have taken much longer had this not been a collaborative effort.

LESSONS LEARNED AND
WHAT I WOULD DO DIFFERENTLY

I have learned that to do this right requires much more time and energy than any of us anticipated. Collaboration is hard work and very time-consuming. I have not ruled out rejoining the project after a one-year sabbatical. However, I plan to do so only after reaching an understanding with all the instructors that we are committed to putting in the necessary time and effort. This would particularly mean:

- Thorough planning with clear objectives and assignments for each class.

- Commitment from each instructor to have speakers and assignments correlated.

- Weekly meetings over the distance learning system or email to fine tune plans and coordinate the current week's lectures, activities, and assignments.

- Agreement to focus on capitalizing the fact that we are at different geographic regions and with different student populations. I think we can use this to our advantage in approaching our instructional design.

I have learned that most of the strategies we find useful in our face to face classrooms can also apply to team-taught distance learning classes. For instance, one of the major challenges for this course remains how to utilize and take advantage of the wide range of student backgrounds (graduate and undergraduate students, environmental studies and education majors). In face to face classrooms, it useful to develop major problem solving projects as a mission or goal for the whole class, and then assign students to work in groups to accomplish that goal. This kind of learning activity stimulates active involvement and commitment on the part of the students and simulates an authentic, real-world context. This instructional model could be used effectively in the environmental education collaborative. For instance, one year the mission might be to develop a public awareness campaign about the plight of nesting sea turtles. Each site would then be given an assignment that would contribute to the overall mission of the course unit. The public awareness campaign assignment could be crafted to capitalize on the diversity and strength of the students at that particular site. For example:

- NCS (graduate students in education): Prepare several grant proposals seeking funds for a conference for teachers and the general public.

- ECU (undergraduate education students): Develop activities for conference participants to help them understand the plight of nesting sea turtles.

- UNCW (environmental studies majors): Develop a series of science content lectures and posters to help conference participants understand the fragile nature of the sea turtles' life cycle and why they have been placed on the Endangered Species List.

- UNCC (in-service teachers): Prepare a teaching unit on the sea turtles and correlate parts of the unit with the state curriculum requirements. The sea turtle unit could include geography activities using longitude and latitude as well as math concepts such as the mean, median, and mode.

Having a major class project in common gives the class a mission and focus and the students a common goal. Each year the project could change to a salient environmental issue and continue to take advantage of the backgrounds and strengths of students' diversity. Each site would benefit from the collaborative learning process as well as the sharing of the completed products. Perhaps the final exam could be site presentations of each product. In addition, the sites could work together to host a joint conference related to the mission. This type of assignment is pedagogically and theoretically sound and reflects the current thinking in science education by providing:

- Authentic assessment

- Science that is personal and relevant to students' lives

- Situations in which students must construct meaning and participate actively in a teaching-learning environment

- Environments in which instructors are facilitators of learning rather than disseminators of knowledge

CONCLUSION

I have chosen to take a one-year sabbatical from the course and to reflect on the positive aspects as well as the challenges of this collaborative effort. I am a gregarious person and like working with others. I also like the challenge of experimenting with new technologies and I view teaching as a continual learning process. Additionally, issues in environmental education change rapidly, and it is difficult to stay current in all areas. Therefore, working with others—especially with experts from other campuses—is very valuable. I am confident that the other instructors also realize the need to redesign the course with an eye toward incorporating many of the methods we know work well in face to face instructional environments.

Participating in this collaborative has been a rewarding experience, both professionally and personally. Despite the complexity and challenges of this project, I have had the opportunity to develop valued professional relationships with other environment education specialists and science educators at the three institutions. Through our struggles with this course, we have all grown professionally; furthermore, we shared the complexities of collaboration and our instructional design of the course with colleagues at national and state conferences as well as coauthored refereed journal articles. Finally, it is in my reflection and analysis of this collaborative that I realized how much I learned and that I am willing to venture forth again.

REFERENCES

Comeaux, P. (1995). The impact of an interactive distance learning network on classroom communication. *Communication Education, 44* (4), 353–361.

Driver, R., Asoko, H., Leach, J., Mortimer, E., & Scott, P. (1994). Constructing scientific knowledge in the classroom. *Educational Researcher, 23* (7), 5–12.

Ehrlich, P. R. (1968). *The population bomb.* New York, NY: Ballantine Books.

Hammrich, P. L. (1997). What the science standards say: Implications for teacher education. *Journal of Science Teacher Education, 9* (3), 165–186.

McHenry, L., & Bozik, M. (1995). Communicating at a distance: A study of interaction in a distance education classroom. *Communication Education, 44* (4), 362–371.

Moran, L., & Mugridge, I. (1993a). Collaboration in distance education: An introduction. In L. Moran & I. Mugridge (Eds.), *Collaboration in distance education: International case studies* (pp. 1–11). New York, NY: Routledge.

Moran, L., & Mugridge, I. (1993b). Policies and trends in inter-institutional collaboration. In L. Moran & I. Mugridge (Eds.), *Collaboration in distance education: International case studies* (pp. 151–164). New York, NY: Routledge.

Mottet, T. P. (2000, April). Interactive television instructors' perceptions of students' nonverbal responsiveness and their influence on distance teaching. *Communication Education, 49* (2), 146–164.

Pedagogy and Process: Linking Two Diversity and Communication Courses Through Interactive Television

Deborah Brunson and Nina-Jo Moore

The purpose of this chapter is to chronicle the pedagogical practices used to link two diversity courses in communication studies via interactive television, and the collaborative process employed to successfully construct a positive learning environment for both students and teachers. When trying to decide on ways to create more interest in the classroom, it seems that we are turning more and more to new technologies. This collaborative project was undertaken by two professors from different yet similar campuses in the North Carolina state university system, the University of North Carolina, Wilmington (UNCW), and Appalachian State University (ASU). We designed the course to be networked class sessions, conducted through interactive television that would meet every other week, or seven times in the course of the semester. The courses at each site were not identical, but there were some strong similarities between them, since diversity was the general topic in both settings.

As instructors and team teachers, we found that the interactive television experience was an exemplary one for both the student group and for ourselves. We learned much about applying a collaborative learning model to a course team-taught through the distance learning technology. We therefore offer our experiences in this chapter because we believe they may be of interest to educators who wish to use alternative pedagogical practices with their classes.

RATIONALE

We frame collaborative learning within a social constructivist perspective. Based upon the work of such scholars as Berger and Luckmann (1966), Pearce (1989), and Schutz (1967), the social constructivist perspective examines the importance of unique and shared experiences in framing reality. We come to know through our shared inquiry. Knowledge is therefore not fixed but is interpretive in nature, and includes multiple perspectives. Penman (in Littlejohn, 1999) lists five assumptions that support social constructivism:

1) The communicative act is voluntary.

2) Knowledge is a social product.

3) Knowledge is contextual.

4) Theories create worlds (i.e., theories are not objective; they are developed through scholarly activity which is also a social creation).

5) Scholarship is value-laden. (p. 176)

Penman's assumptions suggest that humans are active participants in the creation of understanding. We frame our lives and our reality based upon our perspectives. These perspectives are developed through interaction with others within our various social groups including, family, religious groups, community activities, mass media, school, and the workplace. Even when we believe that we are purely objective, our objectivity is often based partially or wholly upon the group's collective agreement about some person, idea, value, judgment, or event.

Although we endorse and apply the social constructivist perspective, we also recognize the importance of providing a solid knowledge base (objectivity) from which students can explore and examine complex social issues and realities (subjectivity). Collaborative learning supported by the assumptions of social constructivism greatly alters the role of both teachers and learners.

> The teacher points out the effect of a student's frame of
> reference on his or her understanding of information and
> ultimately the role that culture plays in shaping everyone's
> frame of reference. Although knowledge is often discov-
> ered by objective methods, it is always known, to one
> degree or another, subjectively. (Fried, 1993, p. 126)

In addition to the scholarly research that suggests collaborative learning creates a strong positive environment for teaching and learning, we
decided that it would be a positive learning situation to combine periodic
and selected class sessions over the interactive audio/video network. Since
we attract students representative of similar populations (our two universities of the 16 in the state system have comparable backgrounds), we
believed that combining students from the two campuses would be a
learning experience for both groups. It was our belief that we, along with
our students, would learn more about diversity by sharing ideas, examples,
experiences, and questions with people outside of our own campus populations.

Another rationale for undertaking this project was to allow us to try a
project that was unique to our pedagogical experiences. We had both done
some work in the distance learning environment, yet neither of us had
taught using the interactive video conferencing network with another professor. The uniqueness was found in the fact that we were both teaching
two separate courses, one titled Diversity in Public Communication, the
other, Intercultural Communication. A look at each course description
and objectives will help the reader to better understand the uniqueness of
this project.

COURSE DESCRIPTIONS

Diversity in Public Communication

The UNCW course, Diversity in Public Communication, examines the
rhetorical appeals and strategies of individuals and groups whose voices
have not been equally heard and valued in our society. While Moore's
intercultural communication course is concerned primarily with building
specific relationships across cultures, the diversity course at UNCW takes
a broader approach by focusing upon public presentations that speak to
the unique experiences of various peoples.

The course is designed to introduce the voices of diversity by starting with experiences that may be less threatening to students and easier for them to understand (for example, women and the disabled). We begin by examining and defining the concept of diversity and the process of socialization. The course is then divided into five units where students study the symbolic expressions of various groups:

1) The voices of the disabled

2) The rhetoric of women

3) The speeches and rhetorical strategies of American Indians or Native Americans

4) African Americans

5) The rhetoric of Hispanics and Latinos

We look at public communication primarily through the speeches, essays, documentary, and feature films generated by or for these groups. Students also study and review several rhetorical criticism theories and methods in order to analyze the messages presented through these diverse voices. By midterm, each student is required to write a social identity paper. In it, the person explores how he or she came to know themselves and society through the socialization processes they experienced as a child and adolescent. In other words, the paper assignment requires that students respond to the following questions: What did you (the student) learn about gender, social class, religion, sexuality, or race from your parents, peers, family members, teachers, school, and mass media? How did these learnings adjust the perceptual lenses through which you see, experience, and understand your world?

The final course project involves selecting a rhetorical artifact (e.g., a speech, film, novel, Internet web site, series of newspaper articles), analyzing how the diversity message is communicated through it, and assessing the rhetorical appeal and effectiveness.

INTERCULTURAL COMMUNICATION

The course at Appalachian State University, Intercultural Communication, has been taught since 1992. The course provides students with the opportunity to learn more about diverse cultures they will encounter in the course of their lifetime. It is designed to study intercultural communication theories by way of practical experiences. This includes, but is not limited to, the study of communication between cultures in foreign countries, from other geographical regions of the United States, different racial groups, gender group differences, religious group differences, ethnic group differences, as well as subgroup differences (e.g., handicapped persons, senior citizens, homosexuals, etc.). In the past, guest speakers were invited to talk with students, but with this new model, the collaborative learning experience took the places of many of the guest speakers.

The course objectives are to have students become acquainted with specific communication aspects across many diverse cultures. In addition, the hope is that students will learn techniques to improve intercultural communication across diverse cultures. As part of the course, students choose a culture to which they do not belong and then research that culture for the semester. They are expected to demonstrate knowledge of various cultures by reporting (both orally and in writing) about the communication differences they discover about that chosen culture, and by applying the various intercultural communication theories to that same culture.

It is easy to see how these two courses are very different, yet they possess a common thread that allowed us to collaborate for this project. Since both classes deal with diversity of human beings, and how communication behaviors are affected by culture and socialization, the subject matter set up an excellent platform for the design of the collaborative aspect of the course. Because Moore uses the same text that Brunson uses for a different course, *Bridging Differences: Effective Intergroup Communication* (Gudykunst, 1998), she was more familiar with Moore's teaching materials than Moore was with Brunson's. Since Brunson made all materials she used available to Moore, this issue did not present many problems.

COURSE DEVELOPMENT:
THE PROCESS OF COLLABORATING

One full semester in advance, Brunson approached Moore with the idea of teaching in a collaborative fashion. It had been Brunson's hope to fully teach the course Diversity in Public Communication as a collaborative venture, but since that course is not offered in Moore's curriculum, we sought another way to work together. A natural relationship was found between our two separate courses, and we opted to do the collaborative sessions as part of those courses.

Moore was faced with some outside restrictions for assignments related to her course as it was part of a writing across the curriculum program (designed to meet writing needs of students, as well as accreditation requirements of having writing intensive courses) and part of a cross-disciplinary course (which means it has aspects from several other disciplines). The major project of writing a term paper in a three-step process could not be deleted, so Moore needed to maintain some of her regular course meeting time to teach the theories of Intercultural Communication, as well as to build on their semester-long projects.

Once we determined the common aspect of our courses, the course and schedule then needed to begin to come to fruition. Both campuses have excellent interactive video distance learning facilities; indeed, the University of North Carolina, Wilmington has been recognized as one of the premier (if not the premier) distance learning networks in the North Carolina system. However, scheduling the networked class sessions was challenging. Moore's department has some severe enrollment issues; they are over-enrolled and under-facilitated. The course needed to be fit into already very tight scheduling constraints, due to a paucity of classrooms available to the department. Brunson and her department administration waited until Moore's department had set their schedule, and then set Brunson's course for the same time as Moore's: 9:00 to 9:50 on Monday, Wednesday, and Friday.

The next step was to reserve the distance learning facilities on both campuses, which was easier said than done. Scheduling classes or sessions over the distance learning network is complex and must be done well in advance. Once the course schedule was set, Brunson turned the material over to the video lab administrators, who then reserved the times on both campuses (in the North Carolina system, one campus sets the course reservations). We then were ready to begin the planning of our collaborative sessions.

In the process of scheduling the course meetings, we discovered that the two universities' academic calendars were slightly different. UNCW's spring break is held one week earlier than Appalachian State University's, a problem with which we easily dealt. In addition, both schools have two days off surrounding Easter weekend; however, University of North Carolina, Wilmington's are the Thursday and Friday before the weekend,

Appalachian State's are the Monday and Tuesday after. Our plan was to meet every other Friday, and that Friday was part of the schedule. We rectified that by deciding to meet the Wednesday prior to that weekend. We were also scheduled to meet on the same Friday as our regional professional association (Southern States Communication Association). We were able to work around that also, and our schedule was finally set.

Once it had been determined when we would meet, we then determined how we would cover topics using a collaborative learning approach. After some general discussions by both phone and email, we decided that we would discuss, in between the course meetings, what we had covered in our classes, what had caught our attention, anything we thought might go over well as a good springboard for discussions about diversity and communication, and anything else that might work for our collaborative experiences.

INTERACTIVE TELEVISION: DESCRIPTION OF CLASSROOM SITES

The physical setting of the two classrooms was different, although there were some commonalities. The UNCW distance learning classroom is a fairly large, comfortable area with three long tables for participants anchored to a carpeted floor. There is seating for nine at each table, and the swivel chairs are anchored to the tables. Four cameras operate in the room. Two instructor cameras are mounted from the ceiling in the back and follow the presenter, and one student camera is mounted from the ceiling in the front of the room to capture images of participants. A documents camera is recessed in the ceiling above the desk on the raised platform in the front to get shots of any writing, overheads, or other images placed on the desk's whiteboard. All cameras have pan-tilt capability as well as zoom features for close-ups and long shots.

There are three television monitors, two mounted from the ceiling in either corner at the front, and one monitor raised and mounted on the back wall. The instructor's microphone is a lapel or lavalier device that attaches to the presenter's shirt or blouse and affords mobility throughout the room. In contrast, students had to speak to the Appalachian State classroom through tabletop microphones—five on each table—which limited their mobility.

A large desk sits on the raised platform in the front of the room for the teacher or presenter's use. Two small monitors are mounted into the desk facing the presenter. One screen shows incoming images from the remote site, and the second screen allows the teacher to monitor images being transmitted from her classroom to the linked location. The whiteboard is mounted on the top of the desk and used to write comments and key points, to show overhead transparencies, or to display other visual images. A computer also sits on the instructor's desk. It is capable of launching and displaying files over the network through such standard software programs as Windows 98 and PowerPoint. A scan converter allows any computer desktop application to be transmitted via the network. Rounding out the classroom technology is a ceiling-mounted LCD projector with an eight-foot screen capable of showing any video or still image to participants.

The Appalachian State University distance learning classroom is a small room, at least for the amount of tables it holds. There are four rows of three tables, holding six students per table. The tables are placed very closely together and are pushed against one of the side walls of the classroom; students need to squeeze into each row to get to a seat. In the classroom, there are four cameras mounted on the ceiling (which is about ten feet high) which can capture all activities of the classroom, including panning the room and zooming in on the speaker. There are four monitors in the classroom, one in each of the four corners. The microphone system provides one microphone for every two seats at the tables and is voice activated (and as we also learned, noise activated). The teacher's microphone is also a lavalier style, similar to the instructor's equipment at UNCW. We have access to other video and audio equipment through this classroom, such as the ability to show videos, overheads, and PowerPoint presentations. Also included are a whiteboard and an overhead projector. With the exception of the layout of the room, the equipment is similar in design and capabilities to UNCW's system.

Given these differences, we realized that we needed to have a trial run with the equipment. During the week prior to our first collaborative meeting, we did a short video conference in the distance learning classroom. The equipment seemed to work well, yet we also had many questions about the viability of the classroom situation. The Appalachian State classroom is designed to hold 24 students, and even that would be cramped. Moore's class had 28 students, so bringing in extra chairs would be necessary. Additionally, since ASU's classroom was set up conference style with tables, the students who walked in late would be a major disruption to the class meeting if they needed to climb over other students to get to an available seat. There were fewer questions about these logistical aspects at UNCW since the distance learning classroom was large enough to hold the class comfortably, and the physical set up (being a tiered classroom) was much more flexible than the ASU classroom.

THE COLLABORATIVE ASPECT OF THE COURSE

We believed we had a unique model with this course design. We knew we were not the first to teach collaboratively in a distance learning situation. The uniqueness of it was two separate courses that were team-taught every other Friday.

A major concern of instructors in diversity or intercultural communication courses is to provide a positive, supportive environment where students may explore such controversial issues as prejudice, ethnocentrism, multiculturalism, racism, and sexism. In our typical, contained classrooms, we both spend a considerable amount of time (usually the first part of the semester) orienting the students to the course, and to the importance of collaborative learning.

Building trust between teacher and student as well as among the students themselves is essential in order to advance learning and personal growth. Notes Frederick (1995), "A genuine 'intercultural' education only begins to happen when students of different cultures, classes, ethnicities, ages, sex, and learning styles interact with each other in classrooms and living units" (p. 83). With this philosophy in mind, we set out to design learning experiences where our students could speak openly to each other across the networked classrooms about their backgrounds, values, and perspectives. We also wanted them to feel that the course collaboration would allow space for growth and change.

We approached every networked session asking, How can this class stimulate discussion and interchange across the classrooms? Since we met in the interactive video/audio classrooms two times per month for 50-minute sessions, our focus was not upon theory input through the traditional lecture mode. We wanted these networked sessions to be filled with discussion among the students and our roles to be moderators and facilitators of that process.

Our design to ensure a collaborative process involved checking in with each other typically through email or telephone at least seven to ten days before our next conference to find out where we were content-wise in our respective courses. We would then brainstorm lesson themes and procedures. Once we finalized our design for the upcoming networked class session, we would each share the plan with our students in order to prepare them for our video meeting. After completing the session, we would usually email each other that day, and follow up with a debriefing on the day's activities by telephone later in the week.

For instance, in our first session we were concerned about establishing an open atmosphere where students would feel comfortable speaking. We also were sensitive to the need for our students to get oriented to the technology. They needed to understand the brief delay between sites when speaking, so as not to overlap or speak over those at the other site. Although the technicians at each site were professional and very capable of operating their systems, technology is not a perfect science. There were times when we had to adjust to echoes, volume difficulties, and problems feeding video segments from films across the networked classrooms.

In order to facilitate an educational experience for our students, the topic we chose for our first meeting focused on ethnic identity and ethnic salience. We used this as an introductory activity to allow the students to acclimate themselves to the aspect of learning how to discuss topics through this interactive audio/video medium. Gudykunst (1998) defines ethnic identity to be the part of us that identifies with our ethnic backgrounds and ethnic salience as "the extent to which our ethnicities are an important part of our self-concept in a specific situation" (p. 79). Since both courses challenge students to know who they are according to their ethnic and racial backgrounds, this was an excellent place to begin the journey of the collaborative meetings of the two classes.

It is always interesting to professors who teach in the areas of cultural diversity to find out how many students do not know their ethnic identities, but the more salient issue to most students is when they realize that their ethnic identity really does not have much impact on how they interact with others. This is an aspect of the American culture, however, since we are now becoming a more homogeneous society. Two hundred years ago, most Americans did identify with their ethnic background. This topic set the perfect stage to begin a semester's journey into how culture and diversity affect our communication across cultures.

A second activity asked students to respond to the question, When will we (the United States) have a female president? This question usually sparks spirited debate and highlights how socialization can often affect the way we experience culture, expectations, and stereotypes. This discussion often expands to include reflection upon when the United States will have its first nonwhite president, first non-Christian president, and first openly disabled president. We noted that Franklin D. Roosevelt was disabled and in a wheelchair, but that his disability was not common knowledge during his presidency. We pose the question, How and why would the issue of a physically disabled president be addressed today?

We feel strongly that using such questions as discussion triggers encourages students to combine their personal experiences with related course readings and concepts covered within their respective classes. The cross pollination of perspectives and ideas promote the community-building process called for by Gudykunst (1998): "Communities are not made up of the like-minded; different types of people, ideas, and emotions must be present in a community. Exclusivity is the enemy of community" (p. 305). In sessions two, four, and seven, our classes had common readings to refer to as we shared ideas and opinions. Because the courses had different content and objectives, having common materials greatly facilitated the collaborative spirit among the sites. In fact, in their survey responses submitted to the instructors during the middle and end of the semester, many participants felt that the common readings were a useful way to promote dialogue across the classes.

REFLECTIONS ON COLLABORATING VIA INTERACTIVE TELEVISION

Interacting Together

Not all collaborative processes between professors have been positive ones. This was not the case for us, although there certainly were times when both felt constrained by the fact that we were neither on the same campus where daily interactions are easier to partake in, nor were our schedules such that we had regular contact. We did communicate regularly by email and telephone, checking in with each other and discussing the upcoming joint class activities. This helped smooth what can be an otherwise difficult process. Our personalities are flexible enough to go with the flow of whatever is happening, another positive aspect of this process.

The Distance Learning Aspects

One concern of this experiment in collaborative teaching was influenced by the use of an interactive audio/video network to accomplish the goal. Much research exists in the area of how important interaction within the classroom is if educational goals are to be met. McHenry and Bozik (1995) report that the "literature reveals that creating intentional interaction will be essential to student learning. Studies of traditional classrooms have shown a connection between classroom interaction and student learning and attitude" (p. 362). Knowing this, we set about developing a course that created an environment where the students would feel comfortable participating. As seen in the discussion about how we developed the course, we made it our mission to create an open learning environment. We both felt it important to have the students be interactive, to learn about the materials we were teaching, as well as from each other, and we set about this with the activity we used for our first course meeting.

The Uniqueness of Our Project

Since our model for the project was different than other distance learning models, where there is a teacher in one place and the students are spread out among many satellite campuses, we felt that we probably would be able to bypass some of the problems researchers have consistently found with that model of distance learning courses. For example, Kruh and Murphy (1990) report, "Quality distant education is dependent upon the interaction and participation of the learners, similarly as in traditional face to face instruction. It is essential that the distant educator purposefully designs this essential ingredient into the instructional program" (p. 6). Since we were both present during these class meetings, we did not suffer the problem of having only one facilitator that may or may not be able to answer questions or direct interactions. Garrison (1990) sums up best what we were able to avoid by the model we chose when he said that " . . . education, whether it be at a distance or not, is dependent on two-way communication" (p. 13). Garrison (1990) also observes that simply accessing information is not enough for education to take place; students need to interact with the materials in order to learn effectively. Our model allowed for that interaction to take place, and thus, our students found it to be a positive learning experience. On the campus of Appalachian State University, the director of the distance learning program continually remarked about how much the two classes were willing to discuss topics and issues. If a teacher had not been present in both places, that would probably have not been as true.

As McHenry and Bozik (1995) discovered, we would agree that this technological aspect of the course influenced the students' perceptions, that they adapted fairly well to the technology, and that the large majority of the group viewed it positively. Only one student commented on not really enjoying this aspect of the course and indicated a preference to stay in the classroom and learn "the regular way." The only negative substantive comment we received frequently (comments other than "I did not like to walk across campus to the distance learning lab—especially when it rained") was about the technological difficulties we sometimes experienced, though those that made these comments still rated the experience very highly.

McHenry and Bozik (1995) also confirmed the position that teaching in a distance learning setting does take skill and adaptation by the teacher. We would agree with that position, but would also comment that teaching is a profession of flexibility, and all teachers probably have to be flexible about one thing or another. Our flexibility was just a part of the natural teaching process; we adapted, adjusted, and survived a very positive teaching experience for both of us, and our students' learning has been enhanced by this encounter with distance and collaborative learning.

One positive outcome of our experimenting with this model is that our students had direct access to a professor. Most criticisms of distance learning courses are that the students do not have direct daily (or triweekly or biweekly) access to their professor. This was not so for our class. If there were questions, students would ask and one of us would answer. We would take care of clarifying issues at the next collaborative meeting or in our own individual classrooms. One particularly poignant example was when one of Moore's students asked, "I notice Dr. Brunson uses the terminology 'people of color' when referring to minorities within the United States, yet you use Blacks, Latinos, Asian descent. What is the difference and why?" Knowing part of the reasons why, but not the full answer, Moore asked Brunson about it, received some reasons, and was able to go back to her class and explain differences in language choices when discussing diversity and cultural differences. Both students and professors learned from this example.

REFLECTIONS AND CONCLUDING THOUGHTS

What we set out to do was most assuredly accomplished—to supply our students with a collaborative learning experience. We framed our definition of collaborative learning on the concepts of shared inquiry and social constructivism. That our project had students from two different campuses discussing issues and topics together was a unique feature in that we were teaching two separate courses. We began with the thought that both of our classes would benefit from the sharing of ideas, opinions, beliefs, examples, and perspectives that were unique to themselves and applicable to the course materials they were covering as a part of meeting our separate course objectives. We believe, at least from the students' evaluations, as well as our own, that we met our goal for the project.

That said, we would point out that the project had a few shortcomings, but most were minor. What the students recognized most were the technological difficulties that sometimes occurred. They noticed those because they wanted to converse with each other and hear what the other members had to say, and when the signal was lost or the audio could not be heard for even a short period of time, it frustrated them in their learning process. This would affirm the definition of shared inquiry. The shared inquiry was lost when they could not communicate because of a breakdown in the technology. Interestingly enough, the students seemed to notice it more than the instructors did.

Another issue to consider is the aspect of the two different courses. We saw the relationship between the two, and the students seemed to also, but would they have benefited more by having two classes that were labeled as the same courses? Some of the students seemed to think that might have been more advantageous. We believed that would change the nature of what we were doing. While the ASU students benefited by narrowing the focus for these discussions to look at more subcultural issues, the UNCW students benefited by expanding their focus to include issues outside the parameters of diversity issues within the United States. That factor, at least, allowed the discussion to go in many different directions, from ethnic diversity to racial differences, from gender differences to age group differences. Also, if these two classes had been exactly the same, this model would not have been as unique. Different sections of the same courses are meeting all over the country, albeit with the regular model of distance learning, and our project allowed us to look at something new and different.

To undertake a similar project, we offer some advice to make it as simple and rewarding as possible:

- Plan early, at least two semesters in advance, if possible. More lead time would have allowed us to make better use of collaborating together long before we actually began the course.

- Develop assignments that cause students to be thinking in advance of the actual sessions. For example, we discovered from the midterm feedback that students would have liked the idea of assigning a movie about cultural diversity for both groups to watch in their respective settings and then coming together to discuss their reactions to the movie.

- Find some collaborative reading materials outside of the regular textbook material. We assigned readings of one of two articles on teaching children about diversity and how people respond to culturally diverse populations. It resulted in one of the best networked class sessions of the semester.

- If possible, the instructors should have a face to face meeting to talk about the course and their expectations as team teachers for this learning experience. Although we did not meet in person during the semester, we knew each other previously through the state communication association and had met on several occasions. Having a prior professional relationship was a major benefit to the collaborative process, particularly since we were teaching different courses.

Would we recommend that our colleagues try a similar project? We answer that question with a resounding "Yes!" It allowed us to broaden our teaching horizons, to think outside the box, and we are richer for the experience. When professors are learning along with their students, only positive outcomes can be accomplished for both.

REFERENCES

Berger, P. L., & Luckmann, T. (1966). *The social construction of reality: A treatise in the sociology of knowledge.* New York, NY: Doubleday.

Eaves, M. (1997). Collaboration takes more than e-mail. *The Journal of Electronic Publishing, 3* (2) [Online]. Available: http://www.press.umich.edu/jep/03-02/blake.html

Frederick, P. (1995, Summer). Walking on eggs: Mastering the dreaded diversity discussion. *College Teaching, 43* (3), 83–92.

Fried, J. (1993, Fall). Bridging emotion and intellect. *College Teaching, 41* (3), 123–128.

Garrison, D. R. (1990). An analysis and evaluation of audio teleconferencing to facilitate education at a distance. *The American Journal of Distance Education, 4,* 13–24.

Gudykunst, W. B. (1998). *Bridging differences: Effective intergroup communication* (3rd ed.). Thousand Oaks, CA: Sage.

Kruh, J., & Murphy, K. (1990). *Interaction in teleconferencing: The key to quality instruction.* Paper presented at the Annual Rural and Small Schools Conference, Manhattan, KS. (ERIC Document Reproduction Service No. ED 329 418)

Littlejohn, S. W. (1999). *Theories of human communication* (6th ed.). Belmont, CA: Wadsworth.

McHenry, L., & Bozik, M. (1995). Communicating at a distance: A study of interaction in a distance learning classroom. *Communication Education, 44* (4), 362–371.

Pearce, W. B. (1989). *Communication and the human condition.* Carbondale, IL: Southern Illinois University Press.

Schutz, A. (1967). *The phenomenology of the social world* [G. Walsh & F. Lehnert, Trans.]. Evanston, IL: Northwestern University Press.

Camera Presentation Perspectives and Techniques in an Interactive Audio/Video Instructional Environment: A Rhetorical Perspective

Frank P. Trimble

As a youngster, I recall my father's completion of a correspondence course in mechanical drawing as he advanced his career as a tool and die maker. I was fascinated by the blue books that would arrive by mail every few weeks, the sleek metal drafting tools he used, and the fact that he had homework, too. What I could not comprehend at the time was how he was able, and motivated, to study and learn without the benefit of a teacher nearby.

While distance education has certainly evolved, the challenges faced by both instructor and student have remained relatively unchanged. Ultimately, those engaged in the process strive for results identical to those achieved via face to face instruction. While technological advances no doubt help the cause, it is our effective use of such technology as instructors, facilitators, and students that proves most beneficial.

Based on my background and primary interests as related to distance education, this chapter deals exclusively with interactive audio/video instruction (IAVI, sometimes referred to in academic literature as interactive television, ITV). Practice and research to date in this particular mode of instruction reveal a number of obstacles and challenges for participants, including an intimidation factor sometimes caused by the high technology environment; sending, receiving, and evaluating nonverbal signals; establishing and nurturing rapport with audience members; and psychologically connecting with those physically removed from the presenter and immediate audience.

A review of literature completed by Schlosser and Anderson (1993) indicates that the two-way synchronous, aural, and visual communication made possible by the microphones and cameras of IAVI represent a new paradigm of distance education. This new model attempts to offer to the distance student an experience as much like that of traditional, face to face instruction as possible. While IAVI technology may hold such promise, others are not so readily convinced of its effectiveness in operation.

Swartz and Biggs (1999) note both the physical and emotional distance between IAVI participants. These authors, reflecting on Stoll (1996), quote C. S. Lewis (1955) in recounting that joy is not a concept but an experience which must be lived. They further posit that, to Stoll (1996), education is like joy, which cannot happen over a speaker, a television, or a computer screen. Education comes to children when they experience warmth, human interaction, and the thrill of discovery. Naturally, these sentiments do not bode well for IAVI.

Hackman and Walker (1990) find a midground in discovering characteristics and strategies resulting in effective IAVI processes. According to these scholars, instructors who use techniques for enhancing social presence, such as encouraging involvement, offering individual feedback, and promoting a relationship with off-campus students, are viewed more favorably. It appears that satisfying televised courses are taught by instructors who use humor, ask questions, involve students, praise student contributions, and maintain a relaxed, expressive nonverbal demeanor.

McHenry and Bozik (1995) offer a list of constructive questions to guide further investigation. These inquiries include:

- How do the communication variables such as nonverbal communication and language change in this mediated setting?

- How can we encourage the proper use of equipment?

- What kind of training should be provided to teachers and students?

- Who should provide it? (p. 370)

Overall, it seems that IAVI clearly holds promise. However, participation is not a matter of simply transferring traditional classroom pedagogy to this technology-rich educational platform. Instead, the primary charge to instructors, particularly in terms of nonverbal behavior, is to deliver the constructive signals necessary to generate rapport with off-site students physically removed from the presenter and immediate audience. It seems apparent that a level of comfort, poise, and informed mastery of techniques regarding camera use are needed to accomplish such goals. Thus, I argue that comprehending the rhetorical impact of camera use and planning strategies for use in interactive audio/video instructional environments are paramount for success. To that end, this chapter will focus primarily on camera presentation philosophies. Specifically, how IAVI video images impact an audience, how presenters may plan and manipulate such images, and the resulting dividends with regard to teaching effectiveness. Drawing from the domain of performance studies and media presentation, I will encourage IAVI teachers to explore the unique challenges of conceptualizing, crafting, and executing messages over an IAVI system and the power of the camera lens to effectively carry those messages to distant students.

MY INTRODUCTION TO INTERACTIVE AUDIO/VIDEO INSTRUCTION

My appointment as department chair in July 1994 occurred in the midst of a major pedagogical development at my institution; namely, the university's commitment to an instructional delivery system generically termed "distance education." As such, in addition to my newly inherited curriculum assessment and enhancement responsibilities regarding our program's bachelor of arts degree, I was now also charged with charting our unit's participation in this new teaching mode. The University of North Carolina, Wilmington, perhaps like most universities, continues to negotiate this teaching practice with various criteria in mind, including available resources; the availability of full degree programs versus individual classes, serving degree-seeking versus extended education students; the school's reputation in academic circles given the correspondence nature of this educational genre; and market pressures as we compete, like it or not, with various high-profile, distance-only, degree-granting entities.

Complicating the process on our campus (and, again, perhaps on yours as well) was the fact that, shortly after distance education of the interactive audio/video variety arrived at our institution, computer online education of this nature took us by storm. As a result, conversations concerning distance education must now be qualified: "Excuse me, but are you referring to audio/video, computer online, or both?"

Fortunately, at this same time one of my colleagues was in the process of launching what has become a research passion—investigating the interpersonal dynamics and success of teaching and learning in distance environments. Her work began with scrutiny of classes conducted via IAVI. Our university is fortunate to have two classrooms equipped in such a manner, so she was able to conduct initial investigations in our own backyard. In response to her invitation, I attended a few sessions and was intrigued with the process, not only from a pedagogical perspective but also as a performance act caught, in my estimation, somewhere between a news broadcast and feature film. That is, I was fascinated by the camera's impact on what I believed to be the success or failure of a given instructional moment. The use of camera, at times left to the technician's discretion, at times adjusted according to an instructor's request, clearly shaped the product delivered to the students present with the teacher and, I suspected, those at other sites. In addition, the skill level, experience, and video style of operators at the other location(s) significantly affected the visual and aural signals reaching those at home base.

Shortly thereafter, my pioneering colleague developed and launched a course, now a permanent curriculum offering, titled Training and Development. With an enrollment of on-campus students, this innovative class is taught using both of our university's IAVI classrooms. At times, these individuals also connect live with guest speakers broadcasting from off-campus locations. As a result, the course addresses two concurrent instructional goals. Students are both learning to design and implement effective communication workshops and professional meetings, as well as to deliver this information over an interactive audio/video conferencing system, akin to those they may use in higher education and corporate environments.

Given my response to initial observations of activity in such venues, subsequent conversations, and my background in performance studies, stage and camera acting, and directing, I was asked to assist with the orientation phase of this class. My charge—to acclimate participants to the technology at their disposal, the possibilities and pitfalls of such equipment, the importance of collaboration and effective communication with technicians (both on- and off-site) as teaching partners, and the general influence of camera use for those physically present with an instructor and those at other sites. In addition to training sessions for student participants, I have since designed and conducted numerous workshops for faculty planning to teach in an IAVI environment, quite often for the first time.

Since my initial observations a few years ago, technology has advanced, particularly in terms of microphones enabling improved sound quality and allowing simultaneous conversation. However, the basics of camera operation and, for presenters, camera presence, remain exciting challenges for those communicating in this manner. Beyond comfort level (in and of itself a major component for success), comprehending the rhetorical impact of camera use and planning strategies for such use are paramount in this form of distance education. Like a stage or screen director, an instructor is well served by preproduction planning, a clear system of communication with the production team, accepting and applying advice offered by technicians and, above all else, rehearsal.

DESCRIPTION OF AN IAVI ENVIRONMENT

To begin, I would first like to demystify the IAVI environment, as did Dorothy in *The Wizard of Oz* as she pulled back the curtain to reveal the hidden technology as well as the equipment in full view. During orientation workshops, I have found that, while technicians may at first be somewhat reluctant to share their expertise (believing it is common knowledge), they soon realize their value in the larger educational process, are buoyed by participant questions, and are pleased with their ability to fully address these inquiries.

For those new to a typical IAVI environment, I offer this general description and common equipment inventory:

- Two cameras located in the back of the room that record the presenter, operated by remote from a production room. These cameras can tilt (up/down), pan (left/right), and zoom to capture various renditions of the presenter. Quite often, one camera is dedicated to a long or wide shot, while the other is used for medium (waist up), portrait (head and shoulders), or, on rare occasion, close-ups.

- Two cameras mounted in front to track the audience with features similar to those noted above for the presenter's cameras.

- Several video monitors in back so the presenter may see the off-site audience(s), or an off-site facilitator (standing in the front of his or her IAVI room) may view the presenter and audience members at other sites.

- Several video monitors in front so the on-site audience may view the off-site audience(s), or the off-site audience(s) may view the presenter and on-site audience.

- A computer fully integrated into the system, allowing the projection of images from various sources (PowerPoint, word processing text, graphics, web material) through an LCD data projector (for the benefit of the on-site audience) or direct transmission through one or more video monitors (for the benefit of the on-site and off-site audience(s)).

- Voice-activated microphones to facilitate conversation.

- At least one technician at each site to control the equipment and mix outgoing and incoming signals.

- Video monitors may also be used in numerous combinations to display data, graphics, video, or images on a marker board.

- An overhead camera to capture images placed beneath, for instance, prepared text or graphics (in essence replacing an overhead projector) or those written on a marker board.

THE IAVI AUDIENCE

One challenge of working in an IAVI domain comes in referring to the audience members located at sites other than the presenter's. Descriptors for such populations seem to relegate these groups to disadvantaged or second-class citizens. Whether a remote, secondary, off-site, or simply distant audience, language of this nature, while somewhat derogatory on face value, may actually serve a viable purpose. In the end, such labels remind us that participants at such locations are, at best, still receiving the presenter's message in a flat and (barring an extremely widescreen monitor) smaller than life nature. The same is true with regard to the presenter's view of these audience members. While a variety of productive interactive discussion techniques may generate heated dialogue among members of all audiences independent of the number of sites simultaneously engaged, the physical realities of dimension and presence cannot and should not be denied.

While on-site consumers in an IAVI domain view a presentation in the usual three-dimensional manner, those off-site must process the information in a two-dimensional world. Therefore, the presenter's (technician's, producer's) use of cameras, live-mix editing decisions, and use of special effects (e.g., a dissolve from the presenter to a projected or computer graphic) can significantly affect the experience for all parties involved. In sum, in addition to all factors that enhance pedagogy in traditional contexts, an instructor's skill in utilizing technology while teaching in an IAVI venue may also have a substantial impact on teaching effectiveness.

To that end, I encourage such presenters to consider the use of cameras and peripherals (microphones, data projectors, computer-generated images, video inserts, etc.) as tools in their production of a live documentary for off-site audiences. In addition, the response to this process by the on-site audience should also be acknowledged. A given population of students in our department's Training and Development course often includes those with academic and field experience in public speaking, broadcast journalism, on-camera performance, and organizational communication. This collective knowledge can go a long way toward exploring potential point of view shifts and subsequent perspective changes both on- and off-site audiences may experience via this mode of instruction. A generic orientation to the new world is always in order for a distance education class, regardless of specific course content.

IAVI AND POINT OF VIEW

Beyond a general physical description, the next concept worthy of our attention as IAVI practitioners is that of point-of-view (POV). Depending on the context, this term may describe a variety of phenomena. In performance studies, POV involves the physical and emotional relationship between a performer and his or her text, a performance and the audience, or the literary characters with respect to one another or the plot's events (Yordon, 2002). In television/film production, POV defines camera placement, manipulation, and the resulting composition of single frames or a sequence of shots (searching for a source). Ultimately, these decisions may reflect the same elements of POV noted for performance studies.

Explorations of POV within IAVI cover conceptual and practical territory. However, in both cases, the focus remains the proactive use of cameras (instigated by presenter and/or technician) as well as accidental implementation and the related consequences on participant behavior and learning. I find framing the experience in feature film to be of value. Participants are readily able to reflect on the ways in which overt, aesthetic cinematography (camera angles, editing, special effects) and audio features (musical accompaniment) heighten the experience of viewing a film on the wide screen. They also acknowledge that such choices are made, applied, and often prove quite successful in generating emotional responses among viewers. Through grand examples, the notion of such features on the modest scale of an IAVI production generally becomes clear.

CAMERA USE AND POINT OF VIEW

The next order of business with regard to an IAVI orientation involves the concepts of what cameras (and microphones) in this environment may do for us and to us. Such a foundation results in noting three primary camera perspectives and the resulting influence on POV. It is, of course, a common practice to videotape presentations in a traditional single site venue (in which all audience members are physically present with the orator) for the purpose of self-critique. For this same purpose, I encourage IAVI presenters to screen recorded sessions. The technology in place easily allows for such videotaping and, most significantly, the presenter is able to see and critique a finished broadcast, complete with editing decisions (i.e., what off-site audience members experience, stimuli affecting their POV) and the influence of the finished production (beyond message content).

Presenter-Camera Relationships

In terms of IAVI technology and the issues most pertinent to participants, I cite these three main presenter-camera relationships:

- Camera as third party observer

- Camera as *a* listener

- Camera as *the* listener

Such relationships shift, not only from one presentation to the next, but from one segment of a presentation to the next, and, in some cases, from moment to moment. IAVI presenters must be aware of their instructional and rhetorical goals at any given time, determine the preferred presenter-camera relationship in response to those conditions and objectives, and then subsequently select and enact constructive behaviors.

Camera as third-party observer. Treat the camera as a nonentity. That is, deliver your message as you would in the absence of technology. The range of lateral movement may be a factor, though, given the camera's ability to pan left and right. In general, however, ignore the lens as much as possible, but do not avoid the camera by glancing unnaturally or rapidly across its field. Rather, treat the camera as a typical member of the on-site audience. At times, such an orientation may be most appropriate when your goals relate solely to the audience present and those removed are simply asked to observe. However, speakers sometimes ignore the camera (and thus the off-site audience(s)) without realizing their behavior and its negative impact. Naturally, those in the off-site audience(s) have experienced the alienation firsthand. During the self-critique process, videotape may allow the speaker to also experience the distance caused when the camera lens is ignored and plan to adjust future presentations accordingly.

Camera as a listener. Under these circumstances, treat members of your immediate audience and the camera(s) equally. In essence, execute direct one-on-one contact with the camera lens in a manner similar to your direct focus to members of the on-site audience. In general, linger a bit longer when gazing into a camera lens than when looking directly at any one individual in the on-site audience. Since focus into the camera is time potentially spent with all off-site audience members, this increased duration will help individuals in those groups stay involved. Audience members physically present tend to feel connected not only when a speaker looks directly at them, but also as they observe such contact between the speaker and others present. A presenter is not apt to build rapport with off-site audience members through even quality contact with the immediate audience: "It appears the speaker really cares about the people there, but why won't she spend time (or more time, or more quality time) with us?"

Camera as the listener. This presentation paradigm shifts to a news anchor or television journalist oriented broadcast with the inherent exclusive attention to the off-site audience, though you need not remain static. Depending on the equipment's capabilities and the technician's skill, you may still move laterally (within reason) when speaking solely to the camera(s). While the on-site audience may be considered in terms of message content and style, this group is ignored with respect to delivery, as all focus is directed toward the camera and, therefore, the off-site audience(s). Members of this remote audience become the primary receivers as you send a message to the masses (i.e., come right into their "living rooms"). I am often intrigued by widely broadcast shows (the Academy Awards, the Tony Awards, etc.) and the manner in which presenters and/or directors of these programs deal with the combination of a substantial on-site audience physically present in the auditorium and substantial off-site audience. Whether by direction or personal choice, some presenters seem most comfortable exclusively addressing the home viewer via the camera. Others combine live discussions with the immediate audience as well as those at home. While other verbal and nonverbal elements certainly come into play simultaneously, the dynamic of a given moment is clearly shaped by how the camera is addressed; i.e., as third party observer, as *a* listener, or as *the* listener.

TEACHING IMPLICATIONS OF IAVI

Presentations

Those communicating via IAVI may be tempted to conduct business as usual—to deny the presence of the technology in an effort to maintain current pedagogical design: "I will not allow the cameras and the fact that my entire audience is not physically present affect my teaching!" While this sentiment may be commendable, most will soon face the realization that, like it or not, cameras, monitors, video projectors, voice-activated microphones, etc. will affect their effectiveness. So, embrace the technology and make it serve you. View time on the network as an opportunity for students to learn more about the mechanics of this communication mode along with course content.

For IAVI presenters and audience members alike, it is imperative to acknowledge the following from the outset:

- IAVI will require some additional work.

- At first, the added stimuli may threaten to overwhelm you. For example, hands raised in your three-dimensional world and those appearing in quadrants on monitors can, initially, pose a challenge.

- Harness the power of technology, but do not feel compelled to use it each and every moment. The star of the show should always remain your content, and the basics of sound delivery, with some minor modifications, should remain your strongest feature. Do not spend the majority of your time playing with the toys.

- This can be fun! A refreshing change of pace from the everyday routine for everyone, so enjoy this chance to broaden your own experiences as a presenter and student.

Fielding Questions

A significant challenge of teaching across an IAVI platform is handling questions from audience members. From the outset, it is wise to practice the process generically to discover these obstacles. Among them could be potential audio or video delay, depending on the nature of the technology employed. Groups may consider creating network discussion guidelines, for example, raising hands and not speaking until recognized by the presenter, since multiple, simultaneous voices can overload the system and result in garbled audio. Perhaps all parties can agree that a presenter will entertain a question from various audiences and sites in rotation. While we may not always be able to control these conditions, such guidelines may at least enhance classroom interactions, encouraging students to explore their creation when possible.

The formal practice of handling questions during standard public presentations or interviews are integral to the success of a question/answer session conducted during IAVI. Standard techniques are essential, for instance, in repeating, paraphrasing, or incorporating each question into your response to ensure accuracy. With regard to eye contact, focus, and use of the camera, it is generally best to address all populations with responses to questions. For example, should a question originate on-site, the instructor, while responding, should also make contact (through the camera lens) with those in the off-site audience(s). Of course, if a question emanates off-site, the respondent should not ignore those physically present. Rather, each question should be seen as reflecting concerns held by all audience members, regardless of location.

Checklist of Objectives and Activities

When preparing and delivering presentations in an IAVI environment, keep in mind this checklist of objectives and recommended activities:

- From the outset, acclimate yourself and your students to the technology. Reveal the process by talking them through some of the basics of the equipment and its potential. Again, I urge you to secure the services of a technician or coordinator of distance education to guest lecture or demonstrate on this subject. Once students understand the capabilities and limitations of the technology, they will possess a clearer understanding of some of the do's and don'ts you suggest.

- Check out your presentation spaces: What can/cannot your primary and secondary spaces do for you and the respective audiences? Technology and broadcast/reception options from one site to the next, while similar, may not be identical.

- Build a strong rapport, both technical and interpersonal, with your production team. Discuss your style with your technician (e.g., quantity and manner of movement) and clearly articulate your requests. Eventually, technicians will sense your style and needs and begin thinking for you, customizing the set up and anticipating requests.

- Draw analogies between camera presentations in class and those seen on television or in film. If you cover the basics of how journalists, news anchors, and directors use the camera to interact with audiences and shift our point of view as a listener from moment to moment, students may begin to appreciate the impact camera presentations have on their lives.

- Provide some brief practice exercises for your students so they may experiment with the technology at no risk, with no points or grade at stake. One such assignment involves the videotaping of 30-second speeches of introduction delivered at least three different ways: to the immediate audience exclusively, to both audiences (present and distant), and solely to the distant audience(s). Play back the taped speeches for audience analysis and feedback. If time does not permit screening of each student's video in class, require students to view their work outside of class time and submit a self-critique.

- Animate speeches and presentations as much as you are comfortable in terms of delivery and text. Only in tight close-ups need you worry about being too physically active for the camera and frame dimensions. Use stories. Do not react to the technology with techno-chat of stuffy, formal narratives that are not your style in a typical educational setting.

IAVI AND OUR DEPARTMENTAL MISSION

As chair of a rather diverse department of communication studies, one of our challenges is to define but not stifle our limits and boundaries. As noted in our mission statement, "we investigate numerous styles and modes of interaction." Given the technology awaiting students in the graduate-level academic arena and commercial marketplace, I feel IAVI experience represents a contemporary discipline fundamental. Some students, like their instructors, may embrace or avoid such high-tech communication modes. Ultimately, though, they will likely be affected by them or have exciting opportunities to take advantage of their merits.

I am bolstered by student reaction to our IAVI-oriented course and sessions of other classes held on the system. In addition to broadening the information students receive (via visiting virtual scholars and off-site students), immersion in the technology, along with training and experience, generally tame initial apprehensions. The dividends of an IAVI course include enhanced subject knowledge as well as the development of public address, broadcast media, and audience analysis skills. In the end, successful IAVI practitioners recall that public communication, be it contact with audience members physically present for those at other sites, is primarily an issue of interpersonal communication. That is, at any given moment, all conversation of this type, no matter how many observe firsthand or the number connected through technology, is still a matter of talking to, versus at, a single listener.

Whether a singular or eclectic approach, we encourage students to explore the philosophical and critical variety available to them in our discipline and the related myriad of mediums for applying these tenets and their individual technical aptitudes. Of course, such goals are reached one course at a time and, in my opinion, our Training and Development class, with its substantive IAVI design, and other departmental offerings now in process (with IAVI sessions), are extremely valuable to student learning. My beliefs regarding such benefits extend beyond those for communication studies majors and encompass the general student and, in fact, the general participant. That is, I feel anyone engaged in IAVI dialogue can benefit substantially from the process as well as the product exchanged across the system.

REFLECTIONS: IAVI PARTICIPANT BENEFITS

Benefits for audience members come in many ways and may be categorized as such:

- The need to heighten one's focus as a critical and active listener (as the technology can sometimes mesmerize)

- Experimental growth concerning the impact of technology on communication success

- An exchange of information among diverse audiences

- A means of easing into a presenter's role given the baseline requirements for attention to detail and protocol (for instance, not rustling pieces of paper resting on a desk or tabletop and near a microphone)

For presenters, dividends include:

- Public speaking experience in a challenging, powerful environment

- The ability to offer material to diverse sets of listeners

- The necessity to sharpen listening and observation skills, particularly with regard to balancing attention to audience members physically present and those at other sites

Whether motivated by exhilaration or distress in anticipation of the process, a presenter is typically inclined to thoroughly prepare both message and delivery style. In sum, based on my observation and participation as both audience member and instructor, I find that IAVI educates me in ways beyond the information discussed. Just as public speaking informs the orator and audience member on two general fronts (content and delivery), IAVI serves to promote intellectual growth relative to the subject at hand as well as the enhancement of technical skills in preparation for future use, the utilization of other instructional technologies, and the rhetorical influence of such delivery systems.

REFERENCES

Hackman, M. Z., & Walker, K. B. (1990). Instructional communication in the televised classroom: The effects of system design and teacher immediacy on student learning and satisfaction. *Communication Education, 39,* 196–206.

Lewis, C. S. (1955). *Surprised by joy.* New York, NY: Harcourt Brace Jovanovich.

McHenry, L., & Bozik, M. (1995). Communicating at a distance: A study of interaction in a distance education classroom. *Communication Education, 44* (4), 362–371.

Schlosser, C., & Anderson, M. (1993). *Distance education: Review of the literature.* (Available from Research Institute for Studies in Education, College of Education, E005 Lagomarcino Hall, Iowa State University, Ames, IA 50011.)

Stoll, C. (1996). *Silicon snake oil.* New York, NY: Anchor Books/Doubleday.

Swartz, J. D., & Biggs, B. (1999). Technology, time, and space or what does it mean to be present? A study of the culture of a distance education class. *Journal of Educational Computing Research, 20,* 71–85.

Yordon, J. E. (2002). *Roles in interpretation* (5th ed.). New York, NY: McGraw-Hill.

SECTION III

CREATING ONLINE LEARNING COMMUNITIES: A FOCUS ON COMMUNICATION AND STUDENT-CENTERED LEARNING IN THE VIRTUAL CLASSROOM

PLANET XENO:
CREATING A COLLABORATIVE
COMPUTER-MEDIATED
COMMUNICATION CULTURE

Mary E. Wildner-Bassett

This chapter is a partial chronicle of a graduate seminar whose participants are pursuing degrees in second language acquisition and teaching. My intentions in developing the course were to explore, with a group of motivated graduate students who are also in-service, postsecondary language and culture teachers, new ways of thinking, learning, and teaching, based on a nonfoundational paradigm. According to this model, " . . . knowledge is a consensus among the members of a community of knowledgeable peers—something people construct by talking together and reaching an agreement" (Bruffee, 1993, p. 3). As the class became more familiar with the theories, terminology, and practices of nonfoundational learning and teaching, they became members of a new, transitional knowledge community. We set out to determine if this model of teaching and learning in higher education could be realized within the constraints of a typical institutional setting. While a nonfoundational paradigm of learning and teaching requires a thoroughly collaborative approach, it is not identical with collaborative learning. Collaborative work and communication are the tools which make a realization of the paradigm of a nonfoundational learning environment possible. In the description and analysis that follows, "collaboration" refers to tools and techniques of communicating and learning, and "nonfoundational" refers to the underlying and important paradigm of what ways of knowing and forming a learning community are driving and motivating the collaboration.

My interest in originating and teaching this course came from my developmental work with a team on a larger project funded by the University of Arizona and its College of Humanities to develop the College of Humanities Collaborative Computer Laboratory (COHLab). In our work to create this teaching research facility, our group, led by Susan Bouldin, discussed the ideas of collaborative learning and how its techniques and tools could be expanded to a paradigm of nonfoundational ways of knowing. Forming learning communities using the media of asynchronous and especially synchronous computer-mediated communication (CMC) in the humanities was the overall focus. The COHLab opened its doors on September 8, 1998, and I have taught in the facility ever since. The COHLab project was funded as a research and development site for piloting computer-mediated collaborative learning strategies in foreign language and English studies. The value of the project for our context is that it provides an experimental site for determining the appropriate place in the curriculum for computer-mediated collaborative writing and communication, the basic tools for our nonfoundational approach. One of the project's strengths is that it is cross-departmental and interdisciplinary and has begun to stimulate collaboration among faculty and graduate students who are engaged in designing, developing, and assessing courses. From within this context, I developed the course described here. For further comments about and details of the physical site and its configuration, see http://www.coh.arizona.edu/COHlab/cohlab.htm[1]

The central purpose of this chapter is to describe the process of engaging a class of advanced graduate students of second language acquisition and teaching in cocreating the content and the learning community that would lead us to a learning and research space where knowledge is not transferred from expert to learner but is created and located in the learning community. Establishing and maintaining a community of learners that is a functional realization of a nonfoundational paradigm is rife with frustrations and mistakes for all concerned. The description and reflection here will show how difficult and rewarding it was for the participants to form the new learning community and realize the nonfoundational paradigm of postsecondary education using the tools of CMC.

COURSE AND CONTEXT DESCRIPTION

The COHLab project is a cooperative venture by faculty, graduate students, and administrative staff that provides an opportunity for hypothesis testing, critical reflection, ongoing dialogue, and critique of issues that arise when the tools that enable computer-mediated teaching are joined with pedagogies and paradigms that support collaborative learning. This technology-mediated collaboration among students shifts the focus from a computer lab environment to that of a learning environment in which the computer is a useful tool to support collaborative writing and dialogue, which in turn support the nonfoundational paradigm.

Computer-mediated collaboration has the potential to promote reciprocal and interdependent learning to the extent that it supports learning as active engagement and dialogue rather than as the transfer of knowledge from teacher to student. Faculty and graduate students teaching in the COHLab are engaged in a number of pedagogical research projects to determine ways in which learning can be enhanced through technology-mediated collaboration. The following are some of the questions these researchers are asking:[2]

- How can computer-mediated classroom discussion facilitate the acquisition of communicative proficiency in a foreign language?

- How does working in a computer-mediated environment that promotes collaboration affect teachers' and students' ideas about learning and teaching?

- In what ways do these effects transfer to other teaching and learning environments?

- What effect does computer-mediated collaboration have on the learning process?

In order to answer these questions experientially, I developed the course described here.

Our sojourn together began during one semester at a public land grant Research I university, the University of Arizona, in the class that came to be called Researching the Paradigms: Collaborative Ways of Knowing, Teaching, and Learning, offered within the Interdisciplinary PhD program in Second Language Acquisition and Teaching (SLAT). The course involved synchronous and collaborative computer-mediated discussions as well as somewhat more traditional classroom sessions and asynchronous CMC written conversation. In general, the students met twice a week for a total of three contact hours per week. In one session per week, the class met in a regular classroom and engaged in face to face discussions of the topics in the syllabus, the readings, and the students' research projects, all of which focused on the research questions listed above. The second session of the week met in the COHLab, and was conducted using a mixture of face to face conversation and synchronous and asynchronous CMC. Throughout all sessions, participants were asked to see and construct themselves as learning and knowing subjects rather than to listen to lectures by a teacher. In most class sessions, the graduate students were responsible for the organization and content of the discussions. As subjects responsible to their peers, they bring their own attitudes, positionalities, and perspectives into their own focus and consciousness (Quasthoff, 1993; Rao, 1993; Wildner-Bassett & Meerholz-Haerle, 1999).

The writing and activities involved in all aspects of the class sessions were also aimed to realize basic tenets of critical, feminist, and positional pedagogies which encouraged learners to " ... situate themselves within the complex of linguistic, cultural, and value-laden practices in which they participate ... " (Zuss, 1994, p. 264). The written conversations which result from these assignments show how the learners see and construct themselves as learning and knowing subjects. These assignments asked students to engage in a discussion of their reading assignment, using synchronous and asynchronous CMC conferencing, and to evaluate their own discussion processes at the end of each week. Their processes were documented, as the self-generated final project for the class, as the learners and the nominal instructor presented chosen aspects of self and mutual experience for the assumed audience of interested readers using the World Wide Web and the web portfolio as a medium.

The group engaged in self-examination of what it feels like to be involved in nonfoundational classroom interactions using CMC as a medium for written conversations and collaborative discussions. The class had as its theme the development of technological, functional, and social engagement in the multiple literacies required for a new way of thinking, learning, and teaching, based on the nonfoundational paradigm.[3] The class read assignments and discussed the readings and their own ideas, using CMC via the conferencing and collaborative features of our university's Project for Online Instruction software during the

COHLab sessions.[4] The content of the course became the theories, terminology, and, especially, practices of nonfoundational learning and teaching.

CREATING A COLLABORATIVE CMC CLIMATE: EXPLORING PLANET XENO

During the course of the semester, we worked together to create a new, transitional knowledge community. When we realized how different this was from anything we had experienced before, we decided this was like being on a different planet, which we named Planet Xeno (Kost et al., 1999). Since we spent most of our time traveling back to a more foundational context during the rest of our work and learning contexts in the university, we knew we were not permanent residents of Planet Xeno, but resident aliens there. In the CMC written conversations, which were summarized in the web portfolio of Planet Xeno cited here, we developed and captured the moments that highlighted our class experiences and the processes we engaged in as we moved toward new ways of knowing.

With me as the nominal teacher, the students and I had little idea of the kind of adventure we were embarking on as we assembled for our first class of the semester. With time and some initial guidance from me, the seven individuals together began our acculturation to a new way of thinking, learning, and teaching, based on the nonfoundational paradigm. As the class gained more and more familiarity with the theories, terminology, and practices of nonfoundational learning and teaching, we all became members of a new, transitional knowledge community.

Descriptors of Classroom Culture

Each of us has recollected several important moments which highlight class experiences and processes toward new ways of knowing. These moments are crystallized in the list of nine descriptors below. The descriptors capture our identity as a classroom culture and as a transitional community moving toward realizing the nonfoundational paradigm of collaborative, reciprocally interdependent ways of knowing, learning, and teaching.

Here in the CMC sessions and the regular classroom session, " . . . understanding is created in a community of discourse, not in the minds of competing individuals with differing levels of expertise. Because the sources of knowledge are recognized as multiple, authority is redefined as well" (Maher & Tetreault, 1994, p. 155). These are the primary traits of our discourse community. Here, all voices, including the self, the other, the teacher, the student, and other texts, can be heard in concert and in symmetrical power relationships as well as is humanly possible. These traits and multiple voices are the essence of the interdependent and collaborative pedagogical environment that we came to know as Planet Xeno.

In our collaborative conversations, we ultimately developed the list of nine descriptors which expressed the essence of our identity as a classroom culture. We understood this culture to be one of a transitional community moving toward nonfoundational, collaborative, reciprocally interdependent ways of knowing, learning, and teaching. While the language is very different, the reader will notice that the themes and ideas discussed above are revisited here, expressed and named by the class as it moved toward creating the transitional learning community. The case study approach and the natural limitations of space in this context constitute the need to let the summaries of the descriptors speak for themselves, without further comment.

1) *Communication.* A necessary prerequisite for any collaborative effort. It includes listening to what others have to say (i.e., understanding what they mean and not what one wants to hear) and having the chance to give one's own opinion. It requires mutual respect and trust (negotiation of meaning).

2) *Collaboration.* An interactive and interdependent act of working together in order to generate new ideas, increase knowledge, and achieve common goals which could not be accomplished individually.

3) *Autonomous, active, engaged, interactive, interdependent learning.* These are terms which describe the nonfoundational paradigm. In this new learning environment, the roles of teacher and student change, and students gain a higher sense of responsibility for their own and others' learning.

4) *Process/product.* Focusing on the process of learning and the mutual exchange of ideas, rather than on the outcome, became our model.

5) *Coconstruction and meaning making.* This occurs when people exchange their ideas on a specific topic, collaboratively creating new knowledge, a tangible product, or a common understanding of a

concept, and reacculturating this knowledge into their own belief and knowledge systems.

6) *Community of support.* The power or energy that people give one another when working together to accomplish a desired goal. Such a community involves reciprocal interdependence where one member's output becomes another's input, and vice versa. Members work together and trust each other in a cocreative symbiosis. This community is a safe place for risk taking and voicing opinions without fearing sanctions.

7) *Dialoguing.* The suspension of judgment in the exchange of ideas and opinions. In dialogue, the goal is not to reach a conclusion; rather, it is to foster an environment where multiplicity of opinion is valued.

8) *Ways of knowing.* This challenges the positivist paradigm which values one truth. On Planet Xeno, we value multiplicity of perspectives, the process of sharing, exploring, and hypothesis testing. Practically speaking, teachers who thought they were teaching knowledge that they considered true knowledge will have to unlearn what they thought was true and instead integrate different perspectives into their teaching.

9) *Coloring outside the lines.* Learning without limitations on ways of being, thinking, and knowing, including collaborative writing, CMC, learner-initiated tasks, inclusion of multiple literacies, process-oriented evaluation, interdependence, and coconstruction of knowledge—all examples of moving away from the traditional paradigms of teaching and learning toward a nonfoundational paradigm (Kost et al., 1999).

LANDSCAPING PLANET XENO: STUDENTS' RESPONSES TO COLLABORATING AND THE NONFOUNDATIONAL PARADIGM

Each of us has recollected several important moments which highlight class experiences and processes toward new ways of knowing. These moments are crystallized in the list of nine descriptors, which capture our identity as a classroom culture, and a few more extended excerpts which describe the culture of Planet Xeno. A more detailed account of one key set of learning experiences will be included in the following section.

The voices here include the original voices of some of the students.[5] Adrian summarized the developmental process of exploring/creating Planet Xeno as follows:

> Although we have referred to these snapshots [of our experiences] as moments in class, the records often involve online and in-class discussions that occurred over several days, if not weeks. I have attempted to recreate, with the help of other participants, some of the discussions that were not conducted online, and have cut and pasted CMC for ease of access and reading. . . . I think the picture that emerges from these snapshots is an honest one, one of a gradual and somewhat difficult adjustment over time to new ways of knowing, teaching, and learning.

To show clearly that our engagement with the nonfoundational learning paradigm and with using CMC to realize the paradigm was not always painless, the first response description will show all the warts and wrinkles of a set of experiences early in the semester. This is most generally Adrian's summary, quoting voices of Mary (me, the instructor) and another student participant, Lisa. The task to be accomplished by the group for one class period in the COHLab was developed and named by Adrian and Lisa: Chain peer response to research questions. Adrian's "Post Hoc Commentary" is introduced by his point that " . . . the written comments aren't as important as the oral discussions Mary, Lisa, and I had about this assignment. So I've summarized these discussions below as best my memory allows . . . " I have recounted my own comments of that time early in the semester, marked as "Mary's Comments," as well.

> Adrian's comments: O.K. Here I am a month after the fact, trying to remember the events surrounding our chain peer review lesson. . . . What I remember is that Lisa and I had designed a COHLab activity in which we had the class moving around the computer pod in a musical chair-like fashion, stopping at each console for a gradually increasing amount of time to read [each class member's research] proposal and related peer comments, then add their own two cents [as feedback on each proposal]. Mary

wasn't as enthusiastic about the plan as we were, though. Her objections centered on the use (or lack thereof) of technology. She saw us using the computers as simple typewriters or perhaps data storage centers. She wanted more bells and whistles, so to speak. . . . This criticism was initially hard for Lisa and me to understand (and the lesson proceeded as we had planned and with Mary's blessings, though it was clear she hoped we would consider more technologically and pedagogically advanced lessons in the future). Lisa seemed to take the criticism especially hard, and this was a source of concern for Mary. I recall her (Mary) saying something about our bumping up against barriers, and in retrospect I think this is true. There was some real tension there, tension which may signify the clash of paradigms. This is why I chose to highlight this event in my portfolio, because I think it was a turning point for all of us. We were learning that we could not proceed with business as usual. We had to find new ways of teaching and learning. . . . I think we have found new interactional routines . . . for how to go about teaching and learning in a collaborative class. . . .

Mary's comments: As I recall it (and I clearly recall the affect of the situation, if not all the words spoken), I was less than enthusiastic because of exactly the problem you mention: I was looking for a paradigm shift that was enabled, engendered, or encouraged by the flexibility and multiple literacies and modes of communication that the technology can offer us. The barriers I saw raise up in this first chain review event were more in myself than in your suggestions per se. I had experienced an entire semester of bleeding edge pedagogy in a general education class using the COHLab, where the possibilities of the COHLab technology itself . . . stretched my own boundaries and creativity about how and what to teach. I responded initially to the chain review idea as within old boundaries of interaction—good ones, but essentially without real interdependent opportunities for interaction. Then, after I had growled and barked at Lisa and Adrian, I realized that I was making horrible mistakes as a teacher—assuming you would be where I was in terms of seeing the same possibilities and boundary-stretching opportunities simply by walking into the COHLab. It was a low point in my own teaching/learning dynamics in initiating a course like this. Then another TA from English walked in and said to his class how he and a student had spontaneously changed the way the class would be approaching their task... because they were brainstorming and realized that the COHLab offered opportunities for teaching and learning that neither of them had thought of before its existence. That was actually my message, too. We've certainly come a long way since then, and I realize that I was too far out there for the phase of development that we, the Planet Xeno community, were in as a community of learners. It was indeed an important moment, for me, too. Thanks for bringing it back into our memories, Adrian.

MAINTAINING THE COLLABORATION AND SURVIVING A COMMUNICATION/LEARNING CRISIS: MIDTERM EVENT

The difficulties of creating and maintaining a new learning paradigm using CMC became most clear to all participants when we ran into the constraints of the institutional and foundational paradigm. The pedagogy and curricular design of this course-as-research and experiential-project had been intended to push as many boundaries as possible. We also had the equal and real-life constraints of working within an institutional context of higher education where, as in nearly all such places, the foundational paradigm and power structures were intact. In order to discover whether the foundational and the nonfoundational paradigms could peacefully coexist, my decision was to leave the institutionally encouraged constraint of a midterm exam in place in our syllabus, but to encourage the graduate students to define the content and organization of the midterm examination event themselves. At that particular time in the semester, we were all still struggling to even understand and work within the nonfoundational paradigm. The world of the foundational institutional constraints, represented by the midterm exam that was still on the syllabus, and which we all knew so well, threatened to crash into and destroy our Planet Xeno. I see the midterm events, which spanned over two full weeks and beyond, as major navigational adjustment experiences in the center of our journey to and ultimate maintenance of Planet Xeno. In this ethnography of Planet Xeno, it is critical, then, to provide details about the midterm events.

It is with some trepidation that I reveal here that I was a very frustrated faculty member on many fronts as we neared the midpoint of the semester. I had been attempting, with my own ideals and limitations, to promote a collaborative learning perspective in a nonfoundational learning paradigm, emphasizing as best I could the need to promote self-directed learning by creating opportunities for these graduate students to define their own learning needs. I felt strongly that in order to do this, the group as a whole, and the students in particular, needed to take increasing responsibility for identifying both what they felt they needed to learn and how they were going to learn it. I had written in a general journal I keep that I was "having such a hard time getting my class to come with me to the 'learning space.'" By this I meant that I knew we would need to move to an entirely different set of ways of knowing and learning in order to really accomplish several of the class goals. But I also was at quite a loss at that point as to how to get people to go there, to follow me there, to lead us all there, or whatever combination was most viable. I really was ready to just give up, for a while anyway, and move back into the foundational space. I had originally hoped that the midterm would be a boundary zone for us all. It was a place where the typical institutional needs and constraints could meet what we had been gradually trying to create and then inspect as a nonfoundational and creative, if turbulent, new kind of learning space. I had wanted us to all take the risk of modeling a nonfoundational, collaborative, and learner/learning-centered paradigm with our own class activities, and then to take a step back and look at and research how it was working. There had been, though, no response whatsoever by the students to the call for defining the boundary zone of the midterm event.

It was from this personal and class context that I threw a tantrum in an email to the class:

> If there is no concrete suggestion, collaboratively arrived
> at by the group, as to the form, content, and grading of
> the midterm, I will assume this responsibility. The fact

that the class members were/are hesitant, or passively resistant, or apathetic, or too overworked to have taken any initiative so far, is a matter of great concern to me. What should we do, and how shall this task be organized and accomplished by Thursday, March 4, at 2 pm?

It turns out that my tantrum-like call for engagement in the midterm event became the initiator of an important rethinking of the whole class structure. This is not to say, however, that I was able to anticipate that outcome at the time. I was reacting mainly out of frustration and a lack of trust in actually accomplishing what I had set as a personal goal for the course. This midterm event had as the goal (and, subsequently the result) to encourage the class, as a learning community, to commit to a nonfoundational and collaborative approach to cocreating a graduate class experience. It was discouraging to be teetering on the edge of giving up on this goal. I honestly felt that the midterm might be the end, and that none of us, myself included, were proving to be able to think or interact beyond our institutional and learning habits. In retrospect, it was by hitting what seemed to be a last-straw exasperation moment that enough energy came into the system of our struggles toward collaborative learning to really launch it into a new arena, as evidenced by the remainder of the midterm events.

There were no CMC or other responses to my email, so when we entered the classroom on the day of the preparation for the midterm, I was frustrated. When there was no response to my call for participation, I had started to realize, or talk myself into, the idea that I had wanted to take us all, including myself, too far too fast. I had hoped for more than was possible, I thought, and I had lost the energy to try to subtly guide and irritate the group into discovering it on their own. I felt I was going to give a really traditional, though fair, midterm and let it fall as it would. And if the class decided to sit back and let that happen, then I was just going to read and discuss for the rest of the semester—slip back into a good old foundational paradigm, with one-way knowledge transmission, power, and, especially, the authority of knowledge centered with the teacher. When I sent the perturbed email to everyone, I felt I was drawing a line in the sand as to the future of our class in general and the form and function of the midterm in particular.

I was frustrated and pretty negatively inclined when I entered the room. Suddenly (I think all I said was, "Let's discuss the reading, but first, what do you want to do about the midterm?"), the students launched us to Planet Xeno. There ensued an intense and very earnest discussion about various options for the midterm. One student started the real interaction by making a nonfoundational type of suggestion for what could be done to cocreate the midterm. There was a lot of excellent, engaged, respectful, and creative face to face discussion, with several different suggestions made. Some students were not quite up to the same willingness, or risk-taking behavior, or creative view of nonfoundational thinking that most of the group was getting more and more excited about, but they listened respectfully and voiced their own concerns. I took the role of a (delighted) observer for most of the time. Here and there I raised some more questions in a directive way ("What shall we do about the 100 points?"), but I was mainly able and very willing to stay on the sidelines of the discussion. I was very excited by the way a gradual consensus emerged and how various people took the lead at various points, then passed it on without difficulty when someone else had a series of constructive points. I was utterly delighted that the students were all contributing, even beyond what I had at first imagined, without my having to do any more pushing. There was indeed an entirely changed energy in the room and in the group. On that day, we became a community of learners and teachers (note the plurals— inclusive for all seven participants) in a new learning space—one that was and has remained nonfoundational and coconstructed, collaborative, and connected to computer-mediated communication in several modes. The energy, the changes of perspective, and the willingness for risk taking in a community of people who are open and ready to seriously consider suggestions, content, and process from each other, and with high mutual respect, has been maintained.

In order to finish the development of the midterm event, the students suggested an asynchronous CMC discussion. They suggested, edited, refined, and voted on the final version of essay questions for the exam in that CMC discussion over the next two days. I read the entire exchange but never made a comment. Almost all of the suggested questions were very good, and there were real considerations about choosing the best and most comprehensive questions.

The quality of the actual midterm event was also quite special. The exam took place during a normal class session in the COHLab. As they entered the room, groups of two students were randomly assigned two essay questions from the compiled set of questions. Even though they had all written the exam questions and had decided to answer the questions collaboratively in dyads, using face to face and especially synchronous CMC discussions as the modes of communication during the 75 minutes of the class session, they did not know who their partner would be or which set of questions they would draw until they entered the room. Their responses to the questions took the form of a collaborative CMC discussion, where both the process of negotiation and the product (either a consensus, or occasionally, the agreement to disagree) were electronically saved and summarized. All the participants took the activity seriously, and were engaged with each other and with the process. Two participants especially, Lisa and Claudia, seemed to be having a wonderful time, with much laughter evident. The participants self-organized, passed out gum and drinks to one another, and sat at a pod (an eight-sided group of computers) per pair. These I interpreted as signs of both connectedness and the desire to have a space to spread out intellectually and personally as the dyads. It seemed to be a good sign, in many ways, that our computer technician lab assistant did not recognize this as a testing situation—and commented on the impression he had that this was the most unusual midterm exam atmosphere he had ever seen.

FROM CRISIS TO INTERDEPENDENCE
IN THE MIDTERM EVENT

In some ways, the best part for me of the midterm events was that I had a chance to read all the parts of the products of the midterm process. The students evaluated each other's products (or to use foundational language, graded the exams themselves) and gave feedback, again using CMC, so I was not involved in that aspect except as an observer. As I read the results of the midterm event, though, I was struck by a very high quality of answer, of engaged discussions that complemented each other in many instances, and of a collaborative and coconstructed event and set of products that was certainly much more than the sum of its individually contributed parts. I was so pleased to see that this had, for my own interpretation, been a real formative assessment event, where several voices had a chance to pull together what we had discussed in class and read about so far. All participants also had a chance to synthesize several of the ideas in ways that we had not managed to do previously.

The participants wrote and posted on the CMC discussion area their own process evaluations of the event, from the development of the exam, to the production of the collaborative responses, to the judgments and responses to quality of responses of other dyads. I was surprised, in a way, to read in the evaluations that some students expressed a concern, or feelings of mild disappointment, because they had trouble equating our process with their other experiences in graduate classes of midterms. It would have seemed to be obvious, and it underscores the idea that this was indeed a nonfoundational event. From my perspective as a graduate program faculty member, I saw a higher level of quality (and even quantity) of response than I think would ever have been produced in a more foundationally approached midterm. The events of the midterm supported what I have always firmly believed: At the graduate level, the process of getting ready for, thinking about, and synthesizing ideas for an exam of any kind is equal to, or much more important than, the actual product of what is written.

My biggest challenge throughout the entire midterm event was to keep my mouth shut. It was not that I wanted to redirect any part of the process, but rather that I was (and am) so thoroughly delighted with what was going on that I kept wanting to say things like, "Did you hear what you just said?" "Did you notice how that interaction just moved from a foundational to a nonfoundational moment?" "Did you all hear the insecurity in participant X's last comment? What is the source of that, do you suppose, and what can we do to redirect the insecurity?" The observer/teacher in me was being deluged with teachable moments, yet I didn't want to interrupt the wonderful process as it was unfolding in order to comment on it online. In sum, it was a delightful and very successful process. I consider it the turning point in our class and in my own understanding of what interdependence can mean in a classroom setting. It remains in my thoughts, in affective as well as in cognitive terms, as a key event, a top-of-the-mountain experience, and one of the most important sets of events in my long and checkered career as an educator and learner.

REFLECTIONS AND LESSONS LEARNED:
MAINTENANCE OF PLANET XENO

In conceiving of this course, it was important to me to explore and push the boundaries of possibilities for addressing the web of relationships among the concepts of collaborative learning; the paradigm of nonfoundational graduate education; collaborative language, literacy, and culture learning; and the multiple literacies necessary for this kind of learning, including all those possible in CMC. I was hoping to engage a class of advanced graduate students in cocreating the content and the learning community that would lead us to a learning and research space that had some of the following characteristics:

- Both teachers and learners are active in and cocreators of the educational setting.

- The culture of the learning environment is a transitional community of support.

- Knowledge is not transferred from expert to learner but created and located in the learning community.

- The power or energy that people give one another when working together to accomplish a desired goal is the key motivation for the community, rather than the institutional constraints of instrumental motivations.

Those hopes were certainly fulfilled, and a new learning community was created and sustained due to the engagement and adventuresome spirit of all the participants. A learning community involves reciprocal interdependence where one member's output becomes another's input, and vice versa. Members work together and trust each other in a cocreative symbiosis. This community is a safe place for risk taking and for voicing opinions without fear of sanctions. In this learning environment, the roles of teacher and student change, and students gain a higher sense of responsibility for their own and others' learning.

Establishing and maintaining a community of learners that is a functional realization of a nonfoundational paradigm is rife with frustrations and mistakes for all concerned. As the instructor, I surely made the most mistakes of anyone as we all explored the learning space on the way to discovering Planet Xeno. But I could also reap the enormous benefits of this risk-taking exploration without permanent, negative repercussions. Instead of repercussions, I experienced growth and excitement as we formed the learning community. Those of us who have created Planet Xeno still travel back there as often as we can, to maintain that community which, while transitional, is still an exciting and rewarding place from which to view and cocreate learning and teaching.

REFERENCES

Bruffee, K. A. (1993). *Collaborative learning: Higher education, interdependence, and the authority of knowledge.* Baltimore, MD: Johns Hopkins University Press.

Kost, C., Wildner-Bassett, M., Gunder, P., Wurr, A., Jurkowitz, L., Ackan, S., & Abella, J. (1999). *Planet Xeno—A web-based learning portfolio* [On-line]. Available: www.coh.arizona.edu/planet-xeno/

Maher, T., & Tetreault, M. K. T. (1994). *Breaking through illusion: The feminist classroom.* New York, NY: Basic Books.

Quasthoff, U. (1993). Ethnozentrische Verarbeitung von Information: Zur Ambivalenz in der Funktionen von Stereotypen in der interkulturellen Kommunikation. In P. Matusche (Ed.), *Wie verstehen wir Fremdes? Aspekte zur Klaerung von Verstehensprozessen* (pp. 37–62) [How do we understand the 'foreign': Towards an explanation of the processes of understanding]. Munich, Germany: Goethe Institut.

Rao, N. (1993). Verstehen einer fremden Kultur. In P. Matusche (Ed.), *Wie verstehen wir Fremdes? Aspekte zur Klaerung von Verstehensprozessen* (pp. 110–121) [How do we understand the "foreign": Towards an explanation of the processes of understanding]. Munich, Germany: Goethe Institut.

Wildner-Bassett, M. (2001, Fall). Multiple literacies, CMC, and language and culture learning. *Academic Exchange Quarterly, 5* (3).

Wildner-Bassett, M. E., & Meerholz-Haerle, B. (1999). Positional pedagogies and understanding the other: Epistemological research, subjective theories, narratives, and the language program director in a 'web of relationships.' In L. K. Heilenman (Ed.), *Research issues and language program direction* (Vol. 9, pp. 203–243). Boston: Heinle & Heinle.

Zuss, M. (1994). Value and subjectivity in literacy practice. In B. Ferdman, R. M. Weber, & A. Ramprez (Eds.), *Literacy across languages and cultures* (pp. 239–272). Albany, NY: State University of New York Press.

ENDNOTES

[1] The description here was taken, with some personalization and editing, from the referenced site.

[2] From http://www.coh.arizona.edu/COHlab/mission.htm, the COHLab mission statement. The current version of the COHLab project mission statement was developed by Susan Bouldin, Julian Heather, Lisa Jurkowitz, Ron Scott, Hale Thomas, and Mary Wildner-Bassett, Fall 2000.

[3] For a more thorough discussion of the multiple literacies and complexity issues involved in this paradigm, see Wildner-Bassett (2001, Fall).

[4] Copyright 1996–2001 Arizona Board of Regents. POLIS is an experimental instructional support system created in the University of Arizona Communication Collaboratory (http://www.u.arizona.edu/ic/polis/).

[5] In contrast to the usual conventions for data citations, the real names of the authors are used here. We were all aware of the public nature of our comments as we developed the web-based portfolio for Planet Xeno.

Designing and Implementing an Interactive Online Learning Environment

Mahnaz Moallem

As an educator, I have been a proponent of social learning theories. Interaction is a vital element in the educational process, and a collaborative interactive learning environment can lead to deeper understanding. I believe that interaction differentiates a course from being an independent and self-directed study to a course that maintains a community of discourse and helps to define and reconstruct the body of knowledge. I argue that while learning ultimately is an individual enterprise, the support of a group with a common learning objective can produce a synergistic facilitation of learning. Sound educational practice demands that learners communicate effectively, ask meaningful questions, formulate their own ideas, and discuss what they are doing.

As an instructional technologist, I have also tended to question the instructionist definition of interaction that emphasizes learner engagement with instructional systems. I argue that such definition essentially focuses on individualized learning (presenting the curriculum effectively to the individual student), and tends therefore, to marginalize the role of social interaction in the process of learning. The instructionist view, I believe, fails to notice that the most significant factors that contribute positively to learning among students are students' interaction with one another and with teachers.

175

In the fall of 2000, I took the challenge (and accepted a university stipend) of designing, developing, and delivering an online graduate course, Instructional Systems Design: Theory and Research, for students in the Instructional Technology Master's program at the University of North Carolina, Wilmington. My immediate reaction was to ask myself, 1) How can I use the web as a knowledge construction tool and not as an information delivery system? and 2) How can social and interpersonal interaction occur in this course? I must admit that although I was aware of the communication options on the Internet and have used some of these tools in my previous courses effectively, I was not able to predict what could happen in a completely online course where social interaction and collaborative learning were to be the primary learning methods. Furthermore, as I began reading the literature and listening to the experiences of some of my development team members who had already designed and developed online courses, I became even more anxious.

My literature review revealed that researchers who studied online courses (e.g., Hiltz, 1997; Kearsly, 1995; Sherry, 1996) repeatedly reported that Internet-based instruction (online courses) was focused mainly on student content and self-study lessons and materials, an approach that I have always criticized and did not desire to follow in my graduate-level courses. Researchers also claimed that asynchronous web-based instruction did not produce the sense of immediacy (verbal and nonverbal interpersonal communication behaviors that reduce physical distance between people) that is an important part of teaching and learning in face to face instruction (e.g., LaRose & Whitten, 1999). However, my investigation assured me that although researchers reported that individual learning was a salient characteristic of existing distance education courses, they thought interaction was crucial for real understanding and for the quality of learning.

The experienced faculty in my development team, who had designed and developed online courses, were also arguing that simply making communication tools available to online students did not mean that students could and would use it. They were further suggesting that if the interaction is not an integrated, essential, and graded part of an online learning environment, the majority of students will never use it at all, and those who start to use it will generally decide that nothing is going on there and will stop using it.

DESIGN AND DEVELOPMENT OF AN INTERACTIVE, COLLABORATIVE, ONLINE COURSE

As I began thinking about the design of the course more seriously, I realized that in order to develop an interactive and collaborative online course, I needed to answer a few questions:

- What instructional design model would be most appropriate for an interactive and collaborative online learning environment?

- How would I make interaction and collaboration the core aspect of the course design?

- How should I facilitate group conversation?

- What is an optimum size for a collaborative learning group?

INSTRUCTIONAL DESIGN MODEL: A FOCUS ON COLLABORATION

What instructional design model would be more appropriate for my interactive and collaborative online learning environment? How would I make interaction and collaboration the core aspect of the course design?

Answering these questions was not difficult. Given my teaching philosophy, it seemed obvious that my instructional design would have to allow for a multiplicity of perspectives so that learners have a full range of options from which to construct knowledge. It would also have to provide learning opportunities which asked students to bring their own relevant mental models and integrate external information within the personal framework. Finally, the learning activities should be designed in a way that students can express their conception of an idea, reflect on the opinion of others, and revise their initial conceptions.

After reviewing several instructional design models, a problem-based learning approach due to its emphasis on active construction of knowledge through inquiry and social negotiation through work with peers (e.g., Jonassen, 1999; Savery & Duffy, 1996; Schwartz, Xiaodong, Brophy, & Bransford, 1999) seemed ideal for my purposes. In a problem-based learning environment, personal relevance is stimulated by authentic problems without lowering the degree of cognitive complexity. Problem-based learning transfers control over the learning process from the teacher to the students, as well as structures, and supports a carefully planned series of collaborative learning activities which constitute the content and assignments of the instruction. Problem-based learning uses a problem as a starting point for learning in contrast to other traditional models that use a problem as a culminating activity or assessment for students once facts and concepts have been presented to them (Savery & Duffy, 1996). Moreover, since problem solving tasks are similar to the challenges that students face in the real world, they are more engaging and provide more opportunities for learners to explore all possible relevant perspectives through interaction and dialogue.

After identifying the content of my weekly lessons for each unit of my instruction, I developed a problem that simulated a situation that instructional technologists encounter in everyday professional practice. Problems were to be used as starting points for learning the content of the lessons and for achieving their objectives. I designed the problems so that they were content specific, but ill defined. In other words, each problem required students to set their own goals and discuss the solutions within a specific content or domain of knowledge (e.g., learning theories and research, instructional design theories and models, etc.) that was the core content of that unit of instruction (weekly lesson). Also, the problem statement did not present all information that students needed in order to solve the problem. They were open-ended in the sense that students had to fill the information gaps, to make judgments about the problem, and to defend their judgments by expressing personal opinions or beliefs. Figure 11.1 shows an example of such problems.

In order to cognitively support students during their problem solving process or social negotiation, I used two strategies. My first strategy was to provide a set of related cases or work examples that could help students explore how a similar problem has been solved. Upon developing or locating such examples, I linked them to the problem statement page. Related cases or worked-out examples, I thought, could provide learners with an example of the desired performance and simultaneously demonstrate actions and decisions involved in the performance. In order to facilitate students' access to experts' opinions during the problem solving process, in addition to making myself available, I also linked the problem statement page to an active online forum where experts in the field of instructional design responded to students' questions and discussed emerging theories and issues in the field of instructional technology.

Figure 11.1

Example of an Ill-Defined Problem Solving Task

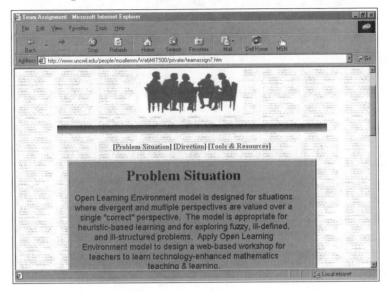

Figure 11.2

Example of an Individual Assignment

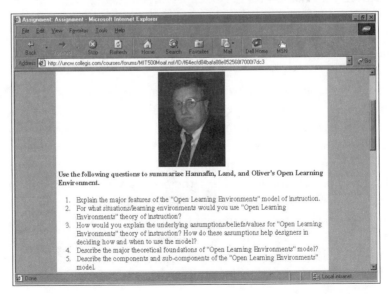

My second strategy was to assist students in their effort to construct individual understanding and to interact with their own prior experiences before presenting, defending, and discussing them with their peers. To that end, I developed an individual assignment for each lesson in which I asked students to read the suggested materials and resources, synthesize their understandings of the readings in a summary format, and post it in the course individual assignment area. Students were required to complete this individual assignment before they would begin discussing and solving the weekly problem or collaborative activity. Again, to provide scaffolding strategies (scaffolding is a temporary support that is removed when no longer necessary), I developed a list of open-ended questions for each individual assignment and asked students to use those probing questions to synthesize their understanding of the reading (see Figure 11.2 for an example of such assignment). At the beginning of the week, once students submitted their responses, I would read them and provide feedback. This feedback most often included summaries of discussion, guidance about resources, and thought-provoking questions to stimulate their thinking.

Once I had designed and developed the problems, my next task was to decide what kind of information students needed in order to understand the problem and to develop personal knowledge. I had two choices: Either link relevant information to the lesson page or provide students with a list of reading resources (textbooks and other readings). I decided to do both. I developed information pages (slides, lecture notes, links to informative web sites) and linked them to each weekly lesson. I also suggested a list of reading materials (textbook and reading package) for each lesson and recommended that students read those materials before beginning to work on the problem.

Another design issue was to identify the activity structures required to solve the problem. This was the most difficult part of the task because it could either advance or discontinue student interactions or conversations. I needed to decide how I wanted to scaffold the learners to perform the task. In a face to face learning environment, I am able to observe students' confusion and lessen it by providing the necessary scaffolding strategies needed at a particular time. However, in an online environment, due to the lack of social context cues, providing the necessary scaffolding strategies was not easy. Furthermore, as some researchers observed (e.g., Ruberg, Moore, & Taylor, 1996), students' misunderstanding or lack of understanding of the task in an online environment could continue without resolutions in the absence of the teacher's directions and guidance, and such loss of understanding might eventually result in suspending the discussion and waiting for the teacher explanation or intervention. In order to guard against this problem, I decided to include a list of focusing questions, product specifications, and procedures for completing the problem solving task or collaborative activity. By providing guidance, my hope was that my directions in the task would allow spontaneity and experimentation during the problem solving process while lessening the confusion.

FACILITATING STUDENTS' COLLABORATION AND GROUP WORK

How should I facilitate group conversation and what is the optimum size for a collaborative learning group?

I strongly believe that the use of collaborative learning promotes higher achievement, higher-level reasoning, more frequent generation of ideas and solutions, and greater transfer of learning than does individualized or competitive learning strategies (see Brandon & Hollingshead, 1999; Webb & Palincsar, 1996). I have regularly used collaborative learning strategies in my standard face to face classes. Nevertheless, I questioned how well I could translate those strategies to this online class.

Given the importance of working jointly on the same problem, the size of the collaborative group was an important issue for me. Both my readings and experiences with collaborative activities indicated that small groups of three to four students would be a better idea because it could 1) reduce the likelihood that members would free ride on the contributions of other members (Shepperd, 1993), 2) make it easier for me to monitor individual contributions and to scaffold teams' progress, 3) provide more opportunities for quality interaction, and, thus, improve commitment to the group, 4) improve each student's social skills to interact smoothly with others at the group level, 5) help team members by developing needed behaviors and eliminating deferring behaviors to facilitate the productivity of the group, and 6) help teams see the value of working together.

I decided to form small groups (four members) for weekly problem solving tasks and apply the following research-based strategies to support and promote collaboration within the team members. First, research on group theory in computer-mediated environments (e.g., McGrath, 1991) suggests that change in the group's membership affects the group interaction process, member reactions, and group task performance. This is because groups are continuously and simultaneously engaged in three major functions: production, member support, and group well being. Any major change imposed on the group will, at least temporarily, alter its previous patterns of attention to various aspects of its work (e.g., more time to solve technical issues, more time and effort to set group norms regarding task focus and participation). Computer-mediated communication research claims that an imposed change in group membership causes more perturbations in computer-mediated communication than it does in face to face instruction. Given these results, I decided to keep the groups the same and not change the team members for the entire semester. I also asked team members to introduce themselves to one another in a "getting to know each other" activity, create an email address list for group members, and use each other's names all the time (I also modeled these behaviors myself). When forming the teams, I tried to consider the personalities and learning styles of individual members.

The research on group theory also shows a positive relationship between successful task performance, team members' perceptions of effective group processes, and the level of satisfaction with the task performance and communication (McGrath & Hollingshead, 1993). In order to help the teams perceive less difficulty with the process of completing the task and feel more satisfied, I applied several strategies. First, I explicitly described the procedures for collaborative work and spelled out the responsibilities of the team members (established social norms) in a separate web page that was linked to the lesson's collaborative activity (see Figure 11.3 for an example). Second, I recommended that each team use a team assessment tool to evaluate its collaborative work and to use the results as a means to improve its collaborative work. Third, I asked each team to identify one member as a team leader and one member as a team recorder for each problem solving task, and to rotate the responsibilities so every member would get a chance to serve both as a leader and a recorder. Finally, I used conversational style (spontaneous and informal with comments directed to individual students or to individual comments) when I participated in team discussions.

Figure 11.3

Example of Guideline for Cooperative Work

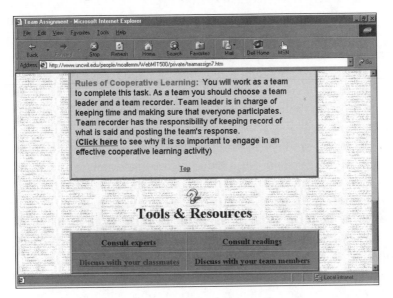

CHALLENGES DURING THE IMPLEMENTATION PROCESS

Before using technology as a sole medium of instruction, I enjoyed and appreciated that computer technology and the Internet tools provided more opportunities for communication and discourse and expanded students' experiences beyond space, resources, and time. However, as I began teaching my online course with its heavy emphasis on social interaction and collaborative work, I realized my limitations within such an environment and faced several challenges.

While the adopted database tools (Eduprise) for the design, development, and delivery of the course provided some degree of communication (forums—team and common, chat rooms, email, and electronic file sharing), the system was limited for an interactive and collaborative course in several ways. First, the system was slow for a course that had conversation and discourse as its core pedagogy. Students and I had to spend many hours managing a discussion that we would have been able to complete within 30 minutes' time in a face to face situation. Second, students had to go from one database (course site—lesson page) to another database (forum) to communicate or converse with their peers. Uploading and downloading files for the purpose of sharing ideas or adding to other members' ideas was not only a slow process, but also difficult to manage especially when students began sharing images and graphics. Students also needed to know basic html language in order to work effectively and creatively within the system. Although most students in my course had basic technology skills, the nuance of the interface (i.e., the time that it took to learn how to share files and other materials and resources during discussion and navigate through the course site) combined with the complexity of the problem solving task demanded more time to complete the problem solving tasks than I had anticipated. Furthermore, technical difficulties forced teams to spend some time helping one another learn how to work within the system. My analysis of students' interaction logs revealed that, as McGrath (1991) observed, the change in the medium (technology) of communication did affect students' interactions. For the first two problems, students spent considerable time trying to help one another learn how to work and adjust to the new technology. Moreover, it appeared that when groups began working collaboratively (at the beginning of the semester), they still had to spend some time sorting out how they wanted to use the communication tools and how they wanted to work together, in spite of my written guidance for group participation, task focus, and group norms. During later weeks of the semester, however, the group process showed more stable patterns, suggesting that even with technically capable students, change in the medium of communication causes perturbations both in the group process and group interaction.

Time was a challenge not only for students, but for me as well. Compared to my face to face classes, I also had to spend many more hours reading students' postings, responding to their ideas, participating in each team's discussion for the collaborative activities, providing just-in-time scaffolding, both in the team area and common forum, and giving immediate feedback both to individual assignments and group works. If I add the slow speed of the system to the hours that I had to spend online, I could easily say that managing this online collaborative course was equal to teaching two similar standard face to face graduate courses.

Another challenge was, indeed, a pleasant surprise. Students' desire for doing the best collaborative work and their willingness to spend as many hours as it required in order to produce their best solution was above and beyond my expectations. In addition to exploring issues, sharing resources, and coaching one another in understanding the underlying concepts and theories, students tended to spend tremendous amounts of time working on the product or the response as they tried to include everyone's ideas in the team product. This result was very impressive. I was pleased with the teams' products or responses, and after the first two collaborative activities, my coaching and scaffolding strategies decreased and I became a team member, for the most part, during the teams' discussions. However, while I was pleased with what I was observing, I knew that the time and effort that students were putting into their work would eventually frustrate them and might, in fact, have a negative effect on their overall performance and satisfaction. Therefore, it was a challenge to help teams understand that I valued the process of social interactions and negotiations more than what they would develop as the end product. Students' investment of time on their products also made it harder to critique the final responses and to provide constructive feedback.

In sum, while I tried my hardest to turn students' attention to the process of learning during the problem solving tasks, I was not completely successful in this effort. This particular group of students seemed to be task-oriented, and therefore, were highly focused on the product. They became frustrated in their attempt to perfect the product to the extent that they lost the value of appreciating shared knowledge through discussion as I had intended. The unlimited time, the absence of interruption, and the opportunity to reflect on one's and other's ideas and opinions seemed to provide an excellent environment for conversation for a group of graduate students who seemed to be highly motivated and wanted to show their best performance.

My last challenge was to establish a collaborative work environment in order to help teams learn how to work effectively and collaboratively. Independent and task-oriented students seemed to get distressed with one another easily and appeared to be more concerned about completing the task, rather than exploring alternative solutions and negotiating multiple perspectives. At the end of the semester, students learned to use verbal communication effectively and did not have to spend much time rephrasing what they wanted to say and how they wanted to say it whereas, at the beginning of the semester, it was a challenge that most of them had to face and learn.

LESSONS LEARNED FROM THIS EXPERIENCE

When I decided to design, develop, and deliver this highly interactive and collaborative course, my fears were real. Even though I had taught graduate-level courses in which interaction and dialogue were the core pedagogy of the courses, in each of these situations both the students and I were physically present in a place and were restricted by time. While these factors somewhat limited us in what we wanted to accomplish in these courses, the rich environment of face to face interaction provided us with the opportunity to quickly redirect our attention and change our dialogue by recognizing the boundaries of one another's tolerance, our content, task, and objectives. Furthermore, in a face to face environment, I was able to begin the task with no structure, and then gradually advance to as much structure as students desired to have. However, with the online course the situation was different. While students and I were not constrained by time and place, we were separated by distance. Therefore, I was uncertain how my previous successful classroom strategies would work in an online environment. My experiences with designing and implementing this online course taught me several valuable lessons.

Lesson #1

The organization and the visual metaphors employed by the course authoring tools (Eduprise) create constraints on the organization of the course content and learning strategies and encourage the faculty to follow the linear structure imposed by the interface. As I began thinking about my online course around the concept of problem-based learning and collaborative learning tasks, I realized that I was somewhat in contrast with the organization that was imposed by the interface. The interface mimicked the organization with a syllabus by providing a template for course information, course content, course resources (library), and a calendar for a timeline. Utilizing such organization could lead me to a course design in which the content was instructor-generated and generally stable, leaving students little or no input in the organization or generation of the course content. Therefore, I learned that it was a challenge to rethink this imposed organization and apply other approaches (such as problem-based learning) to organize the content and the course.

Lesson #2

Course design is the most critical factor in creating an online interactive learning environment. During the design and development of this online interactive course, I realized that developing an online course that does not simply provide students with information, but rather requires them to accept the data as truth, demanded much more time and effort than I had previously anticipated. I also learned that just because I had taught several graduate-level courses with similar pedagogical approaches did not mean that I was able to use all my experiences in an interactive online course. Some of my experiences were not simply transferable to an online learning environment. As I was thinking about the course design specifications, I found it very useful to review the literature and learn from the experiences of others. Although incorporating the workload into my current and busy academic calendar was a major challenge, and I had to give up on some of my dreams and ideals during the development process, I think the time spent on the design of the course was worth it. I am convinced that designing an interactive and collaborative course for online delivery is more of a pedagogical issue than a technological issue. Although it is important for a faculty member to learn to work with the course software and to develop some expertise in multimedia, graphic arts, and html formatting, it is even more important to learn to adapt and design instructional activities that are functional within the courseware, while being able to facilitate student learning, communication, and resource sharing.

Lesson #3

Task structure and organization influence the nature and quality of student interaction. Teaching this course demonstrated to me that a successful interactive and collaborative online course requires well-designed and well-thought-out collaborative tasks or activities that stimulate peer interaction and encourage peer collaboration. I also realized that in contrast to collaborative activities in face to face classes, online collaborative tasks should be structured enough to diminish student confusion. Due to the flexibility of time and place and the problem posed by the absence of rich, nonverbal communication in online collaborative tasks, developing a focus, timeline, clear expectations, well-defined roles for each participant, and clear evaluation format for the online tasks is very important in improving interactivity and preventing confusion and frustration. Furthermore, I learned it is important that domain knowledge be well integrated into the problem.

This is essential to online problem solving tasks because it helps students understand the problem and remain within the knowledge domain as they are solving it.

Lesson #4

Designing collaborative learning tasks should become the focus of learning content in interactive online courses. My experience in this course echoes previous research in collaborative and interactive learning pedagogy. Collaborative interactive learning is the development of shared meaning among group members, a perspective that emphasizes the social creation of knowledge as the basis of learning. This shared meaning needs to occur within a learning activity that provides means for both individual development and collaborative construction of knowledge. Such learning activities should be carefully designed to be suitable for group work, and should be designed in such a way to encourage learners to explore and make use of new knowledge and skills in order to solve the problem at hand. The collaborative activities should also carefully structure positive interdependence to ensure that students are committed to each other as persons and to each other's success. The structure of the collaborative activity should promote individual accountability while simultaneously requiring coordinated efforts to complete joint response.

Lesson #5

Augmenting group activities with individual assignments improves the quality of interaction and encourages student participation. My experience taught me that I could not expect learners to know enough about the knowledge domain to constructively participate in the problem solving task. I learned that I needed to prepare learners for an intellectual discussion. Supplementing group activities with individual activities was a good idea. Asking students to individually explore the underlying concepts and issues in advance and connecting them with their own previous experiences helped them better understand the collaborative task and be prepared to formulate ideas and participate in the team discussion as well as large group discussion. Furthermore, by providing individual feedback to each student, I was able to not only encourage students to think more, but also to examine alternative perspectives and resources.

Lesson #6

The instructor of an interactive online course should prepare students for discussions. Part of my instruction as a facilitator during the team and large group discussion was to remind students of some norms (netiquette) for an online discussion, such as how to reply to each other's comments (e.g., not just say "I agree" or "I disagree" but expand upon what they were agreeing or disagreeing), how to disagree respectfully, how to reflect and reformulate ideas, and so on. As I tried to face the challenge of preparing students for a text-based online discussion, I learned that the best way of coaching students was to model the behaviors myself. Modeling what I expected students to do as a team member was more effective than telling students how to manage online discussion.

Lesson #7

Students in an interactive online course need time to adjust to their new technology. During the delivery of the course, I soon realized that the newness of the medium and the learning environment required that students learn about the software, adjust to a text-based communication environment, and become accustomed to less rich information (compared to rich face to face communication). Therefore, I learned to be patient, encouraging, and considerate of the fact that the initial discussions are not indicative of student performance.

Lesson #8

The immediacy behavior (behaviors that enhance closeness to and nonverbal interaction with others) affects students' motivation in carrying on the discussion and discourse. As a teacher, I agreed with my students that online text-based discussion was not as stimulating and interesting as face to face discussion. However, we were able to include some of the interactive immediacy cues, such as praising students and peers, addressing them by name, digressing to respond to their comments, and prompt feedback. These practices seemed to influence students' perceptions and attitudes and increased their willingness to participate in the discussion and interaction. Although I was not able to incorporate videotape recording and video conferencing in this course, I could see how these technologies can improve online discussion and produce nonverbal cues that are absent in our existing online courses.

CONCLUSION

I will take the above eight lessons that I have learned with me into the new year, and for what I have learned, become a better teacher and online facilitator. I have validated my belief that technology cannot teach—that teachers teach—and that the Internet communication tools do not, by themselves, enhance learning, but provide avenues for learning when placed in the capable hands of a skillful teacher and designer of instruction. I have learned that taking risks with technology and learning can be thrilling and anxiety inducing. Most of all, I have learned that I must continually reflect, evaluate, and adjust my instruction when using technology.

REFERENCES

Brandon, D. P., & Hollingshead, A. B. (1999). Collaborative learning and computer-supported groups. *Communication Education, 48* (2), 109–126.

Hiltz, S. R. (1997). *Impacts of college-level courses via asynchronous learning networks: Some preliminary results* [Online]. Available: http://eies.njit .edu/~hiltz/workingpapers/philly/philly.htm

Jonassen, D. (1999). Designing constructivist learning environments. In C. M. Reigeluth (Ed.), *Instructional design theories and models: A new paradigm of instructional theory* (Vol. III, pp. 215–241). Hillsdale, NJ: Lawrence Erlbaum Associates.

Kearsly, G. (1995). *The nature and value of interaction in distance learning* [Online]. Available: http://www.gwu.edu/-etl/interact.html

LaRose, R., & Whitten, P. (1999). *Websection: Building web courses with instructional immediacy* [Online]. Available: http://www.telecommu-nication.msn.edu/faculty/larose/websectionlite.htm

McGrath, J. E. (1991). Time, interaction, and performance (TIP): A theory of groups. *Small Group Research, 22,* 147–174.

McGrath, J. E., & Hollingshead, A. B. (1993). Putting the "group" back in group support systems: Some theoretical issues about dynamic processes in groups with technological enhancements. In L. M. Jessup & J. S. Valacich (Eds.), *Group support systems: New perspectives* (pp. 78–96). New York, NY: Macmillan.

Ruberg, L. F., Moore, D. M., & Taylor, C. D. (1996). Student participation, interaction, and regulation in a computer mediated communication environment: A qualitative study. *Educational Computing Research, 14* (3), 243–268.

Savery, J., & Duffy, T. M. (1996). Problem-based learning: An instructional model and its constructivist framework. In B. G. Wilson (Ed.), *Designing constructivist learning environments* (pp. 135–148). Englewood Cliffs, NJ: Educational Technology.

Schwartz, D., Xiaodong, L., Brophy, S., & Bransford, J. D. (1999). Toward development of flexibly adaptive instructional design. In C. M. Reigeluth (Ed.), *Instructional design theories and models: A new paradigm of instructional theory* (Vol. III, pp. 183–215). Hillsdale, NJ: Lawrence Erlbaum Associates.

Shepperd, J. A. (1993). Productivity loss in performance groups: A motivation analysis. *Psychological Bulletin, 113,* 67–81.

Sherry, L. (1996). Issues in distance learning. *International Journal of Educational Telecommunication, 1* (4), 337–365.

Webb, N. M., & Palincsar, A. S. (1996). Group processes in the classroom. In D. C. Berliner & R. Caffee (Eds.), *Handbook of educational psychology* (pp. 841–873). New York, NY: Macmillan.

Communicating: The Key to Success in an Online Writing and Reading Course

Ele Byington

My colleagues in the English department are generally skeptical about teaching English courses online. Some claim that virtual classrooms cannot create a climate for discussions about literature equal to those in traditional literature courses, or equal to discussions of student writing in writing courses. They fear that an essential process in learning about literature and writing, the dialectic of classroom discussion, will be lost. By "dialectic" they mean the collective understanding of texts that comes from hearing and questioning a range of possible responses to those texts. And they may be right. But these assumptions about online teaching are untested. We need to test the assumptions, unless we think we can resist, indefinitely, the advance of technology. To begin a descriptive study of online courses in English and to test assumptions about differences between classroom interactions in traditional courses and online courses, I chose to develop and teach a writing course online.

Testing assumptions was not the only reason for developing the course examined in this chapter. I find my life as a university professor is changing faster than anyone could have predicted. Although I have years of experience in computer-assisted instruction, word processing skills alone are not enough to survive the teaching and administrative demands of the modern university. When I must participate in bureaucratic processes within my department or the university, I visit various web sites to fill out forms. The need to record, retrieve, or respond to information online happens almost on a daily basis. I like the convenience, and I do not miss the tedium of the old way of dealing with bureaucratic processes, namely, with paper. But in the beginning, I often experienced new technology overload.

This was especially true when I returned a few years ago from a summer of fieldwork in Scotland, two weeks before the first day of classes, to find that the system for locating information in the library databases had completely changed. During that one summer, the system went online. No instructional handouts on how the system worked were yet available to help me or students navigate it. As a member of the graduate faculty who teaches linguistic courses in language and culture to students enrolled in the critical literacy emphasis of the Master's of Arts program in English, study of this rapidly evolving culture of online teaching and research seemed essential.

Fortuitously, the Office of Academic Affairs at the University of North Carolina, Wilmington (UNCW) made it easy for me to begin the study.

In October 1999, academic affairs sent out a request for proposals for online courses in basic studies. The administration needed to offer these basic studies courses online to students in the new Technology College. Successful proposals would receive a grant of $5,000 and instructional support in online course design.

The opportunity to satisfy my research and teaching interests, the prospect of gaining support in learning and practicing online technology, and the promise of $5,000, proved irresistible. (I did not know then that, in addition, each member of the development team would also get the use of a brand-new IBM ThinkPad.) I proposed an online course in what used to be called Advanced Freshman Composition, and which is now titled College Writing and Reading (Advanced), a basic studies course. Entering students placed in this course are exempt from one of the two course requirements in freshmen composition. All other students take College Writing and Reading I and II, to satisfy the requirement. As I anticipated, the proposal was successful.

In the fall of 2000, a total of 34 students registered in the two online sections of College Writing and Reading (Advanced).

The purpose of this chapter is to show that online writing courses can provide student writers with multiple opportunities for interaction and discussion about reading and writing processes, perhaps more so than in traditional writing courses. What students might lose in class and small group interaction in traditional courses can be offset by increased opportunities for one-on-one online interaction between instructor-student and student-to-student. Because the medium of interaction is writing rather than speaking, students write more online than in traditional courses to get the information they need to complete their work—for real audiences and for real purposes.

But the shift in the medium of online instruction, from oral to written language, means the dynamics of such courses change significantly. These changes place new demands on the communication skills of both instructors and students. I believe that strong students, those with effective technical and interpersonal communication skills, will succeed whether or not the medium of instruction is the written language of online courses or the mostly oral and nonverbal language of traditional courses. Students who lack effective communication skills will do poorly in both.

DEVELOPING THE ONLINE COURSE: INSTRUCTIONAL DESIGN WORKSHOP

As a member of an instructional design team funded and supported by the university administration, I attended weekly workshops for two months in the summer of 2000, along with instructors who, like me, were developing courses for the first time, and with others who were experienced in teaching online courses. Members of the design team met in two types of sessions: small group sessions and demonstration sessions for the whole group.

Small Group Sessions

In the small group sessions, expert and novice worked together in true Vygotskian (1978) fashion, and I was able to experience the "positive interdependence" described by Johnson & Johnson (1990, pp. 27–28). That is, I could easily see the value in this collaboration and was, therefore, eager to learn from my partners. For example, they described the need for communicating meticulously in online courses. One experienced instructor stressed another need—what she called "cheerleading" online. I knew what she meant immediately at the beginning of my course: The instructor needs to establish an encouraging persona online, more so even than in the traditional classroom.

But there was no explicit discussion in the small group sessions about the central shift an instructor has to make in beginning online teaching: the shift in the medium of instruction from oral to written language. It is because of this shift that a compelling need exists to create meticulously written directions and to cultivate cheerleading capabilities.

In fact, teaching through written language as the medium of instruction changes everything. Written language does not allow for the kind of shortcuts in communication that oral language does. Online, writing is the sole medium of communication: the medium for assigning and responding to reading and writing, for managing the class, and for creating the character (the ethos) of the class (with some photographs and a variety of icons). Although, after the fact, all this seems self-evident, my attention during the development period was devoted to gaining technical proficiency to teach online, not to understanding the consequences of the shift in the medium of instruction.

Demonstration Sessions

During the design workshops, I initially found the demonstration sessions less useful than the small group sessions. We had instruction on writing html code and demonstrations of interactive technology. In these sessions, experts seemed to talk only to other experts. Several sessions were incomprehensible to me, a novice at that stage in developing an online course. I could not imagine then, for example, why I would need to be familiar with html. I was not ready, either, to design intricate chat rooms with roving avatars to help online class discussion.

Of course, as it turned out, being familiar with some html code was essential in teaching my course online. I needed that means of working with text to highlight information on the course web site and to provide links to other web sites. Without knowing how to write this code, I would not have had the means to create variations in color and font size on the web site to emphasize important information for my students, or to create links to the library databases and online writing labs.

Also, once I started teaching the online course, I recognized immediately the advantages of creating special discussion areas in such courses. I had neither the expertise nor the time in the middle of the semester to create such areas and had to manage with what was already provided by the course management service. But I wished that I had those skills and was sorry I had not recognized the value of the demonstrations in the design workshops. Interestingly, in discussing collaborative learning, Brandon and Hollingshead (1999) also refer to positive interdependence and, further, state that "group members must see the value in working together for collaborative learning to occur" (p. 114). They refer to conditions for learning which were present in the small group sessions but absent in the demonstration sessions. I mention this positive interdependence again because getting online students to work together successfully depends on instructors finding ways to communicate the value of collaborative work.

One-on-One Sessions

During the same period that I attended the design workshops, I also worked one-on-one with technology consultants in the Center for Teaching Excellence at UNCW. They helped me reach the level of technical proficiency needed to manage the web site and actually teach online. The consultants had superior interpersonal communication skills equal to or surpassing their technological skills. It was from them that I learned how to manage rudimentary technology with some degree of comfort and be creative with online technology.

COLLEGE WRITING AND READING (ADVANCED): GENERAL CHARACTERISTICS

All sections of College Writing and Reading (Advanced) which I teach, either in traditional classrooms or online, share the same objectives, collaborative structures, and course materials.

Objectives

The course has mainly two integrated objectives. One is to develop analytic reading skills through practicing various critical responses to readings: interpretation, analysis, and synthesis. These multiple responses are meant, first, to introduce strategies of close reading and, second, to show the possibilities for deriving multiple readings from the same text. Students compare and analyze responses to the readings and reading strategies in groups, either online or in the classroom.

As students work on analytic readings skills, they also work on improving their writing skills. This is the second objective in the course. To work toward it, students complete four graded essays, with multiple drafts, and various informal response exercises.

Collaborative Structures

I have developed instructional practices in college courses which appear, at first glance, to rest on two competing theories of teaching writing: 1) Students can learn to write by working collaboratively without instructors, and 2) students can learn to write through direct instruction both in whole class groups and individual conferences with writing instructors. These are not competing but complementary practices that operate at different points in the reading and writing processes. For example, students learn a lot about their writing process in peer groups. I have found that student reviewers are more than capable of pointing to or summarizing the positive or negative aspects in each other's drafts, or telling what was in their minds as they read a draft (Elbow, 1973). To model the kind of interaction I want to see happen in writing groups, I show a videotape which follows Elbow's (1973) model for writing groups and demonstrates the process described in his book, *Writing Without Teachers*. I encourage students to follow the model and point to or summarize what they see, good or not so good, in the drafts of the other writers in their groups. I steer them away from trying to actually rewrite someone else's draft during the group sessions. Students who attempt to do so account, often unwittingly, for some of the problems writing groups experience. In "Learning to Write: Computer Support for a Cooperative Process," Neuwirth and Wojahn (1996) present a clear sense of the complex process of revision. They refer to a number of studies that analyze the cognitive processes involved in revision. Neuwirth and Wojahn (1996) claim that the difficulty in revising is not so much with the detection or even the diagnosis of particular problems but with students' "inability to fix them" (p. 149). Citing Sitko (1992), Neuwirth and Wojahn (1996) raise yet another problem: "students may simply be unable to see fault with problems in the text that caused great difficulty in reading and interpreting. Instead, students may attribute the problem to inadequacies on the part of the reader" (p. 149). The rewriting, at this point, is best left to collaboration between the instructor and writer and best accomplished in one-on-one conferences or by written comments on drafts, or both.

Students in College Writing and Reading (Advanced) collaboratively brainstorm topics and development of topics in large groups. They exchange and discuss drafts in small groups in the early stage of revision and exchange later drafts individually with me. In both the traditional course and the online course, we exchange drafts electronically. My comments appear throughout the student papers in pop-up dialogue boxes using the Microsoft Word "insert comment" feature. In the traditional course, I have conferences in my office. Commenting on papers and individual conferencing become part of one process online. This combining of commenting and conferencing was an unexpected result of the change in the medium of instruction.

Course Materials

For each College Writing and Reading (Advanced) course, computer-assisted or online, I select four or five articles, sufficiently complex to serve the aims of the course, and place these on electronic reserve in the library. The reading and essay assignments for the course are based on these four articles.

I also put on reserve short excerpts from work on the power of language to "create, highlight, and distort reality" (Lakoff, 1990, p. 12), excerpts on fundamental differences in the way men and women view the world (Tannen, 1990), and reader response theory (Rosenblatt, 1983). These excerpts give students some ways to account for markedly different responses to readings from the same set of facts.

Students extend the final essay they write in the course by adding ideas and information from articles they find in the library. This gives them experience searching online and in citing sources electronically both in the text and on a works cited page.

TEACHING ONLINE

A commercial company, Eduprise, provided the course management system, which included course development software. The UNCW web course development team used the software to develop a template for the courses. Within this development framework, instructors could customize the design scheme to fit their individual courses. For students and instructors, the site is not difficult to navigate even with minimal Internet skills. In my course, the web site consisted of a course front page (with my photograph and a letter of introduction to me and to the course), a navigator column to the left, and a line of icons at the top. I posted daily bulletins and special messages on the front page throughout the semester. Students could click on links from this front page to the syllabus, assignments, calendar, or special topics all listed on the navigator column to the left. Or they could click one of the icons at the top of the page and go to the class forum or team forum area. In the class forum area, students could ask or answer questions or contribute comments in response to a question or answer from other students. In the team area, students, arranged in groups of four or five, could only communicate with members of their teams and the instructor. These teams could easily be rearranged during the semester.

Class Forum Area: Special Advantages

Our collaboration in the class forum area was the most useful of the online activities. When I needed to alert students to a problem I was seeing in the writing (a lot of asserting and little developing, for example), I posted examples to instruct them as they were writing. Students could read the examples almost as quickly as I posted them or, if they wanted to, read the examples at two in the morning if that suited them better. They told me that these examples were quite helpful in understanding the assignments. Students also posted questions and made comments about the assignments—if they were unsure of what an analysis was, or a synthesis, or what I meant by an unusual reading of the articles. I responded to the questions and comments, as did other students in the class. Students found useful the continued availability of class discussion, questions, and comments about sample introductions or conclusions or other features of their writing throughout the semester. These discussions stayed in the class forum area for the rest of the semester and could be revisited at the click of a mouse. The main points of the discussion were not wiped off the blackboard, taken away on a transparency never to be seen again, or forgotten on handouts stuffed in backpacks. Every time we went online, any piece of writing could be put up on the screen for discussion and instruction. These mini-workshops were retrieved and referred to for class discussions by students or instructor throughout the course, not just on workshop days. The opportunity for extensive interaction between student-instructor and student-to-student was the most interesting feature of the class forum.

Further Advantages of Online Collaboration

As I mentioned earlier, I commented on individual drafts of student papers using the "insert comment" feature of Microsoft Word. Comments appear in the body of the text, not simply as footnotes or endnotes or in the margins. An annotation number appears on the page wherever a comment is inserted, and a splash of yellow color also marks this place. A student moves his or her cursor on the yellow mark and the instructor's comment appears in a pop-up dialogue box. When the student removes the cursor, the pop-up box disappears. I find this feature useful for the following reasons:

- I can type faster than I can write.

- I find I can give more extensive comments, when needed, with less effort than writing long comments in the margin.

- I can edit those comments easily—no laborious erasing and rewriting.

- My comments, especially the long ones, seem less intrusive in the pop-up boxes, than when I write too much in the margins of a student paper.

Neuwirth and Wojahn (1996) present a more elaborate collaborative commenting process called the PREP editor that lets teachers and students respond to each other's comments directly on the student paper. As we become skilled in this medium of instruction, the PREP editor and other processes like it, I imagine, will become just one in an array of possible processes instructors will be able to use in collaborative conferences with students.

In the online course, unlike the computer-assisted courses I teach, students sometimes asked for clarification of my comments. They also asked for my response to their revisions because it was easy to do so; we were always connected. The online interaction reminded me of the one-on-one experience in basic writing courses I taught for four years at the University of Michigan. Students in these courses met with instructors each week for 30-minute conferences on their papers. This personal connection to the writers was central to the instruction. The regularity of one-on-one talk about writing seemed central to the writing instruction online.

The online students had an added benefit that the students in Michigan did not. Each student had a written record of any discussion of my comments and any further suggestions or explanations of those comments. They had a record of the entire response process: my comments, their questions, my responses to their questions and, in addition, my responses to other students' questions about the current assignment in the class forum. Harasim (1990) points out, "'the 24-hour classroom' is always open; this facilitates self-pacing and self-directed learning. Asynchronicity expands user control over the time of the interaction, and increases the time available to read or reread a message and formulate a comment" (p. 46). She asserts that "the need to verbalize all aspects of interaction within the text-based environment can enhance such metacognitive skills as self-reflection and revision in learning" (p. 49). I would add that this need to verbalize in writing will enhance the learning process in online writing courses. By necessity, students will have increased opportunities to write purposefully.

Writing Groups Online: Different Dynamics

It was difficult in the beginning to set up and monitor writing groups online. Although my observation during the semester was that just as many students responded well to working in writing groups in the team forum area as they did in traditional classrooms, the dynamics changed. Introducing the workshop model for group work, and more important, monitoring the groups, became extremely labor-intensive for me, and I had difficulty keeping current with the work of the groups.

In the traditional classroom, I use a video that demonstrates a particular model of writing groups. Students see a writing group in action and also hear other students on the video raise frequently asked questions about how and why that particular model works. Before the first writing workshop in the traditional classroom, it is relatively easy to introduce the model then work within that model throughout the semester. Written online instructions that introduce the model and elaborate on the how and why of the model can get the teams working together online but not with the same ease.

Monitoring the groups in the traditional classroom is not labor-intensive. Monitoring online is extremely labor-intensive by comparison. Some groups in the team area worked well with little online supervision. Others did not when one or more students in the group gave either little or no response. In traditional classes, I was all too familiar with those students in small group situations who do not collaborate if they can avoid it. They have long been identified in the collaborative literature as social or intellectual loafers (Latane, Williams, & Harkins, 1979; Salomon & Globerson, 1989). It could take several days to coax a few students to read and respond to their peers online. Even when grades for participation in writing and reading groups depended on evidence of response, some students did not participate. I had to rearrange groups when I discovered that two of the four students in one group had not completed their own drafts. This kind of rearrangement can be made on the spot in the traditional classroom with little or no effort. Not so online. The medium of instruction makes a big difference here. There is a negative time lag in rearranging groups online. I will be investigating ways of working with discussion groups and collaborative learning processes in great detail before teaching another online course. Further advances in technology and my ability to use discussion chat-type rooms online will allow me to work better with writing groups in future classes.

LESSONS LEARNED

Teaching Online

In many ways, we are learning to teach all over again when we go online. The creation of a curriculum for the online course demands meticulous attention to detail in every aspect of that curriculum. This medium also demands skilled communication and organization on the part of both instructor and students. Although there have been enlightening studies published for decades on collaborative learning in writing courses, among others, online collaboration is relatively new and untested. I find myself thinking about all the courses I teach in a new light because of this online experience. Assignments, syllabi, and other instructional material could benefit from the kind of scrutiny I have given these online course materials.

I learned a lot about my own communication skills, both technical and interpersonal. I experienced the exhilaration of discovery, the discovery that learning to manipulate this new medium was not a matter of mostly learning Internet navigational skills. For me, it was analogous to learning to speak French in this one respect: There is a moment when learning a foreign language becomes a matter of understanding the language at a level beyond the simple exchange of information. The struggle to acquire new vocabulary and grammatical structures never stops, but, if that moment occurs, it feels as if a solid obstruction to internalizing the language has been reached and passed, a wall has crumbled. The result is a lessening of strain in speaking the language and comfort in having some control over the medium. You are out of the dark. The rest is a matter of practice.

Comfort in this online medium came to me with a similar breakthrough. Learning to communicate online is more than learning technical tricks. It is about being familiar with a system, an evolving communication system replete with technical glitches that occur often and demand solutions. When I understood the basically unstable nature of the system and could respond to technical problems with some novel solutions of my own, I was no longer in the dark. I felt in control of the medium rather than at its mercy. The rest is a matter of practice.

Students Online

Some of the students enrolled in my online course had reached that level of comfort with this medium of instruction. Others had not. They lost work online and struggled to redo it, they crossed their fingers when sending attachments, or they (literally) sent along a prayer with the attachment for its safe delivery. I learned to give meticulous instructions, repeated at different locations on the course web site, to help lessen the struggle and help avoid unnecessary glitches.

Before the end of the semester, all but a few students reached a reasonable level of control of the online medium of instruction, beyond the basics needed to navigate the web site, and their grades reflected their success. The most successful students in the course were those who began the semester with good technical control and effective interpersonal skills, in addition to strong intellectual skills they had acquired so far in their education. These students used all avenues for interpersonal communication on the web site. They asked the most questions on the class discussion site (the class forum), read and responded to their peers' writing in the team discussion sites, zipped around in the library databases in order to complete the final writing assignment, and posted questions when they needed information and used the information relayed back to them. If they did not get a response as quickly as they needed it, they followed directions posted on the front page of the web site to call my office or home.

Others learned the necessary technical skills as they went along fairly easily, and did well as long as they kept connected to the whole class activities and small group activities. But they sometimes had to be reminded to read the drafts from their team and give feedback to their team writers. However, when they were in a group with strong writers and communicators, they benefited. They asked questions on the open forum discussion and asked for help from time to time in finding or checking information.

They—and this is important—stayed up-to-date on daily announcements.

A few really struggled. When the struggle became too much, apparently, one dropped out. He disappeared without a word by midterm. Another stayed and passed the course, but she told me that she hated technology even more than she had before she took the course. I asked why she enrolled in an online course, and she said the only other open class was too early in the morning. When it came to getting up early in the morning, pragmatic concerns overruled good sense.

Others failed to reach a level of comfort with the technology and did not have the communication skills to help them as they struggled. They managed to fulfill the requirements, but barely. These few were never able to gain control of the medium on their own or even work out how to ask for help in a timely fashion. Their interpersonal communication skills seemed, at times, to be nonexistent. They had to be cajoled to respond online. They never communicated with anyone about their problems until after a deadline had been passed and they reached crisis point. They seldom read messages posted prominently on the course front page and even missed questions directed to them in green 14-point font. They would log onto the course wherever they happened to have logged out. If that did not happen to be the front page where all class bulletins were posted, they missed changes or additions to the work. They almost never checked the daily headlines on the course front page.

Of course, I learned that social and health problems do not go away with online courses. It is possible that at least some of these students were not struggling but playing too much, and I know some were dealing with health problems. Every first-semester freshmen course has students who cannot manage unlimited opportunity to play and successfully manage their classes at the same time. One student who barely passed the course told me at the end of the semester that he had been suspended for the following semester for having an illegal drug in his possession. One was taking medication for depression; she dropped out. Another never got over the time lost to allergies early in the course.

CONCLUSION

I found that I spent much more time—hours and hours online getting the work assigned, completed, and graded—than I do in the traditional classroom. I discovered the hard way that the shift in medium of instruction, from mostly oral to mostly written, changes the way I need to introduce assignments and manage group work and other reading and writing activities.

Until I learn new strategies and build a body of class material online, this work will continue to be labor-intensive. Will I teach online again? Yes, I cannot wait.

At the end of the day, standard evaluations of student perceptions of my online course—instructor, material, teaching, and grading practices— all suggest that I managed well enough this first time. The evaluations showed that the students perceived the course as successful. The mean score overall for the course, on a five-point scale, five being excellent, was 4.23 in one section and 4.00 in another (the section with the student who hated technology). Their comments on the evaluations gave me generous credit for managing the course.

My perception of student learning is harder to quantify since we have no standard evaluation of instructors' perceptions of student learning practices other than grades. But my strong impression is that the writing produced in the course reflected as good or better quality and effort as the writing produced in the computer-assisted sections I taught in traditional classrooms.

REFERENCES

Brandon, D. P., & Hollingshead, A. B. (1999). Collaborative learning and computer-supported groups. *Communication Education, 48* (2), 109–126.

Elbow, P. (1973). *Writing without teachers.* New York, NY: Oxford University Press.

Harasim, L. M. (1990). Online education: An environment for collaboration and intellectual amplification. In L. M. Harasim (Ed.), *Online education: Perspective on a new environment* (pp. 39–64). New York, NY: Praeger.

Johnson, D. W., & Johnson, R. T. (1990). Cooperative learning and achievement. In S. Sharan, (Ed.), *Cooperative learning: Theory and research* (pp. 23–37). New York, NY: Praeger.

Lakoff, R. T. (1990). *Talking power: The politics of language.* New York, NY: Basic Books.

Latane, B., Williams, K., & Harkins, S. (1979). Many hands make light work: Causes and consequences of social loafing. *Social Psychology, 37,* 822–832.

Neuwirth, C. M., & Wojahn, P. G. (1996). Learning to write: Computer support for a cooperative process. In T. Koschmann, (Ed.), *CSCL: Theory and practice of an emerging paradigm* (pp. 147–170). Hillsdale, NJ: Lawrence Erlbaum Associates.

Rosenblatt, L. (1983). *Literature as exploration.* New York, NY: Modern Language Association.

Salomon, G., & Globerson, T. (1989). When teams do not function the way they ought to. *International Journal of Educational Research, 13,* 89–99.

Sitko, B. M. (1992). Writers meet their readers in the classroom: Revising after feedback. In M. Secor & D. H. Charney (Eds.), *Constructing rhetorical education* (pp. 278–294). Carbondale, IL: Southern Illinois University Press.

Tannen, D. (1990). *You just don't understand: Women and men in conversation.* New York, NY: Ballantine Books.

Vygotsky, L. S. (1978). *Mind in society: The development of higher psychological processes* (M. Coles, V. John-Steiner, S. Scribner, & E. Souberman, Trans.). Cambridge, MA: Harvard University Press.

Fostering Intellectual Development in a Learning Community: Using an Electronic Bulletin Board

Mary Bozik and Karen Tracey

The introduction of new technologies in education is resulting in what the International Society for Technology in Education (1998) labels new learning environments. As a result, instructors are increasingly seeking ways in which these tools can contribute to the development of learning communities. This chapter investigates the impact of an electronic bulletin board on a group of first-year students taking a general education cluster course. The goal was for the students to form a learning community consistent with the definition offered by Lenning and Ebbers (1999): "an intentionally developed community that will promote and maximize learning" (p. 8). Such communities, they argue, will be effective if they "emphasize active, focused involvement in learning and collaboration that stimulates and promotes the group's and group members' learning" (p. 8). In the class described here, an electronic bulletin board was intended to facilitate student interaction, an element long recognized as contributing to learning. In fact, researchers have noted the superiority of student discussion to other instructional methods for achieving high-level cognitive objectives (Althaus, 1997; Bloom, Englehart, Furst, Hill, & Krathwohl, 1956) and affective goals (Krathwohl, Bloom, & Masia, 1956).

McKeachie (1994) adds that student talk is considered valuable as a means of both monitoring and promoting student learning. This chapter extends the arena of student talk to include an electronic bulletin board, explores how one student learning community in an interdisciplinary general education course used it for discussion, and offers recommendations for maximizing positive outcomes.

THE COURSE

The University of Northern Iowa (UNI), with a student enrollment of just under 14,000 and a faculty of 850, is a regional comprehensive university that takes teaching seriously. In fact, an often-heard campus slogan is "Great teaching makes the difference." Overall excellence is also a goal, and the entire campus takes pride in the fact that UNI has ranked second in the *U.S. News & World Report* category "Midwest top public universities" for four consecutive years. All students take the same general education program and there is considerable concern among faculty that the series of courses contributes significantly to the liberal education of students.

The interdisciplinary course reported here is being piloted as a way to help students see connections among their general education courses. For descriptions of the cluster model, see Lenning and Ebbers (1999, p. 21) and Shapiro and Levine (1999, pp. 23–30). This cluster emerged from a grant funded by the University of Northern Iowa's Center for the Enhancement of Teaching and Learning. The grant supported an eight-week effort by four faculty members to design a general education cluster that packages four courses: Oral Communication, College Reading and Writing, American Civilization, and Humanities II. It was designed to offer a cohort group of 27 first-year students (all but one of whom were recent high school graduates) 13 hours of their required 47 hours of general education in a block. The class is team-taught by four faculty members and meets four afternoons a week. The researchers and authors were two of the four members of the faculty team, one a professor of Oral Communication and one of College Reading and Writing. The research reported here is from the first time the class was offered.

This course clusters four courses seeking to integrate intellectual skills of critical thinking, reading, writing, speaking, listening, and viewing with the study of European and American culture, history, civilization, and ideology since 1500. The course aims to:

- Enhance the level at which students meet goals of individual general education courses

- Create a learning community that enables students to develop the knowledge, skills, and values necessary to live thoughtful, creative, and productive lives

- Provide faculty and students with intense intellectual stimulation by making a variety of connections among historical movements, intellectual theses, and communication concepts and practices

- Help students understand the role of communication in structuring, shaping, and changing the world

In light of these goals, the choice of computer-mediated communication as a supportive pedagogy seems especially appropriate because it can, as McComb (1994) points out, ". . . support a pedagogy that aims to increase student responsibility and autonomy in the hopes that students will grow to be active, critical members of society" (p. 169). The cluster course was a unique attempt at interdisciplinary education. It was intended to more directly help students see connections among their college classes and was designed using a definition of interdisciplinary as instruction that "refers to instructional activities that involve two or more disciplines in a way that all areas are meaningfully addressed simultaneously..." (Hillman, Bottomley, Raisner, & Malin, 2000, p. 92). The above goals and definition are consistent with Eastmond and Ziegahn's (1995) description of a good learning experience as one in which a student can "master new knowledge and skills, critically examine assumptions and beliefs, and engage in an invigorating, collaborative quest for wisdom and personal, holistic development" (p. 59).

THE TECHNOLOGY

The professors incorporated a web-based classroom environment into the course with the aim of enhancing the accomplishment of these goals. Previous classroom researchers from a range of disciplines have determined that asynchronous computer communication can enhance student learning in a variety of ways. Mowrer (1996) concluded that the electronic forum in a phonetics class helped with instructional goals by extending instructional time, promoting student-to-student and student-instructor communication, and providing the instructor with feedback throughout the semester. Collins (1998) studied the incorporation of asynchronous communication into large biology courses and concluded that "the electronic bulletin board is an extremely useful educational tool whose uses are seemingly unlimited" (p. 87). Morley and LaMaster (1999), reporting on physical education methods courses, found that "use of our bulletin board extended students' experiences beyond the traditional classroom walls, enabled professional networking, and provided students an opportunity to express their beliefs and concerns... in an open forum outside of class" (p. 16). Stith (2000) found a correlation between student grades in a web-enhanced college biology course and the number of articles on the class bulletin board that were read. Positive results have also been reported by Allen (1994) for a first-year writing course, Wernet, Olliges, and Delicath (2000) for nontraditional social work students, and Cole (2000) for introductory chemistry.

WebCT, a system supported by the university, was selected, and faculty received training in its use during a summer workshop prior to the first course offering in the fall of 1999. Researchers have since reported positive experiences with WebCT for student learning, student bonding, and classroom logistics; the ease of use for both instructor and student is also stressed (Cole, 2000; Morley & LaMaster, 1999; Stith, 2000; Wernet, Olliges, & Delicath, 2000).

These positive outcomes are consistent with the three goals faculty had for incorporating WebCT into the cluster course. First, it was hoped that this format would provide students an additional discussion setting that would be nonthreatening and encourage them to process and connect information and content from the four courses. Brandon and Hollingshead (1999) reported such a result: "the opinions generated by the group induce cognitive conflict within the individual who may then contribute an elaboration of his or her own point of view back to the group discussions" (p. 122).

Second, the establishment of a community of learners might be encouraged and the social environment of the class strengthened. Althaus (1997) found that "Students who participated in the CMD [computer-mediated discussion] groups not only performed better on first papers and final exams, but they also attended class more regularly and were more active in face to face discussions than other students" (p. 165). Their experience is consistent with that of Riel and Fulton (2001), who maintain that

"...today's learning communities are evolving tasks, activities, and practices of shared value for their members...[that make] it possible for students to participate in the construction of knowledge and products" (p. 523).

In addition, it was thought that the logistics of the course would be facilitated. Other instructors have reported that computer-mediated communication provides an additional means of keeping in touch with students and demonstrating that professors care about and are willing to communicate with students (McComb, 1994). In our class, the schedule was designed to be fluid to accommodate special needs, such as when one teacher needed a three-hour block of time to show and discuss a film or one member of the team was out of town and others used the time for their class. Students were often assisted by being advised of such details as what textbooks to bring, where to turn in an assignment that would be read by more than one teacher, and when class meetings would be held in a computer lab or the library.

The use of an electronic bulletin board is consistent with a constructivist view of education where learning is seen as occurring in an environment that fosters both personal development of meaning and a sharing of interpretations. In addition, constructivists aim to develop learning environments where learners "are required to examine thinking and learning processes; collect, record, and analyze data; formulate and test hypotheses; reflect on previous understandings; and construct their own meaning" (Crotty, 1994, p. 31). As Edens (2000) points out,

> ... the new focus on constructivist theories of learning have [sic] given rise to constructivist information processing views that propose a conceptualization of the individual as an active constructor of knowledge. This view highlights the significant role of the social dimensions of learning acquired through active interactions and communal sharing in collaborative environments. (p. 22)

In the cluster course described here, the 27 students and four professors used the bulletin board in a variety of ways and at various levels. The second day of class, students attended a workshop run by a member of the instructional technology staff who explained the technology and how it would be used in this class. Then the students explored its uses and were assigned tasks that would help them get acquainted with each other and begin a pattern of use.

ANALYSIS OF THE ELECTRONIC BULLETIN BOARD

The data we examined from the class bulletin board includes all the entries made during the class semester, and those made in the semester following when the class was over but the board remained active and in existence. Thus, the data consist of a total of 1,252 entries: 931 posted during the class and 321 posted in the following semester. Of those, 1,120 were posted by students, 132 by faculty. Students were even more active consumers of the bulletin board's contents, with a total of 26,656 items read. The average number of posts was 41 and the average number of items read was 987. Not all students used the resource equally; items read ranged from 34 to 1,252 and items posted from 10 to 158. A thematic analysis revealed that the bulletin board functioned in a range of ways within the cluster course.

We read the contents of the bulletin board to determine whether it contributed to the development of the learning community and to the intellectual development of individual students. We found that the bulletin board most definitely contributed to the development of group rapport and cohesiveness, and that, apparently as a result of that cohesiveness, meaningful and extended discussions emerged that suggest the bulletin board also aided in the development of intellectual growth of individual students.

Evidence of how the bulletin board contributed to group cohesiveness comes from three areas: comments students offered in class assessments, both during and after the class; the postings themselves; and the ongoing use, sporadic but warm, of the bulletin board, which remains in occasional use a full three semesters after the end of the cluster course.

The group of first-semester students who took the pilot cluster course and produced the discussions analyzed in this chapter have now completed their second year of college, and at least a third of them still visit the bulletin board from time to time to offer holiday greetings, give updates on major events in their lives, invite others to their band gigs, and tease each other. The bulletin board does not retain its function as discussion facilitator, yet it still serves as a site where many of the students check in on each other, suggesting that many of the bonds formed in that first-semester learning community have lasted.

Student surveys verified enthusiasm for WebCT and indicated their belief that the bulletin board contributed to their learning. Surveys at the end of the course included the following comments:

- One of most memorable things about the class was WebCT.

- WebCT is a great tool that we have to interact with students and professors.

- The bulletin board is a nice addition to the class, giving students a forum to express themselves. I think the cluster course will help students become better learners and students. And even the single critical comment about the bulletin board was linked to a positive response.

- The WebCT was a great resource, but it is difficult when some assignments require going on it.

All 16 responses about WebCT submitted in a later survey were also positive, including comments such as "I love WebCT" and "WebCT rocks!" Students commented on both social and educational benefits: "I like chatting with other people," "It adds to the camaraderie," and "I thought it was great when we debated, because it gave us an opportunity to clearly think about what we want to say and hear what others our age had to say."

This final student comment captures our own conclusions about the bulletin board. It did indeed give students the opportunity to think, compose their ideas, and listen to their peers. In other words, it provided a venue whereby the students could benefit from many of the advantages of student discussion as outlined by McKeachie (1994):

> Discussion helps students learn to think, gives them opportunities to formulate applications of principles, helps them become aware of and formulate problems using information gained from readings or lectures, provides them with the resources of the group, encourages them to accept information or theories counter to their previous beliefs, and in general motivates their learning. (pp. 31–32)

Berrill (1991) also investigated discussion among undergraduates and found that "students can generate alternative viewpoints, can evaluate them and can come to individual synthesis or group consensus" (p. 143). She observed that students "become increasingly aware of their differences and the areas in which their understandings are shared" (p. 155). This she claims "typifies the talk of university undergraduates" (p. 156). Every one of these positive results of student discussion can be identified in the bulletin board discussions.

The bulk of bulletin board postings are not intellectually stimulating discussions; rather, they announce class assignments or student activities, respond to brief assignments, and, most of all, contain banter between students. But all of these postings, which may seem relevant only to the daily running of the class or to student socializing, in fact appeared to build a comfort zone for this student learning community within which several rich and risky discussions emerged. We will examine two of these in some detail. First, a discussion about Christopher Columbus and his contemporary, Bartolomé de las Casas, and second, a debate about the controversial film *Blue Velvet*.

Analysis of Columbus and de las Casas Thread

The first true discussion on the bulletin board evolved from assigned posts into a spontaneous debate about how we should judge history and its prominent figures, and about the level of responsibility individuals might have for large-scale crimes against humanity. The discussion drew the participation of 14 students and one professor and consisted of 41 posts, 23 of which offer discussion of substance while the remainder include banter related to a class party inspired by the discussion. The bantering students were also the debating students, and the students who did not write posts were, for the most part, following the bulletin board debate and participated in the resulting class party.

The Columbus discussion began when students were asked to post the results of their research about one aspect of their American Civilization or Humanities II course and to respond to two other posts. Two students chose to follow up on material the class had read that criticized Christopher Columbus (throughout this chapter we have retained the students' original typography):

> My research question was about Columbus and how different people viewed him [in 1492, 1892, and 1992]. . . .

He wasn't looked upon as the scum that [our textbook writer] thinks he is.

Well in this little episode of research I decided to delve into the realm of Columbus and his biological warfare that he unleashed. He may have killed hundreds of thousands by the sword but he was also the root of MILLIONS of deaths due to the diseases the white man brought to the new world. . . . I personally don't judge the man at all. . . . Why should he be held accountable by todays standards when the "crimes" he persecuted 500 years ago weren't all that bad?

At this point, the American Civilization professor intervened to challenge the students to think more deeply about the issue:

Someone who lived at the time [Bartolomé de las Casas] in fact saw just what we now see—that the Natives were fully human, and deserved better. . . . I'd like to declare October 12 de las Casas day, when we should celebrate the real hero of that era.

Students responded both to the possibility of a celebration and to the challenge to think harder, and all the rest of the posts in this thread were voluntary rather than assigned. One group of students, eager for a class party, began to argue about who made the best cookies:

Wait a second, I just want everyone to know that I spent all day baking these wonderful, chocolatey cookies that were just the most perfect things in the world

Apparently [student name] was trying to poison the class with her "wonderful chocolately cookies." So I expect a big thank you from all you guys on de Las Casas Day because I just might have saved your lives. . . .

You guys might as well quit arguing because I am a better cook than any of you. My cookies are the best, especially my monster cookies (sorry I'm not bringing that kind on Tuesday).

Meanwhile, three other students forged connections between the Columbus problem and other material: a quote from Albert Einstein, a sociology lecture, and Holocaust author Elie Wiesel:

> A quote From Albert Einstein: "The world is too dangerous to live in—not because of the people who do evil, but because of the people who stand by and let them."

> In my sociology class, my prof told us that when something bad happens and there is a group of people there, it is more likely that no one will help because everyone is expecting someone else to do something about it.

> This reminds me so much of Elie Wiesel... one of my favorite authors. I'm sure that when you guys read "Night" [...] you will understand what I mean.

The move from bulletin board to in-class activity and back to bulletin board underscores the valuable dynamics between the electronic classroom and the traditional classroom. The bulletin board discussion helped students to struggle with information from class readings and lectures, and to become aware of different viewpoints held by class members, just as McKeachie (1994) and Berrill (1991) suggest good discussions should. Students also drew links between their cluster courses, introducing a contrast between Columbus and Hitler that anticipated issues that would be studied in their Humanities II class later in the semester. As the debate progressed, the students wrote longer posts, working harder to make their ideas clear to their classmates and to counter objections. The strength of the learning community bonds is evident both in the honesty with which students shared their beliefs and feelings, and in their evident concern at maintaining civility:

> i'm getting a little upset because of how everyone is bashing columbus. i still like the guy, and i know he made mistakes, but so does everyone else.

> Well I for one, loved Las Casas Day! I know that you guys won't all agree with what I have to say next, but I honestly believe Columbus was a greedy terrible person. ... Maybe it is true that we would not be here today if it

> wasn't for Columbus, but I'm sure more native Americans would be...

> I'm not saying that he and Columbus are in the same league, but I'm curious as to your opinion of Hitler. Did that have a purpose? I guess I can't figure out why anyone, including God, would have purposely and knowingly unleashed Hitler on the world...

> i guess i don't think it is fair to try to compare the two. . . i know that what hitler did was wrong, and i have to stick to my belief that i think everything in this world happens for a reason that we don't know

> The point I'm trying to make with all of this is that a person must look at the issue from both perspectives before passing judgement on whether a leader was heroic or tyrannical. There's always two sides to a story, and I'm sure both Hitler and Columbus had valid justifications for their actions.

The stage was set for the Columbus discussion by the writing professor who assigned the research and by the American Civilization professor's prompts for deeper thinking, but the students themselves controlled the debate from there. Once the debate had taken off, students left behind the assigned task; they were interested in hearing each other's opinions and arguments:

> Wow! Thanks everyone who has given their opinions on this! I was neither condemning or supporting either Hitler or Columbus, but I do see some parallels between the two, and it is interesting to hear what you guys think.

One clear advantage of bulletin board discussions is that while the board is an extension of the class, students can claim the space as their own in a way they cannot in a classroom where the professor is physically present. In a conventional classroom, lighthearted banter about cookies could not intermingle so successfully with earnest arguments about faith and values to produce a multifaceted discussion that simultaneously validated social bonds and fostered intellectual growth. These students directed their comments primarily to each other rather than to the professors. Furthermore, students whose opinions were less popular, or even ran counter to the professor's point of view, used the bulletin board to express them. On the bulletin board, students know professors will read and perhaps respond to their posts, but they are most interested, as the final comment makes explicit, in hearing each other's thoughts. These trends continued into the spontaneous discussion of the film *Blue Velvet,* which began shortly after the Columbus thread ended.

Analysis of *Blue Velvet* Thread

After two students left the viewing of *Blue Velvet,* which they considered an immoral film, one of them posted the one-line entry, "I must say that I was not impressed with this movie," launching a discussion that developed quickly into a serious debate about education, personal values, and the relationship between art and reality. Many of the posts are several thoughtful paragraphs in length and demonstrate both the strength of the learning community that had developed by midterm and the capacity of first-year students to challenge each other and contribute to one another's learning. These excerpts demonstrate how the bulletin board can become a space for effective discussion that achieves learning aims by facilitating non-threatening exploration of class content among a community of learners. This series of 81 postings was written by 13 students (several of whom were not normally frequent contributors) and three professors. In other words, although the discussion was not assigned, half the students in the class participated, and most of the others read the posts.

The *Blue Velvet* entries show the students working hard to express their opinions and respond to the challenges of their classmates with stronger evidence and logic, while maintaining their learning community bonds. One student framed her critique of the walkout with concern about maintaining bonds:

> I've got something to say about all this, so at the risk of alienating half the class, here goes . . . [She goes on to explain how in her view their behavior was troubling and inconsistent] So, in closing, if you've made it this far, I'm not condemning either of you (gives their names here). I'm trying to explain the "other" point of view, or at least one of them.

Other students were inspired to share their points of view as well, and to defend them:

> My personal feeling is, when you come to college you have to expect certain things which will stretch your mind. You might get uncomfortable, but it is important to stop and think about why. That's where growth comes from. If I was never challenged—never made uncomfortable by some thought or image or notion—I'd never grow as a person. I'm not saying that all things are appropriate to sit through, but "Blue Velvet" is a film; it's not even like it's a documentary on a real event.

> I am all for the stretching of my mind; however, I do not think that polluting my mind is the same as stretching it. Learning from the mistakes of the past (like the holocaust, the witch trials, and the guillotine) in my mind is not the same as watching sexual acts involving a pair of scissors.

> No offense to [student names] or anyone else who didn't like Blue Velvet, but IT'S JUST A MOVIE!! For example, if you saw a movie with people drinking beer in it, would you get up and leave because you don't agree with it? . . . If you look at the movie, as a whole, it's actually got a plot. It's not people having sex all the time. You can't just single out the 1 or 2 bad parts of the movie and slam them, look at the whole picture, then comment on what you liked and disliked.

> [Student name]-i don't see how you can say the 'sex' scenes in blue velvet promotes sexual violence. it is a very disturbing, offensive, and violent depiction of a sexual event. but i have notice that not one person has brought up, is that the sexual encounter between Dennis Hoper, and Isabella Rossilenie was not two people having sex. it was a sexual assault, rape. . . . Do you think that director David Lynch made that scene with the hopes of it uping the number of rapes in this country? NO, he wanted to show how extremly F**ked up Frank really was.

The *Blue Velvet* thread also demonstrates how students used the bulletin board to make their own connections among the content of different classes, which was a central goal of the cluster course. Several students drew on course material they studied in European and American history and literature to strengthen the arguments they were developing. The references to guillotines, death camps, witch hunts, Martin Luther King, Jr., and John Stuart Mill demonstrate students not merely recollecting material studied, but drawing connections and using those connections to advance their own arguments:

> To the people who dislike the film so much—why did you sit though discussions of guillotines and WWII death camps? *That* makes me sick to my stomach. That was real. Tortures so cruel that we can't even begin to fathom them occurred . . . but no one walked out. Why?

> i understand where you are coming from, and i thank you for posting your point of view. i think of ww2 and the witch trials as part of history, and by educating ourselves on those points in history will make us sure not to repeat ourselves and our terrible acts. 'blue velvet' is a movie that may have some good points that i'm sure we will discuss tomorrow after you finish watching the movie.

> I think the movie speaks for itself in how disgusting it was. I need not embellish or detract. If according to my view the scene was sick, do I have the right to express my views? Where is the spirit of nonviolent protest (ie boycott) for which we so readily commend MLKJ? If the black community would have never spoken up about what they felt was wrong, what would have happened? I believe that watching this movie is wrong. That is the reason I left.

> How do we "know" our beliefs if we can't face the fact that they might be wrong, or at least might change/ If at the beginning of blue Velvet I had believed that the film and the things portrayed in it were immoral, by the end of the movie I would have had a stronger convection of it

than I had before! Like [John Stuart] Mill would say, the
more argument you have the more truth you will reveal.

Despite the intensity of the debate over the film and the issues it raised
for students, the debate did not become hostile. A few students were bait-
ed, but refused to respond in kind. Many of the posts acknowledged the
value of varying opinions, or thanked other students for their input
despite disagreements. Social bonds between students that developed over
the semester seemed to help them resist the urge to attack each other and
to focus their arguments on the issues.

The final comments students made on the *Blue Velvet* thread emphasize how valuable they found the discussion, underscoring how the bulletin board did help meet course goals. The following comments come
from students on all sides of the issues:

> I think it's great that we're watching this movie. I've never
> seen so many posts on the bulletin board. Whether we
> like it or not, it's great that everyone is discussing the film.

> Right on!! That is, right on about us discussing it, and
> that being neat.

> I do love a good discussion. This has been a great use of
> the message boards, and I hope that we can carry this
> conversation into class.

> i know we are all entitled to our own views and opinions,
> and most of us have voiced them over this topic. i think
> that this discussion has brought up a lot of good points
> for and against what i did, but i am going to stick behind
> my actions [the choice to leave class during the film].

These closing comments also convey a sense that students feel an
ownership in the debate: "everyone is discussing" and "us discussing it"
and "most of us have voiced them [our views]." This ownership, and the
pride that goes with it, are possible because the bulletin board is a space
primarily for the students themselves. Professors participated in the discussion, but as in the Columbus debate, most of the student comments
are directed to other students, not to professors. In fact, throughout the
semester, students showed a strong inclination to keep professors on the
outskirts of bulletin board discussions.

RECOMMENDATIONS

The results from this class clearly indicate that the electronic bulletin board enhanced the learning experience in the cluster course, fostering learning community bonds and student learning through discussion. We offer several recommendations for incorporating an electronic bulletin board into a class in such a way as to maximize the potential for such a positive outcome and increase the possibility that vital discussions will emerge. Based on our experience and on the analysis of bulletin board content, we offer the following suggestions for using the electronic bulletin board productively:

- Require students to attend a hands-on orientation session run by an expert, and ensure that every student can successfully access and use the electronic bulletin board before the end of the first week of class.

- Insofar as possible, make it convenient for students to access the electronic bulletin board regularly. Make certain that students are aware of the location and hours of computer labs and university-sponsored training sessions that would be of value.

- Use the class management functions of the web classroom software to track student involvement on the bulletin board.

- Make the bulletin board participation a factor in student evaluation, perhaps simply with credit/no credit marks, but do not criticize students' grammar, usage, and punctuation.

- Assign postings regularly, especially early in the semester, to help students become comfortable with the technology, to encourage habits of checking the bulletin board, and to lay the groundwork for a variety of uses of the bulletin board.

- Require students to respond to each other's postings in order to facilitate discussion. This strategy helps ensure that students see the bulletin board as a space for interaction and not simply reporting, and it works particularly well in facilitating the transition from routine postings to true discussion.

- Maintain a regular, but not dominating, professorial presence on the bulletin board. Students like knowing that teachers read their posts, but too much teacher involvement in discussions tends to reduce student comfort and voluntary participation. The electronic bulletin board seems to work best when it is a space primarily populated by students.

- Do not be afraid to be provocative. Placing your comments and/or the words of others (or links to online articles, etc.) on the board for reaction encourages students to offer thoughtful opinions and to quickly see that others view the world differently than they do—a valuable insight for undergraduates.

- Do not assume that only those posting frequently are learning. In our experience, many students were frequent readers and less frequent posters. (You can easily assess this using the course management tool.) Some of the best comments came from students who read often, then replied with insight gained from hearing the others out before responding. Both the quick and frequent posters and those who read and think before responding play an important role in the use of the board as an interaction tool.

CONCLUSION

The use of an electronic bulletin board as a support tool offers a rich opportunity to enhance many of the academic and social goals of the college classroom experience. We found that an analysis of its use in an interdisciplinary set of courses for first-year students showed it served multiple purposes. A closer examination of two of the discussion threads evidenced student cognitive development and insight. Our experience leads us to concur with Riel and Fulton (2001): "one of the most promising uses of technology is as a vehicle for building and supporting learning communities that will help students thrive in the new millennium" (p. 519).

REFERENCES

Allen, M. (1994). Adventures with "Robin Hood": Gender and conflict on a first-year bulletin board. *Journal of Teaching Writing, 13* (1–2), 169–196.

Althaus, S. (1997). Computer-mediated communication in the university classroom: An experiment with online discussions. *Communication Education, 46* (3), 158–174.

Berrill, D. (1991). Exploring underlying assumptions: Small group work of university graduates. *Educational Review, 43* (2), 143–157.

Bloom, B., Englehart, M., Furst, E., Hill, W., & Krathwohl, D. (1956). *Taxonomy of educational objectives. Handbook I: Cognitive domain.* New York, NY: Macmillan.

Brandon, D., & Hollingshead, A. B. (1999). Collaborative learning and computer-supported groups. *Communication Education, 48* (2), 109–126.

Cole, R. (2000, July). Chemistry, teaching, and WebCT. *Journal of Chemical Education, 77* (7), 826–827.

Collins, M. (1998). The use of email and electronic bulletin boards in college-level biology. *Journal of Computers in Mathematics and Science Teaching, 17* (1), 75–94.

Crotty, T. (1994). Integrating distance learning activities to enhance teacher education toward the constructivist paradigm of teaching and learning. In A. Yakimovicz (Ed.), *Distance Learning Research Conference Proceedings* (pp. 31–37). College Station, TX: Texas A&M University, Department of Education and Human Resource Development.

Eastmond, D., & Ziegahn, L. (1995). Instructional design for the online classroom. In Z. L. Berge & M. P. Collins (Eds.), *Computer-mediated communication and the on-line classroom, Vol. 3: Distance education* (pp. 59–80). Cesskill, NJ: Hampton Press.

Edens, K. (2000, Summer). Promoting communication, inquiry and reflection in an early practicum experience via an on-line discussion group. *Action in Teacher Education, 24,* 14–23.

Hillman, D., Bottomley, D., Raisner, J., & Malin, B. (2000, Summer). Learning to practice what we teach: Integrating elementary education methods courses. *Action in Teacher Education, 24,* 91–100.

International Society for Technology in Education. (1998, June). *National educational technology standards for students.* Eugene, OR: Nets Project.

Krathwohl, D., Bloom, B., & Masia, B. (1956). *Taxonomy of educational objectives: Handbook I: Affective domain.* New York, NY: Longman.

Lenning, O. T., & Ebbers, L. H. (1999). *The powerful potential of learning communities: Improving education for the future.* (ASHE-ERIC Higher Education Report Volume 26, No. 6). Washington, DC: The George Washington University, Graduate School of Education and Human Development.

McComb, M. (1994). Benefits of computer-mediated communication in college courses. *Communication Education, 43* (2), 159–170.

McKeachie, W. (1994). *Teaching tips: Strategies, research, and theory for college and university teachers.* Lexington, MA: D. C. Heath.

Morley, L., & LaMaster, K. (1999, August). Use electronic bulletin boards to extend classrooms. *The Journal of Physical Education, Recreation & Dance, 70* (6), 16–20.

Mowrer, D. E. (1996). A content analysis of student/instructor communication via computer conferencing. *Higher Education, 32,* 217–241.

Riel, M., & Fulton, K. (2001). The role of technology in supporting learning communities. *Phi Delta Kappan, 82* (7), 518–523.

Shapiro, N. S., & Levine, J. H. (1999). *Creating learning communities: A guide to winning support, organizing for change, and implementing programs.* San Francisco, CA: Jossey-Bass.

Stith, B. (2000, March). Web-enhanced lecture course scores big with students and faculty. *T.H.E. Journal, 27* (8), 20–23.

Wernet, S., Olliges, R. H., & Delicath, T. A. (2000, July). Postcourse evaluations of WebCT (Web Course Tools) classes by social work students. *Research on Social Work Practice, 10* (4), 487–504.

BUILDING A COMMUNICATIONS LEARNING COMMUNITY

Patricia Worrall and Brian Kline

> *... embedded in the process of communication is the fact that we live in and search for community. In fact, our attempts to communicate are attempts at community building.*
>
> —Palloff & Pratt

Turoff (1995) asserts, "...we can use the powers of the computer to actually do better than what normally occurs in the face to face class" (p. 1). As we developed our learning community, the question constantly examined was, What can we do in a learning community with web support that we cannot do in our traditional classrooms?

RATIONALE FOR THE LEARNING COMMUNITY

During the fall 1999 and spring 2000 semesters, students in the Composition and Introduction to Human Communication courses took part in a learning community that was developed for several reasons. First, the college was supportive of the learning community concept. Research indicates that learning communities can help students by providing additional emotional and academic support. Hiltz (1998) indicates, "Despite earlier fears to the contrary, online communities can provide emotional support and sociability as well as information and instrumental aid" (p. 2). The

226

learning community was the project of Physics Professor J. B. Sharma, the 1998–1999 Gainesville College Distinguished Professor. Distinguished professors are asked to develop a project in which faculty from different disciplines can participate. Professor Sharma attended a conference on learning communities and decided on this as his project because of the potential for involving faculty and for showing students the connections between courses in a liberal arts education.

Second, the Department of Speech and Fine Arts was an independent department until an administrative decision was made to collapse it into the Humanities Division. One of the outcomes of this merger was a communications component consisting of English and speech.

The final rationale for the learning community was the common concepts and assignments in these introductory courses. Until recently, the English Composition course was a prerequisite for the Introduction to Human Communication course. The prerequisite seemed unnecessary; the skills learned in either course would help students in the other.

PLANNING FOR THE LEARNING COMMUNITY

The initial planning for the learning community was done a semester before teaching the course. Professor Sharma conducted an on-campus workshop explaining the requirements and incentives for doing a learning community. In order to create a learning community, faculty had to:

- Define core values
- Identify thematic linkage between courses
- Define expected student learning outcomes
- Decide how student learning would be measured
- Define grading criteria
- Decide how the learning community grade would factor in course grading
- Obtain the approval of the division chair

After the faculty developed these aspects, they were posted on the Gainesville College home page (www.gc.peachnet.edu) under the heading of "GC Learning Communities."

Faculty who participated in the project were entitled to one semester hour of reassigned time, which is equivalent to a stipend of $750. Faculty were expected to put a minimum of 15 hours into the project during the course of the semester, though it took more than 15 hours to develop and teach the learning community. Of these 15 hours, eight were for planning, and seven were for direct contact with the students in the learning community. At least three to five of the seven contact hours were expected to be completed in the classroom.

After obtaining division approval, we developed the course syllabus. Four guiding values were established for the communications learning community:

- To have students understand the importance that verbal and nonverbal communication plays in their daily lives

- To emphasize the connections and shared strengths of verbal and nonverbal communication

- To develop an appreciation for the spoken and written word

- To have students understand that an effective communicator must develop his or her written and oral skills

Three learning community activities were identified. First, students in both courses would meet for joint classroom sessions and to form project groups. Students would also be connected using WebCT. In order to ensure all students could meet during the joint session, their individual courses were taught on the same day and time. We also obtained a room on campus large enough to hold 50 students.

Second, students would work together on two projects. The first would be an informative presentation for the communication students and an informative essay for the English students. The second project would be a persuasive presentation for the communication students and a persuasive essay for the English students. Students would work together in groups on topics for these projects.

Third, Kline, the speech professor, would present lectures on delivery and using visual aids, and Worrall, the English professor, would present lectures on language and organizational strategies. Both would co-teach sessions on informative and persuasive communication. Because both disciplines are based upon rhetorical theory, the areas for inclusion in combined classes were easy to develop. Students could understand and help one another with the WebCT assignments and discussions because the rhetorical elements of an essay and a speech are quite similar.

We both established how the learning community grade would be incorporated in the final individual course grade. The learning community grade was based on the following percentages for the class assignments:

Intro. to Human Communication		English	
Informative presentation	10%	Informative research paper	15%
Persuasive presentation	10%	Informative presentation	5%
WebCT assignments	10%	Persuasive essay	10%
		WebCT assignments	10%

IMPLEMENTATION OF THE LEARNING COMMUNITY

Although students knew they were going to be part of a learning community with another class, the first combined class did not take place until the third week of the semester. This first joint class was team taught and focused on informative communication. Before meeting the combined classes, we divided students into eight groups, each with a representative from both classes. The groups were given a name—society, health, education, transportation, jobs, food, government, and defense—based upon the topic they would focus on for the persuasive presentation and essay. When the students arrived for the first class, they sat with their groups. As Clark (2000) notes, "A sense of community and some basic knowledge about fellow students is something that is usually present in face to face classrooms" (p. 5). Thus, students were given 15 to 20 minutes to introduce themselves to their group members in order to begin establishing their own community. Follow-up communication would take place with the first WebCT assignment dealing with introductions and a response to an introduction. Class discussion focused on defining information theory, patterns of organization appropriate to informative communication, topic categories, and requirements for the informative project. Students also watched a sample student presentation and discussed the merit of the speech as informative communication.

Because students in the English class are assigned a presentation with one of their papers, visual aids and delivery were discussed. Thus, the second joint class determined why visual aids are important in a presentation and the different types of visuals a speaker could use. The delivery portion of the class, taught by Kline, focused on ways to present a speech, areas to evaluate, and how to deal with nervousness. Students watched clips of professional speakers and evaluated the positives and negatives of the presentations.

Worrall taught the third joint class dealing with language and double-speak—language that pretends to communicate but really does not. Students were assigned to read two articles on the use of language, which were placed on reserve in the library before class. The class began with a discussion on words, and four types of doublespeak were examined. Students then watched a video on doublespeak and also had the opportunity to decipher doublespeak by taking a nongraded quiz.

The fourth joint class was team-taught and centered on persuasive communication. The differences between informative and persuasive communication were examined. Patterns of organization, motivational appeals, as well as needs and audience analysis were also discussed. The class then watched a student speech dealing with car repair. Students were assigned a paper or speech dealing with any topic under their group name. For the next joint class, students worked with their group in the library.

Later in the semester, students had the opportunity to listen to some of the finished presentations. One class was devoted to the English presentations, and another to speech presentations. It was, however, too time-consuming to listen to all the presentations from both classes. During the entire process, students were encouraged to visit either professor for help in completing their projects.

The in-class and WebCT assignments were designed around the idea of collaborative learning. Hiltz (1998) explains, "the role of the teacher changes from transferring knowledge to students (the "sage on the stage") to being a facilitator in the students' construction of their own knowledge (the "guide on the side")" (p. 4). We wanted the students to be more active participants in the learning community, which meant that the focus or role of the teacher had to change. The in-class and WebCT assignments also helped achieve the goal of collaboration in the learning community.

Pedagogical Strategies

To facilitate collaboration among the students in both courses, we used WebCT to engage students in computer-mediated communication (CMC). For the purpose of the learning community, we chose three of the applications provided by WebCT: the calendar, email, and the bulletin board.

The Calendar

The calendar enabled us to post assignment due dates, meeting places, and other important information, ensuring that students from both courses had access to relevant information in one convenient, central location. An additional benefit was that it emphasized the shared requirements of the two courses. Students also had the option of using the calendar to post private entries. We encouraged them to do so, which, in turn, encouraged students to check the calendar frequently. Thus, they stayed up to date with what was going on in the learning community.

Email

WebCT also provides a closed email system that students used to email each other. This system made it easy for students to communicate with their group members from both classes and easy for us to communicate with individual students. Using the email system was another means of creating community and encouraging communication between students.

The Bulletin Board

The bulletin board, however, provided the core of the online collaboration for the learning community. The bulletin board allows for the posting of entries under topic headings and for conducting threaded discussions. We used the bulletin board to post assignments; the students used it to respond to the assignments and to each other. During the course of the learning community, students had to complete three bulletin board assignments, each designed to facilitate collaboration and emphasize the shared goals and requirements of the two courses. Using the bulletin board for assignments enhanced collaboration within the learning community and was "premised upon a learner-centered model that treats the learner as an active participant" (Harasim, 1990, p. 43).

Palloff and Pratt (1999) note,

Another means by which to deliberately promote collaboration in the electronic classroom is to create teams for the purpose of small-group discussion, completion of group assignments, and engagement in small-group activities and simulations. This can be particularly useful when working with a large group or when a group needs an extra push in working collaboratively. (p. 115)

The communication learning community was both large (47 students) and needed an extra push because the students were only working together on two relatively short projects rather than semester-long projects.

Assignment #1

The first WebCT assignment occurred early in the semester. After the initial meeting with their group members, students posted an electronic introduction and a response to an introduction on the bulletin board. Palloff and Pratt (1999) suggest, "Not only does this practice [posting introductions] enable students to begin opening up to each other but it begins creating a safe space in which they can interact" (p. 114). Topic areas were created on the bulletin board that corresponded to the group designations. Under a group's topic area, each member posted a 200- to 250-word introduction giving the other group members general information about himself or herself, such as classes the student was taking, if and where he or she worked, and any hobbies or areas of interest he or she might have. Palloff and Pratt (1999) note that

> [t]he posting of an introduction is the first step in revealing who one is to the remainder of the group. Because participants feel more comfortable revealing parts of themselves in this medium that they might not reveal elsewhere, it is critical that they feel acknowledged so they can continue to do that safely throughout the duration of the course. This is the first point of connection—the point where these important relationships begin to develop. (p. 114)

In order to ensure that each student would receive an acknowledgement to his or her introduction and to facilitate interaction among students in the different classes, each student was required to post a 100- to 150-word response to one of his or her group members who was not in the same class. For example, a student in the English class would respond to a group member who was in the communication class. These introductions and responses provided students with general information about their group members and often established shared interests and mutual friends. These introductions and responses could also be read and responded to by students in other groups, which frequently happened. Thus, students in both classes learned about and responded to students who were not members of their specific groups. As a result of this first assignment, when students met again face to face with their group members, they already had conducted numerous virtual conversations. The range and variety of these personal conversations would not generally have occurred in a traditional classroom setting because of time and place constraints, and certainly not in a class that only met face to face several times during a semester.

Another approach we used to create community was through collaboration. We chose to create assignments that would emphasize the rhetorical connections between written and oral communication and provide opportunities for students to help their group members with their topics.

Assignment #2

Thus, the second WebCT assignment focused on the informative speech for the speech class and the informative essay for the English class. Students in the communication class prepared presentations on a notable speaker, while students in the English class prepared informative essays about a person who made national or international news in the year 2000. The second assignment had two parts, and was designed to help students in both classes with their research topics as well as encourage collaboration and communication among the group members. The first part of the assignment asked students to go to their topic area on the bulletin board, post their research topics, and indicate a problem they were having, such as finding information, narrowing the topic, or organizing the information about the topic. The posting needed to be specific and about 200 words. The second part of the assignment required students to respond to a group member's posting. The response needed to address the problem and offer suggestions about how to approach it. The response, as with the topic posting, needed to be specific, but only about 100 to 150 words. Through this assignment, students shared their research problems and gained assistance from other group members. Sharing problems and offering assistance with the informative speech and essay reinforced the similarities in experiences among the students, as well as the connections between written and oral communication.

Assignment #3

The third WebCT assignment followed a pattern similar to that of the second assignment, but this time students focused on the persuasive speech and the persuasive essay. As mentioned earlier, each of the eight groups was designated by broad subjects, and it was under these subjects that students selected their topics for either the persuasive speech or the persuasive essay. For example, students in the health group selected topics within that subject area. Thus, all the group members were researching similar topics. The third assignment also had two parts. First, students were required to post a description of their topic and then to note several points they planned to discuss that supported their point of view. They were also to ask for comments about these points. This posting needed to be about 200 words. The second part of the assignment was to respond to a posting from one of their group members. In their response, students provided comments about the group member's points and then provided several points in opposition to the group member's position. By providing opposing points, students helped their group members plan and organize their persuasive speeches or essays. This assignment also promoted collaboration among group members through shared topics.

The following exchange between three students is an example of postings for the third assignment. They show students working together to offer suggestions and support and illustrate community and collaboration:

> Student A: Hey There! This is . . . and I need some help writing my persuasive essay. I am writing on teenage smoking and how it is increasing in the world today. This essay is going to be directed towards a teenager as far as the audience goes. First, I am going to find a resource at the library and get some facts on how it will affect someone not just now but in the future. Then, I want to give a personal experience. My grandpa died of cancer and it was a very sad experience. My grandma gets up and coughs every morning because of the many years of secondhand smoke. Last, I am not sure how to end it, the paper, or

anything else to write. Most of all I plan for this to hit the young adults that do not realize what really can happen to them when they are older. I will try not to offend anyone but sometimes you cannot help it. So how can I end my paper? Is there anything else that I can put in my paper to make it better. I am really against smoking; I hope that I did not offend anyone who reads this. Thanks for helping.

Student A's initial posting asking for help with her topic illustrates several positive aspects of communication and community. Her posting is focused on the topic, her tone is informal, and she shares personal information with her group members that is within the context of the topic. Student B's response follows:

Student B: Hey . . . How are you? Good I hope. I read over your ideas for your paper. I think that it sounds good. Especially the part about your grandpa because sometimes it takes something really emotional like that to open up someone's eyes and realize how dangerous smoking is. I'm like you, i [sic] hate smoking. It think that if you end your paper with something emotional that will really make the audience stop and think, they are more likely to remember it and hopefully be affected by it. For instance, you could say that "Smoking is not a game. Either you can put away the cigarettes now, or I will visit you at the funeral home in a couple of years. The decision is yours." I know that sounds really stupid but I hope that you get what I am trying to say. In my opinion [sic], getting someone to quit smoking is one of the hardest things a person can try to do. Both of my parents smoke and I stay on them all the time. Good luck on your paper and I hope that maybe this has helped you a little.

Student B's response indicates that she has carefully read Student A's posting and has thought about ways for Student A to approach her topic. Student B stays focused on the questions, indicates her agreement, and offers encouragement. Student C's response to Student A follows:

Student C: Hey . . . I think the smoking topic is a good idea. Smoking can harm not only the person who smokes but also the people who are around the smoker. Another problem deals with the tobacco growers who are getting slammed by the lawsuits that hit their buyers, the cigarette manufacturers. Maybe you could include something about the people and their problems too. P.S. thanks for the help with my topic.

Student C also focused on Student A's questions and adds another suggestion for the essay, the inclusion of the tobacco growers. The student closes her response by thanking Student A for her help.

The responses of these three students show a sense of community and productive collaboration. Students B and C offer concrete suggestions to Student A about her topic. Also, the tone of the initial posting and the responses is informal and friendly, thus reinforcing a sense of community among these students.

The three WebCT assignments discussed above proved to be invaluable as a means of building a sense of community within these two classes. The assignments and the conversations that resulted extended the learning community beyond the physical space of the classroom and, in turn, increased communication and interaction among students.

Personal Issues

For the most part, this interaction was positive and enhanced collaboration, as shown by the above exchanges, but there were times when communication broke down among students. In their discussion of computer-mediated communication, Palloff and Pratt (1999) note that "one of the concerns about conflict in this medium is that with the absence of face to face contact and cues, many people feel less socially constrained" (p. 27). They also note, "We need to be able to make space for personal issues in an online course. This must be done deliberately and fostered throughout the course. If this space is not created, it is likely that participants will seek out other ways to create personal interaction, such as through email or by bringing personal issues into the course discussion" (p. 29).

Unfortunately, we did not provide a space for informal discussions of personal issues, and the following series of exchanges illustrate how one student responded to the third WebCT assignment by inappropriately using the bulletin board for personal issues, which in turn, resulted in a flurry of emotionally charged postings:

Student D: I don't know what I am going to do on my persuassion [sic] speech. By the looks at the people in my class the only possible topic I could do would be to persuade them not to inbreed. It is bad! I don't know for real what I am going to do. I haven't decided. I am not focused on doing this right now anyway. I don't have a hard time B.S.'ing my way everyday so I don't think I'll have a problem in this speech. I got man troubles anyway. Hey maybe I'll do my speech on how to get a man and what and what not to say to him to get him to stay. Men are so hard [to] tell things too. Well I take that back men that you like sexually are hard to tell things too. All my friends are guys and I talk to them just fine, but of course I don't have feelings for them. Help me ladies! Tell me how your [sic] suppose to carry on a conversation with a guy you work with and you have a crush on? Is it possible? Oh well, we'll find out today in fact. Gook [sic] luck with your topic!

Fiksdal (2001), citing the work of Deborah Tannen, notes that "women use language to make connections and establish and maintain relationships" (p. 184). She concludes that "[s]peaking in one's own voice means using a particular conversational style that may not be shared by others in the group" (p. 184). Student D's posting illustrates these aspects. Her group members were all female, and she uses the posting to establish a relationship with the other women in her group. Responses to her posting, however, were confrontational and posted only by women both in and outside her group. These female students came to the defense of their peers and the college as the exchanges below illustrate:

Student E: I have read two recent entries from you that are absolutely outrageous!! Basically, between the two messages, you have called all of us Gainesville College students "[inbred] rednecks"!!! Is that what you meant to say? I am not sure of who [sic] you are referring to, but I am neither a redneck nor [inbred] and do not by any means appreciate your comments. You really need to watch what you say in here because believe it or not, people do read these entries!! Do you really think you are any better than the rest of us?! If so, I would LOVE to hear why! Also, there are a lot of people who love Gainesville College. And you must have had some bad experiences with teachers because I will graduate soon and I have liked almost all of my teachers. If you are so unhappy here at Gainesville College, then by all means, LEAVE!!

Student D responded in her own defense with additional accusations:

Student D: Let me ask you something? Are you in my group? I do not think so, but you seem to be interested in all that I say! Hum! I wonder why? If you had read my [posting] carefully and completely you would have known that I said what I said should not be taken personally and that I have had a bad experience with Gainesville College. But you have seemed to completely ignore that fact. Typical of someone who is trying to start an argument over nothing. Well, I [don't] want [to] start a battle of the wits with an unarmed person. But I will tell you the last time I checked my opinions were guaranteed by the Constitution of the United States of America not you. All I can suggest is if you don't like my opinions don't read them. Otherwise don't comment about them because you will have no ground to stand on. Next time show a little more class and write an intelligent letter with correct punctuation.

The rhetoric continued to escalate into even more insults directed toward Student D. Student F responded:

Student F: Where did you address your so called message to anyone specific? HELLO this is an open bulletin board format. Try using all two of your brain cells and maybe you will notice that every message is public to everyone. Well, that's not true, you certainly have more than two brain cells. But your previous post proves your pathetic, moronic ineptude [sic] at utilizing more than two. And sorry to break the news to you, but a free country means everyone has the right to criticize you into oblivion for idiotic, stupid ideas that you fail to keep to yourself.

This deterioration in communication and community was resolved by the students themselves without our intervention. Once confronted with the immediate barrage of responses, Student D retreated from her confrontational stance and was reconciled with her group members, although there remained some tension within the group. The above exchanges also illustrate the attitude of some students about the public space of the bulletin board postings. Some either forget that the bulletin board is a public forum or they are uncomfortable with the fact that it is. What we found, however, was that most students responded with the awareness that their postings were public, and they appreciated having access to the comments of other students in and out of their groups.

STUDENT FEEDBACK

Student surveys concerning the communication learning community were conducted, and the responses were encouraging. When asked if the interaction with students in the other learning community course enhanced their learning experiences, the majority responded that it had. Although they did not articulate the reasons why their learning experiences were enhanced, Harasim (1990) suggests, among other reasons, that "[a]synchronous group learning can also reduce competition for air-time among participants" and "[i]nterpersonal contact among members of the group is extended, since interaction is not limited to a finite period, as in face to face or telephone contact" (p. 47). We suspect that these two aspects certainly contributed to the enhanced learning experiences of the students. The majority of the students also responded that they would take another learning community course and that they would recommend learning community courses to other students. A number of students responded that they felt the learning community course required more work than a traditional course. Their perception was perhaps due to the number of collaborative assignments, which they would not necessarily have had in a completely face to face course. On the other hand, some students felt they needed more time and interaction with the other students in the learning community. Overall, however, the responses were positive.

LESSONS LEARNED

We have learned a number of valuable lessons from our experiences teaching the communication learning community:

- First, there is a need for space on the bulletin board for informal chat and discussion of personal issues. There is also a need for a written disruptive virtual behavior policy to prevent exchanges such as the one presented earlier. The policy would address the use of inappropriate language, the posting and discussing of inappropriate subject matter, and the participation in personal attacks. It would also set forth the consequences for violations of the policy, such as a student's removal from his or her group.

- More emphasis is needed on the WebCT assignments in the form of a higher percentage of the course work. These assignments must comprise a substantial part of the overall grade for the course or students will tend not to take the assignments seriously, which works against the goals of communication and community.

- Third, we became aware that we needed to reinforce the interconnections between our two disciplines. What is quite obvious to us is not so obvious to the students. Thus, we need to emphasize the shared rhetorical aspects between oral and written communication through our discussions of the materials and the assignments we give students.

CONCLUSION

As we prepared and taught the communication learning community, we formed a learning community ourselves. We collaborated on assignments, course material, and lectures, a collaboration that would not have happened without the creation of the learning community. We shared our knowledge and expertise in our disciplines, and in turn, gained as colleagues.

REFERENCES

Clark, J. (2000, October). Collaboration tools in online learning environments. *Asynchronous Learning Network Magazine, 4* (1) [Online]. Available: http://www.aln.org/alnweb/magazine/Vol4_issue1/Clark .htm

Fiksdal, S. (2001). Voices in seminar: Ideologies and identities. In B. L. Smith & J. McCann (Eds.), *Reinventing ourselves: Interdisciplinary education, collaborative learning, and experimentation in higher education* (pp. 179–194). Bolton, MA: Anker.

Harasim, L. M. (1990). Online education: An environment for collaboration and intellectual amplification. In L. M. Harasim (Ed.), *Online education: Perspectives on a new environment* (pp. 39–64). New York, NY: Praeger.

Hiltz, S. R. (1998, November). *Collaborative learning in asynchronous learning networks: Building learning communities* [Online]. Available: http://eies.njit.edu/~hiltz/collaborative_learning_in_asynch.htm

Palloff, R., & Pratt, K. (1999). *Building learning communities in cyberspace: Effective strategies for the online classroom.* San Francisco, CA: Jossey-Bass.

Turoff, M. (1995, March). *Designing a virtual classroom* [Online]. Available: http://www.njit.edu/Department/CCCC/VC/Papers/Design.html

TEACHING AND LEARNING WITH INTERACTIVE TECHNOLOGIES: WHAT HAVE WE LEARNED AND WHERE ARE WE GOING?

Patricia Comeaux

When we venture outside our academic discipline, we expand our knowledge, our perspective, and our understanding of other disciplines as well as our own. This is similar to what anthropology professor and scholar Edward T. Hall (1977) recommends individuals do for survival and for understanding of self and others. As he cautions, "That means that if one is to prosper in this new world without being unexpectedly battered, one must transcend one's own system [culture]" (p. 51). This collection, in effect, illustrates the value of transcending one's own discipline.

SECTION I: PROGRAM DEVELOPMENT

The four chapters in Section I are case studies in which the authors describe and analyze their efforts as part of a design and planning team charged with adapting and developing a graduate degree program for distance education.

The themes of Section I are:

1) A clearly defined need must be the basis for developing a distance learning program.

2) Cross-disciplinary planning and sharing of resources contribute to successful collaboration in cross-disciplinary projects.

3) Successful distance education programs must offer degrees rather than individual courses.

Clearly Defined Needs

Motivations or incentives play a large part in any decision-making situation. To be successful, distance education programs should be based on clearly identified needs. While this seems obvious, it does not always happen, especially with the push to try out new interactive technologies. The four chapters all identified pressing needs as they developed their programs:

- To correct a deficiency in an MBA program (Chapter 1)

- To remedy declining enrollments in an on-campus graduate project management degree program as well as a desire to be the first fully online asynchronous project management degree program in the United States (Chapter 2)

- To address state-mandated certification purposes for a graduate degree in instructional technology and to share resources among three state universities (Chapter 3)

- To reach potential graduate students who could not leave families or careers to obtain an advanced degree (Chapter 4)

Collaborative Cross-Disciplinary Planning and Resource Sharing

Three of the four chapters in Section I articulate the value of collaborative planning. In two of the case studies (Chapters 1 and 2), the teams included cross-disciplinary faculty from the business schools as well as administrative representatives and instructional design and technology experts. Since the focus for the instructional technology degree (Chapter 3) was to develop seven courses to meet state certification mandates, seven teams of three individuals (combining content, technological, and distance education expertise) were formed, with each team responsible for developing a course. Clearly, the success of these programs is intricately linked to the development processes and the ability of the team members to collaborate effectively. In addition, the authors of these case studies describe how they developed and followed a systematic plan based on sound instructional designs and the perceived needs of the distance students.

In contrast, Chapter 4 illustrates what happens when collaboration is not part of the planning process. In this case study, faculty responsible for teaching in the distance education program were locked into a top-down decision with a pedagogical model not of their design nor consistent with their teaching philosophy or methodology.

Graduate Degree Programs

All four chapters in Section I describe case studies of graduate programs. The most significant thing they have in common is the agreement (both stated and implied) that to be successful it is better to offer a degree program rather than individual courses. As evidenced in these chapters, the real power of distance education can be realized from degree programs because they have the potential to change institutional practice and to capture the interest and imagination of the university as well as the public.

SECTION II: PROFESSIONAL COLLABORATIVE ENDEAVORS

Section II presents case studies of faculty electing to teach with colleagues from different institutions across the distance via interactive technologies. Teaching and presentational strategies in an interactive audio/video environment focusing specifically upon the impact that video images have in a teaching environment mediated by technology is also considered.

The themes of Section II are:

1) Team teaching provides multiple benefits culminating in professional development.

2) Successful professional collaboratives require advance planning and productive communication.

Team Teaching as Professional Development

All eight authors in Section II state that their most compelling reason for electing to collaborate with faculty from institutions across the distance is for professional development. A teaching collaborative allows individuals to expand their knowledge base, enhance their teaching methodologies, and explore new technologies in a professional support network. Furthermore, professors realize the value of diverse perspectives in a learning environment. Thus, there is a distinct advantage to teaming with other professors (and their students).

Other advantages of a professional collaborative articulated by the authors in Section II include:

- Sparks interaction and interest among the students

- Enacts (demonstrates) the uses of interactive technologies

- Offers a wider range of instructional materials

- Adds credibility and diversity

- Gains assistance and support (comfort—we are in this together) with technical difficulties

Successful Collaboration: Advance Planning and Productive Communication

All authors agree that collaborating with others requires preplanning and hard work; it is time-consuming and risky, but for the most part, worth the effort.

Not only is advance planning necessary for teaching and learning successes but it serves to potentially avoid conflict or misunderstandings among the partners in the collaborative. The most successful collaborative endeavors, as evidenced in these case studies, are characterized by frequent, direct, open, and honest communication.

It is also important to note that too many partners in a collaborative add a level of complexity and complication that can make it extremely difficult to manage the communication and the instructional environment (see Chapter 7). In such cases, the partners must agree upon both specific course goals and common objectives, and how they will achieve them. In addition, they must both plan and prepare their students in advance for the collaboration. In sum, they must be willing to engage in frequent, productive communication about what is working and what is not working. Productive communication can enhance the professional relationship as well as the instructional design and implementation.

Section III: Creating Online Learning Communities

The five chapters in Section III all detail the efforts and pedagogy involved in creating online learning communities. Although the authors in these case studies use different software packages, their educational objectives are similar: to create an online communication and learning environment as an integral part of an online course (Chapters 11 and 12), or in combination with the face to face classroom environment (Chapter 10), or as an extension of the face to face classroom environment (Chapters 13 and 14).

The themes of Section III are:

1) Instructors are willing to investigate their online courses and, furthermore, they are being internally funded by their institutions to develop their courses for online instruction.

2) Online instruction (computer-mediated communication) produces noteworthy effects on the communication skills of instructors and students.

Online Teaching Initiatives as Research and Internally Funded Projects

Significantly, all five case studies represent a major effort on the part of higher education faculty to not only develop innovative approaches to teaching, but most important, to test assumptions regarding online learning. Furthermore, all five projects were funded by their respective institutions to support their teaching initiatives or teaching-research endeavors. Thus, these teacher-scholars were actively engaged in teaching and examining their classroom practices.

Computer-Mediated Communication: Noteworthy Effects

Although there is agreement that adapting a course (or a portion of a course) to an online environment and managing the communication and learning in that environment is labor-intensive, there is also agreement among the authors in this section and, for that matter, throughout the whole collection, that the effort and the risk involved is worth it. What is particularly instructive, especially considering the communication focus of this collection, is the effect that computer-mediated communication (CMC) has on instructional design and interpersonal communication. First, it is necessary to have clear, precise instructions online. Second, it is necessary to understand the characteristics of the new communication environment. Whether implied or explicitly stated, the distinct advantage of an online learning community is that the communication exchange stays online (for the duration of the course and sometimes longer) and can be revisited by students and examined by instructors. Indeed, the authors of these case studies not only used their students' learning community to enhance their instructional design but also to examine the effect of their teaching practices and the nature and quality of their students' communication. Because of the permanency of the written and recorded exchanges in an online learning community, instructors have data available to examine.

Chapters 13 and 14 provide a detailed examination of the nature and quality of the online communication. Although only a limited representation, it seems appropriate to speculate from these reports that students are more comfortable confronting each other on difficult issues online than they are face to face. In my over 20 years of mostly undergraduate classroom teaching, I find that students rarely confront other students who sometimes make offensive statements, for example racial, ethnic, or gender slurs (see Chapter 14). It seems that they assume it is the role of the instructor standing (or sitting) in authority in the classroom. In these online communities, students apparently feel more ownership in the communication and learning environment.

OVERALL THEMES OF THE COLLECTION

The Introduction revealed three major themes:

1) Dialogues about teaching and learning with interactive technologies are increasing and supported by major initiatives, such as the Carnegie Academy for the Scholarship of Teaching and Learning.

2) There is agreement among the literature that teaching is a complex communicative process, and furthermore, collaborative learning philosophies and methodologies have been historically strongly advocated for face to face classroom instruction in higher education.

3) Collaborative learning and similar learner-centered philosophies and methodologies are also strongly advocated by scholars as effective and essential for classrooms mediated by interactive technologies.

The case studies in this collection support and extend those themes. The increased dialogues about teaching and learning are evident not only from the case studies in which these teacher-scholars examine and discuss their classroom practice but also from their reports of interdisciplinary dialogues on their university campus and among universities. It is important that with the evolution of interactive technologies, these interdisciplinary dialogues about teaching and learning continue.

All the authors in these case studies describe their teaching philosophies and practices as a type of learning in which students and teachers are actively and reciprocally engaged in the process of knowledge construction, creating and sharing meaning, theory-based applications, and situational problem solving. Although they use different terms—collaborative learning, problem-based learning, social constructivism, small group learning—they are essentially describing teaching and learning as reciprocal processes in which knowledge is created and negotiated in a communal space by members of groups involved in authentic real-world situations.

Given that understanding of teaching and learning, it should be no surprise that scholars strongly advocate collaborative learning (and similar instructional methodologies) for effective online teaching and learning. If lecture-based (information-dispensing) instruction is static (and tends to promote rote learning) in a face to face instructional environment, then it is fair to say that it is deadly in an online instructional environment.

REFLECTIONS AND LESSONS LEARNED

This collection is a culmination of almost two decades of my teaching and research interests in observing and examining communication and learning in institutions of higher education. I began, in 1983, with the belief that effective communication in the classroom increases the potential for learning. That philosophy and belief remains, to this day, the center of my teaching and research endeavors. Since the 1990s, my particular interest has been in the qualitative assessment (observation and examination) of the interpersonal nuances involved with communication and learning in distance education settings. Furthermore, I believe that faculty across disciplines, as teachers and scholars, must critically assess the characteristics and the quality of instruction, especially as these new technologies continue to affect education.

In reflecting on these case studies, as well as my own investigations of communication and learning with interactive technologies, there are three striking lessons or observations that come to the forefront:

1) The boundaries between the traditional face to face classrooms and the distance education classrooms are collapsing or coalescing as interactive technologies continue to evolve and merge.

2) Teaching successfully in the audio/video interactive environment is mainly a matter of adapting one's communication style to the environment.

3) Teaching online requires a paradigm shift in instructional design and challenges instructors and students alike to understand the communication requirements of this new environment.

Merging of Interactive Technologies Collapses Instructional Boundaries

When I accepted a stipend to examine the new distance learning classrooms in the "Vision Carolina" project, I was asked to compare teaching and learning in the traditional classroom with the distance learning classroom. While I understood that policymakers and vendors selling the technology wanted to prove that distance education was just as viable as traditional education, I also understood that the comparison is not a valid one. Furthermore, my research interests are in the qualitative assessment of the processes of teaching and learning, not of the effects (which can only be measured by outcomes and requires control of many variables to achieve reliability). However, that was the beginning of my experience with the plethora of terms (language) used on our campus (and, I am sure, many others) in an attempt to distinguish the two instructional settings. In addition, it was a challenge for those teaching in that environment to know how to refer to students at the different sites. Such terms as "originating site" or "home site" were used to distinguish from the "remote site" or the "distant site." The implication of remote or distant students had a negative impact on the communication and learning climate as students "felt like 'intruders in the classroom'"(Comeaux, 1995, p. 360).

With online instruction developing on our campus and others, new terms became part of campus dialogues and were appearing in the literature. This was particularly evident as I began reading the case studies for this collection. Many authors observed and discussed differences, as well as similarities, of their teaching experiences in the regular classrooms with those of their online classrooms. Examples of attempts to distinguish the two are:

- Onground versus online classroom

- Face to face instruction versus online instruction

- Traditional classroom versus virtual classroom

More than likely, as interactive technologies continue to evolve and merge (e.g., desktop video conferencing), not only will our terms change but the efforts to distinguish face to face classrooms from the virtual classrooms will become moot. From my observations (and as is evident in these case studies), more mainstream educators are teaching via interactive technologies. Furthermore, online instruction is an option for on-campus students as well as distant students; indeed, this is the case at UNCW. These observations are supported, and in fact more strongly asserted, by Moran and Mugridge (1993) in the concluding comments of their study of interinstitutional collaboration in distance education:

> . . . economic and ideological pressures for rationalization, coupled with the educational possibilities of new information technologies . . . are breaking down the distinctions between conventional face to face teaching methods and forms of distance education that became entrenched in the 1970s and 1980s. . . . With the emergence of new technologies and the demand for new programs, distance education is not only changing—it is also converging with conventional education. The boundaries between 'distance education' and classroom-based teaching are now disappearing. We are heading toward 'virtual classroom' electronics and a completely open conception of design and teaching, in which both learners and teachers can choose the media and location best suited to the subject and their own needs. Traditional boundaries of knowledge and of institutions will be strongly challenged by this change. (p. 163)

Many faculty and administrators in higher education remain understandably skeptical of such assertions. Universities thrive on the uniqueness of their institutional culture and the reputation of their curriculum and programs. Moran and Mugridge (1993) acknowledge that skepticism as they remind us, "One should not, however, underestimate the countervailing pressures to retain institutional uniqueness and ownership of curriculum and pedagogies, and to maintain a sense of individualism and human scale in relationships between teacher and learner" (p. 164).

Teaching in an Interactive Television Environment: An Adaptation of Communication Style

Because the interactive audio/video environments (IAVE) that I have observed closely resemble variations of the traditional classroom (see Chapters 7, 8, and 9 for details), successful teaching in this environment is a matter of adapting one's communication style. This observation, of course, assumes that one's teaching approach actively involves students in the learning process as espoused throughout this collection. As I stated earlier, static instruction in the traditional classroom becomes deadly in an interactive audio/video environment. There are valuable benefits to teaching in this environment (see Chapter 9). Furthermore, success in this environment requires instructors to use engaging and interactive styles that can positively affect their teaching.

While teaching in this environment is challenging and requires adaptation to the nuances of the audio/video technology, it does not, in my opinion, require a paradigm shift in instructional design.

Online Instruction as a Paradigm Shift: The Challenges of Communication

In my first visit to an online classroom (1998), I was baffled, disoriented, and overwhelmed. Of course, I did not have the benefit (as the students did) of an orientation to this environment. I entered the course about three weeks after it started as a visiting professor for research purposes (see Comeaux & Nixon, 2000). I eventually learned to navigate my way through the course; however, I distinctly remember trying to reconceptualize and envision the space or the teaching-learning environment. The experience, in effect, challenged my previous models of the teaching-learning environment. Because collaborative learning theories and methodologies informed the instructional course design, the assignments were largely team-based. I was impressed with the quality and depth of interactions that occurred in these assignments. Of course, the participants were graduate students (and full-time professionals), and so I questioned whether this kind of online collaborative learning environment would work with undergraduates. In essence, although I agreed in principle, I had not experienced it in practice. In other words, I philosophically and logically agreed with the scholarly literature that constructivist learner-centered philosophies and methodologies are the key to quality instruction in the virtual classroom. It was not until I experienced it firsthand (in my continued research as a visiting professor in virtual classrooms), and most significantly, until I read and reread the case studies in this collection, that I considered the possibility that what we are experiencing, with the influx of interactive technologies in computer-mediated education, is indeed a paradigm shift. It is because of this shift, from a mainly oral to written medium of instruction, that a paradigm shift is required in instructional design and in consideration of communication and learning in a computer-mediated environment (see, in particular, Chapters 11 and 12).

One of the main concerns or fears that is often expressed about online teaching is the potential loss of the interpersonal dimension that face to face (nonmediated) communication allows. It is true (and reported in these case studies and the literature) that in online instruction, much of the richness of nonverbal communication (e.g., tone of voice, facial expressions) is not possible. However, the interpersonal dimension of the teacher-student relationship as well as the student-student relationship is quite possible and potentially heightened through computer-mediated communication in an online teaching environment.

The case studies in this collection report and imply other advantages of CMC:

- The discussion stays online and can be revisited as part of the learning process.

- More students can participate in an online asynchronous threaded discussion than in a face to face classroom limited-time period.

- Students are learning to express their ideas in writing and write purposefully.

- Students have more "think time" in CMC exchanges.

Thus, quality online classroom interaction is possible and is occurring. However, the authors in these case studies, as well as other instructors who teach online courses, claim that managing the communication environment is time- and labor-intensive. The important lesson for all of us is if we want quality instruction, our class sizes must be manageable. This lesson also holds for the interactive audio/video instructional environment: When too many sites or students are enrolled in a course, the quality of interaction diminishes. Given the belief in a learner-centered approach by all authors in this collection, I would claim, on behalf of us all, that the quality of learning would be diminished.

CLOSING REFLECTIONS

In closing, I would like to return to my purpose in writing and editing this collection: to provide readers with a comprehensive understanding of the human communication issues that must be addressed in higher education as interactive technologies continue to evolve and impact instructional design and practice. It is my hope that this collection will be a catalyst for continued dialogues (disciplinary and interdisciplinary) as well as renewed appreciation for the scholarship of teaching and learning.

Finally, I want to remind us all that communication is our primary thinking and socializing tool, and it is through the process of communication that we come to know others (as well as our self) and to understand our environments. Thus, as I continue to explore the impact of interactive technologies upon our lives, I assert that in my explorations, I will arrive at the place where I started: the belief (knowledge and experience) that learning occurs in relationships with others and it is that process, the very human communication process, that will endure. We will continue to explore interactive technologies, but teaching and learning will always be about human communication.

> *We shall not cease from exploration*
> *And the end of all our exploring*
> *Will be to arrive where we started...*
> —T. S. Eliot

REFERENCES

Comeaux, P. (1995). The impact of an interactive distance learning network on classroom communication. *Communication Education, 44* (4), 353–361.

Comeaux, P., & Nixon, M. A. (2000). Collaborative learning in an internet graduate course: A case study analysis. *WebNet Journal: Internet Technologies, Applications & Issues, 2* (4), 34–43.

Eliot, T. S. (1952). *The complete poems and plays: 1909–1950.* New York, NY: Harcourt Brace.

Hall, E. T. (1977). *Beyond Culture.* New York, NY: Anchor Press/Doubleday.

Moran, L., & Mugridge, I. (1993). Policies and trends in inter-institutional collaboration. In L. Moran & I. Mugridge (Eds.), *Collaboration in distance education: International case studies* (pp. 151–164). New York, NY: Routledge.

Bibliography

Abrami, P. C., & Bures, E. M. (1996). Computer-supported collaborative learning and distance education. *The American Journal of Distance Education, 10* (2), 37–42.

Aitken, J., & Shedletsky, L. (Eds.). (1995). *Intrapersonal communication processes.* Annandale, VA: Speech Communication Association and Hayden-McNeil.

Allen, M. (1994). Adventures with "Robin Hood": Gender and conflict on a first-year bulletin board. *Journal of Teaching Writing, 13* (1–2), 169–196.

Althaus, S. (1997). Computer-mediated communication in the university classroom: An experiment with online discussions. *Communication Education, 46* (3), 158–174.

American Council on Education. (1996). *Guiding principles for distance learning in a learning society* [Online]. Available: http://www.acenet .edu/calec/publications.cfm

Amundsen, C. (1993). The evolution of theory in distance education. In D. Keegan (Ed.), *Theoretical principles of distance education* (pp. 61–79). New York, NY: Routledge.

Barker, L. L. (Ed.). (1982). *Communication in the classroom: Original essays.* Englewood Cliffs, NJ: Prentice-Hall.

Barrows, H. S. (1985). *How to design a problem-based curriculum for pre-clinical years.* New York, NY: Springer.

Baym, N. (1998). The emergence of online community. In S. Jones (Ed.), *Cybersociety 2.0: Revisiting computer mediated communication and community* (pp. 35–68). Thousand Oaks, CA: Sage.

Berger, P. L., & Luckmann, T. (1966). *The social construction of reality: A treatise in the sociology of knowledge.* New York, NY: Doubleday.

Berrill, D. (1991). Exploring underlying assumptions: Small group work of university graduates. *Educational Review, 43* (2), 143–157.

Bloom, B., Englehart, M., Furst, E., Hill, W., & Krathwohl, D. (1956). *Taxonomy of educational objectives. Handbook I: Cognitive domain.* New York, NY: Macmillan.

Blumenfeld, P. C., Marx, R. W., Soloway, E., & Krajcik, J. (1996). Learning with peers: From small group cooperation to collaborative communities. *Educational Researcher, 25* (8), 37–40.

Brandon, D. P., & Hollingshead, A. B. (1999). Collaborative learning and computer-supported groups. *Communication Education, 48* (2), 109–126.

Brown, J. S. (1990). Toward a new epistemology for learning. In C. Frasson & G. Guatheir (Eds.), *Intelligent tutoring systems: At the crossroad of artificial intelligence and education* (pp. 4–35). Norwood, NJ: Ablex.

Brown, J. S., & Duguid, P. (2000). *The social life of information.* Cambridge, MA: Harvard Business School Press.

Bruffee, K. A. (1993). *Collaborative learning: Higher education, interdependence, and the authority of knowledge.* Baltimore, MD: Johns Hopkins University Press.

Carey, J. W. (1975). A cultural approach to communication. *Communication, 2,* 1–22.

Chadwick, S. A. (1999). Teaching virtually via the web: Comparing student performance and attitudes about communication in lecture, virtual web-based, and web-supplemented courses. *The Electronic Journal of Communication, 9* (1) [Online]. Available: http://www.cios.org/getfile/Chadwick_v9n199

Chrislip, D. D., & Larson, C. E. (1994). *Collaborative leadership: How citizens and civic leaders can make a difference.* San Francisco, CA: Jossey-Bass.

Clark, J. (2000, October). Collaboration tools in online learning environments. *Asynchronous Learning Network Magazine, 4* (1) [Online]. Available: http://www.aln.org/alnweb/magazine/Vol4_issue1/Clark.htm

Cole, R. (2000, July). Chemistry, teaching, and WebCT. *Journal of Chemical Education, 77* (7), 826–827.

Coles, R. (1991). *Anna Freud: The dream of psychoanalysis.* Reading MA: Addison-Wesley.

(2001, January 17). College of business receives full reaccredidation. *The Western Carolinian,* p. 3.

Collins, M. (1998). The use of email and electronic bulletin boards in college-level biology. *Journal of Computers in Mathematics and Science Teaching, 17* (1), 75–94.

Collins, A., Brown, J. S., & Newman, S. E. (1990). Cognitive apprenticeship: Teaching the craft of reading, writing, and mathematics. In L. B. Resnick (Ed.), *Knowing, learning, and instruction: Essays in honor of Robert Glaser* (pp. 453–494). Hillsdale, NJ: Lawrence Erlbaum Associates.

Comeaux, P. (1995). The impact of an interactive distance learning network on classroom communication. *Communication Education, 44* (4), 353–361.

Comeaux, P., & Nixon, M. A. (2000). Collaborative learning in an Internet graduate course: A case study analysis. *WebNet Journal: Internet Technologies, Applications & Issues, 2* (4), 34–43.

Conquergood, D. (1993). Storied worlds and the work of teaching. *Communication Education, 42* (4), 337–348.

Constant, D., Sproull, L., & Kiesler, S. (1997). The kindness of strangers: On the usefulness of electronic weak ties for technical advice. In S. Kiesler (Ed.), *Cultures of the Internet* (pp. 303–322). Hillsdale, NJ: Lawrence Erlbaum Associates.

Cross, K. P., & Steadman, M. H. (1996). *Classroom research: Implementing the scholarship of teaching.* San Francisco, CA: Jossey-Bass.

Crotty, T. (1994). Integrating distance learning activities to enhance teacher education toward the constructivist paradigm of teaching and learning. In A. Yakimovicz (Ed.), *Distance Learning Research Conference Proceedings* (pp. 31–37). College Station, TX: Texas A & M University, Department of Education and Human Resource Development.

Dance, F. E. (Ed.). (1967). *Human communication theory: Original essays.* New York, NY: Holt, Rinehart, and Winston.

Dede, C. (1996). The evolution of distance education: Emerging technologies and distributed learning. *The American Journal of Distance Education, 10* (2), 4–36.

Dewey, J. (1933). *How we think: A restatement of the relation of reflective thinking to the educative process.* Lexington, MA: D. C. Heath.

Dirr, P. J. (1999). Distance and virtual learning in the United States. In G. M. Farrell (Ed.), *The development of virtual education: A global perspective* (pp. 23–48). Vancouver, British Columbia: The Commonwealth of Learning. Available: http://www.col.org/virtualed/index.htm

Driver, R., Asoko, H., Leach, J., Mortimer, E., & Scott, P. (1994). Constructing scientific knowledge in the classroom. *Educational Researcher, 23* (7), 5–12.

Dunlap, J. C., & Grabinger, R. S. (1996). Rich environments for active learning in the higher education classroom. In B. G. Wilson (Ed.), *Constructivist learning environments: Case studies in instructional design* (pp. 65–82). Englewood Cliffs, NJ: Educational Technology Publications.

Eastmond, D., & Ziegahn, L. (1995). Instructional design for the online classroom. In Z. L. Berge & M. P. Collins (Eds.), *Computer-mediated communication and the online classroom, Vol. 3: Distance education* (pp. 59–80). Cesskill, NJ: Hampton Press.

Eaves, M. (1997). Collaboration takes more than e-mail. *The Journal of Electronic Publishing, 3* (2)[Online]. Available: http://www.press.umich.edu/jep/03-02/blake.html

Edens, K. (2000, Summer). Promoting communication, inquiry and reflection in an early practicum experience via an online discussion group. *Action in Teacher Education, 24,* 14–23.

Ehrlich, P. R. (1968). *The population bomb.* New York, NY: Ballantine Books.

Elbow, P. (1973). *Writing without teachers.* New York, NY: Oxford University Press.

Eliot, T. S. (1952). *The complete poems and plays: 1909–1950.* New York, NY: Harcourt Brace.

Engelkemeyer, S. W., & Brown, S. C. (1998, October). Powerful partnerships: A shared responsibility for learning. *AAHE Bulletin,* 10–12.

Fiksdal, S. (2001). Voices in seminar: Ideologies and identities. In B. L. Smith & J. McCann (Eds.), *Reinventing ourselves: Interdisciplinary education, collaborative learning, and experimentation in higher education* (pp. 179–194). Bolton, MA: Anker.

Finn, J., & Lavitt, M. (1994). Computer-based self-help groups for sexual abuse survivors. *Social Work with Groups, 17* (1–2), 21–46.

Fosnot, C. (1989). *Enquiring teachers, enquiring learners: A constructivist approach for teaching.* New York, NY: Teachers College Press.

Foster, L. (1997). *A degree of distinction: A collaborative model for degree delivery via distance education.* Paper presented at the 49th Annual Conference of the American Association of Colleges of Teacher Education, Phoenix, AZ.

Frederick, P. (1995, Summer). Walking on eggs: Mastering the dreaded diversity discussion. *College Teaching, 43* (3), 83–92.

Fried, J. (1993, Fall). Bridging emotion and intellect. *College Teaching, 41* (3), 123–128.

Garrison, D. R. (1990). An analysis and evaluation of audio teleconferencing to facilitate education at a distance. *The American Journal of Distance Education, 4,* 13–24.

Garrison, D. R. (1993). Quality and access in distance education: Theoretical considerations. In D. Keegan (Ed.), *Theoretical principles of distance education* (pp. 9–21). New York, NY: Routledge.

Garton, L., & Wellman, B. (1995). Social impacts of electronic mail in organizations: A review of the research literature. *Communication Yearbook, 18,* 434–453.

Gatliff, B., & Wendel, G. (1998). Inter-institutional collaboration and team teaching. *The American Journal of Distance Education, 12* (1), 26–37.

Geer, C. (1996). *Interactive distance learning: An impetus for collaboration.* Cincinnati, OH: Clermont County Educational Service Center. (ERIC Document Reproduction Service No. ED 401 874)

Gergen, K. J. (1985). The social constructionist movement in modern psychology. *American Psychologist, 40* (3), 266–275.

Gijselaers, W. (1995). Perspectives on problem-based learning. In W. H. Gijselaers, D. T. Tempelaar, P. K. Keizer, J. M. Blommaert, E. M. Bernard, & H. Kasper (Eds.), *Educational innovation in economics and business administration: The case of problem-based learning* (pp. 39–52). Norwell, MA: Kluwer Academic Publishers.

Gillis, L. B. (1999). *A model for training asynchronous distance education instructors: The virtual College of Texas.* Unpublished master's thesis, Northwestern State University.

Giroux, H. A. (1988). *Teachers as intellectuals: Toward a critical pedagogy of learning.* Granby, MA: Bergin & Garvey.

Glaser, B., & Strauss, A. (1967). *The discovery of grounded theory.* Chicago, IL: Aldine-Atherton.

Goodman, N. (1984). *Of mind and other matters.* Cambridge, MA: Harvard University Press.

Greeson, L. E. (1988). College classroom interaction as a function of teacher- and student-centered instruction. *Teaching & Teacher Education, 4* (4), 305–315.

Guba, E., & Lincoln, Y. (1981). *Effective evaluation.* San Francisco, CA: Jossey-Bass.

Gudykunst, W. B. (1998). *Bridging differences: Effective intergroup communication* (3rd ed.). Thousand Oaks, CA: Sage.

Gunawardena, C. N., & Zittle, F. J. (1997). Social presence as a predictor of satisfaction within a computer-mediated conference environment. *The American Journal of Distance Education, 11* (3), 8–25.

Hackman, M. Z., & Walker, K. B. (1990). Instructional communication in the televised classroom: The effects of system design and teacher immediacy on student learning and satisfaction. *Communication Education, 39,* 196–206.

Hall, E. T. (1977). *Beyond Culture.* New York, NY: Anchor Press/Doubleday.

Hammrich, P. L. (1997). What the science standards say: Implications for teacher education. *Journal of Science Teacher Education, 9* (3), 165–186.

Harasim, L. M. (1990). Online education: An environment for collaboration and intellectual amplification. In L. M. Harasim (Ed.), *Online education: Perspective on a new environment* (pp. 39–64). New York, NY: Praeger.

Harasim, L. M. (Ed.). (1990). *Online education: Perspective on a new environment.* New York, NY: Praeger.

Harnad, S. (1996). Interactive cognition: Exploring the potential of electronic quote/commenting. In B. Gorayska & J. L. Mey (Eds.), *Cognitive technology: In search of a humane interface* (pp. 397–414). The Netherlands: Elsevier Science.

Harper, N. (1979). *Human communication theory: The history of a paradigm.* Rochelle Park, NJ: Hayden Book Company.

Harris, T. E., & Sherblom, J. C. (1999). *Small group and team communication.* Boston, MA: Allyn and Bacon.

Hillman, D., Bottomley, D., Raisner, J., & Malin, B. (2000, Summer). Learning to practice what we teach: Integrating elementary education methods courses. *Action in Teacher Education, 24,* 91–100.

Hiltz, S. R. (1994). *The virtual classroom: Learning without limits via computer networks.* Norwood, NJ: Ablex.

Hiltz, S. R. (1997). *Impacts of college-level courses via asynchronous learning networks: Some preliminary results* [Online]. Available: http://eies.njit.edu/~hiltz/workingpapers/philly/philly.htm

Hiltz, R. (1998, November). *Collaborative learning in asynchronous learning networks: Building learning communities* [Online]. Available: http://eies.njit.edu/~hiltz/collaborative_learning_in_asynch.htm

Hiltz, S. R. (1998). Collaborative learning in asynchronous learning networks: Building learning communities. *Proceedings of WebNet '98 World Conference on WWW, Internet and Intranet, 1* (1), 1–7.

Huba, M. E., & Freed, J. E. (2000). *Learner-centered assessment on college campuses: Shifting the focus from teaching to learning.* Boston, MA: Allyn and Bacon.

Huber, M. T. (2000). Disciplinary styles in the scholarship of teaching: Reflections on the Carnegie Academy for the Scholarship of Teaching and Learning. In C. Rust (Ed.), *Improving student learning through the disciplines* (pp. 20–31). Oxford, England: Oxford-Brookes University, The Centre for Staff and Learning Development.

Husmann, D. E., & Miller, M. T. (1999, Fall). Faculty incentives to participate in distance education. *Michigan Community College Journal: Research & Practice, 5* (2), 35–42.

International Society for Technology in Education. (1998, June). *National educational technology standards for students.* Eugene, OR: Nets Project.

Johnson, D. W., & Johnson, R. T. (1990). Cooperative learning and achievement. In S. Sharan, (Ed.), *Cooperative learning: Theory and research* (pp. 23–37). New York, NY: Praeger.

Johnson, D. W., Johnson, R. T., & Smith, K. A. (1991). *Cooperative learning: Increasing college faculty instructional productivity.* Washington, DC: George Washington University.

Joki, E. (1998). Partnering for success—Maximizing project management value through a strategic partner. *Proceedings of the 29th Annual Project Management Institute 1998 Seminars & Symposium, 1,* 114.

Jonassen, D. (1999). Designing constructivist learning environments. In C. M. Reigeluth (Ed.), *Instructional design theories and models: A new paradigm of instructional theory* (Vol. III, pp. 215–241). Hillsdale, NJ: Lawrence Erlbaum Associates.

Jonassen, D., Davidson, M., Collins, M., Campbell, J., & Haag, B. B. (1995). Constructivism and computer-mediated communication in distance education. *The American Journal of Distance Education, 9* (2), 7–26.

Jordan, B., & Henderson, A. (1995). Interaction analysis: Foundations and practice. *Journal of the Learning Sciences, 4,* 39–103.

Jorgensen-Earp, C. R., & Staton, A. Q. (1993). Student metaphors for the college freshman experience. *Communication Education, 42,* 123–141.

Jutla, D., Bodorik, P., Hanjal, C., & Davis, C. (1999, March). Making business sense of electronic commerce. *Computer, 32* (3), 67–75.

Katz, R. N. (2001, March/April). Archimedes' lever & collaboration: An interview with Ira Fuchs. *EDUCAUSE Review, 36* (2), 17–22.

Kearsly, G. (1995). *The nature and value of interaction in distance learning* [Online]. Available: http://www.gwu.edu/-etl/interact.html

Kellogg Corporation News. (1992). *The show on Broadway: A model for the partnering continuum process,* parts I & II. Littleton, CO: Author. (Note: Kellogg Corporation is now Petersen Consulting, LLP.)

Kolb, D. A. (1976). *The learning style inventory: Technical manual.* Boston, MA: McBer.

Kolb, D. A. (1981). Learning styles and disciplinary differences. In A. W. Chickering & Associates, *The modern American college: Responding to the new realities of diverse students and a changing society* (pp. 232–255). San Francisco, CA: Jossey-Bass.

Kolodner, J., & Guzdial, M. (1996). Effects *with* and *of* CSCL: Tracking learning in a new paradigm. In T. Koschmann (Ed.), *CSCL: Theory and practice of an emerging paradigm* (pp. 307–320). Hillsdale, NJ: Lawrence Erlbaum Associates.

Koschmann, T. (1996). Paradigm shifts and instructional technology: An introduction. In T. Koschmann (Ed.), *CSCL: Theory and practice of an emerging paradigm* (pp. 1–23). Hillsdale, NJ: Lawrence Erlbaum Associates.

Kost, C., Wildner-Bassett, M., Gunder, P., Wurr, A., Jurkowitz, L., Ackan, S., & Abella, J. (1999). *Planet Xeno—A web-based learning portfolio* [Online]. Available: www.coh.arizona.edu/planet-xeno/

Krathwohl, D., Bloom, B., & Masia, B. (1956). *Taxonomy of educational objectives: Handbook I: Affective domain.* New York, NY: Longman.

Kruh, J., & Murphy, K. (1990). *Interaction in teleconferencing: The key to quality instruction.* Paper presented at the Annual Rural and Small Schools Conference, Manhattan, KS. (ERIC Document Reproduction Service No. ED 329 418)

Lakoff, R. T. (1990). *Talking power: The politics of language.* New York, NY: Basic Books.

LaRose, R., & Whitten, P. (1999). *Websection: Building web courses with instructional immediacy* [Online]. Available: http://www.telecommunication.msn.edu/faculty/larose/websectionlite.htm

Latane, B., Williams, K., & Harkins, S. (1979). Many hands make light work: Causes and consequences of social loafing. *Social Psychology, 37,* 822–832.

Lea, M., & Spears, R. (1995). Love at first byte? Building personal relationships over computer networks. Under-studied relationships: Off the beaten track. In J. T. Wood & S. Duck (Eds.), *Understanding relationship processes, series 6* (pp. 197–233). Thousand Oaks, CA: Sage.

Lebow, D. (1993). Constructivist values for instructional systems design: Five principles toward a new mindset. *Educational Technology Research and Development, 41* (3), 4–16.

Leidner, D. E., & Jarvenpaa, S. L. (1995, September). The use of information technology to enhance management school education: A theoretical view. *Management Information Quarterly, 19* (3), 265–291.

Lenning, O. T., & Ebbers, L. H. (1999). *The powerful potential of learning communities: Improving education for the future.* (ASHE-ERIC Higher Education Report Volume 26, No. 6). Washington, DC: The George Washington University, Graduate School of Education and Human Development.

Lesh, S. G., & Rampp, L. C. (2000, October). *Effectiveness of computer-based educational technology in distance learning: A review of the literature.* (ERIC Document Reproduction Service No. ED 440 628)

Lewis, C. S. (1955). *Surprised by joy.* New York, NY: Harcourt Brace Jovanovich.

Lippard-Justice, P. (1989). The relationship between intrapersonal and interpersonal communication patterns. In C. Roberts & K. Watson (Eds.), *Intrapersonal communication processes: Original essays* (pp. 444–455). Scottsdale, AZ: Gorsuch Scarisbrick.

Littlejohn, S. W. (1999). *Theories of human communication* (6th ed.). Belmont, CA: Wadsworth.

Luck, A. (2001, January/February). Developing courses for online delivery: One Strategy. *The Technology Source* [Online]. Available: http://horizon.unc.edu/TS/beta.asp

Machiavelli, N. (1981). *The prince* (D. Donno, Trans.). New York, NY: Bantam.

Maher, T., & Tetreault, M. K. T. (1994). *Breaking through illusion: The feminist classroom.* New York, NY: Basic Books.

Martin, G. I. (1997). Getting personal through impersonal means: Using electronic mail to gain insight into student teachers' perceptions. *Research and Reflection: A Journal of Educational Praxis, 3* (1) [Online]. Available: http://www.gonzaga.edu/rr/v3n1/martin.html

Matheson, K., & Zanna, M. P. (1988). The impact of computer-mediated communication on self-awareness. *Computers in Human Behavior, 4* (3), 221–233.

McComb, M. (1994). Benefits of computer-mediated communication in college courses. *Communication Education, 43* (2), 159–170.

McCormick, N. B., & McCormick, J. W. (1992, Winter). Computer friends and foes: Content of undergraduates' electronic mail. *Computers in Human Behavior, 8* (4), 379–405.

McGrath, J. E. (1991). Time, interaction, and performance (TIP): A theory of groups. *Small Group Research, 22,* 147–174.

McGrath, J. E., & Hollingshead, A. B. (1993). Putting the "group" back in group support systems: Some theoretical issues about dynamic processes in groups with technological enhancements. In L. M. Jessup & J. S. Valacich (Eds.), *Group support systems: New perspectives* (pp. 78–96). New York, NY: Macmillan.

McHenry, L., & Bozik, M. (1995). Communicating at a distance: A study of interaction in a distance education classroom. *Communication Education, 44* (4), 362–371.

McKeachie, W. (1994). *Teaching tips: Strategies, research, and theory for college and university teachers.* Lexington, MA: D. C. Heath.

Mead, G. H. (1934). *Mind, self, and society.* Chicago, IL: University of Chicago.

Mentkowski, M. (1988). Paths to integrity: Educating for personal growth and professional performance. In S. Srivastva & Associates (Eds.), *Executive integrity: The search for high human values in organizational life* (pp. 89–121). San Francisco, CA: Jossey-Bass.

Milter, R. G., & Stinson, J. E. (1995). Educating leaders for the new competitive environment. In W. H. Gijselaers, D. T. Tempelaar, P. K. Keizer, J. M. Blommaert, E. M. Bernard, & H. Kasper (Eds.), *Educational innovation in economics and business administration: The case of problem-based learning* (pp. 30–38). Norwell, MA: Kluwer Academic Publishers.

Moore, C., Mosley, D., & Slagle, M. (1992). Partnering: Guidelines for win-win project management. *Project Management Journal, 23* (1), 18–21.

Moore, C. C., Maes, J. D., & Shearer, R. A. (1995). Recognizing and responding to vulnerabilities of partnering. *Project Management Network, 9* (9), 20–23.

Moore, M. (1989). Three types of interaction. *The American Journal of Distance Education, 3* (2), 16.

Moore, M. (1993). Is teaching like flying? A total systems view of distance education. *The American Journal of Distance Education, 7* (1), 1–10.

Moran, L., & Mugridge, I. (1993a). Collaboration in distance education: An introduction. In L. Moran & I. Mugridge (Eds.), *Collaboration in distance education: International case studies* (pp. 1–11). New York, NY: Routledge.

Moran, L., & Mugridge, I. (1993b). Policies and trends in inter-institutional collaboration. In L. Moran & I. Mugridge (Eds.), *Collaboration in distance education: International case studies* (pp. 151–164). New York, NY: Routledge.

Morley, L., & LaMaster, K. (1999, August). Use electronic bulletin boards to extend classrooms. *The Journal of Physical Education, Recreation & Dance, 70* (6), 16–20.

Morreale, S. (2001, April). The preparing future faculty program . . . What's in it for communication studies? *Spectra, 37* (4), 13.

Mottet, T. P. (2000, April). Interactive television instructors' perceptions of students' nonverbal responsiveness and their influence on distance teaching. *Communication Education, 49* (2), 146–164.

Mowrer, D. E. (1996). A content analysis of student/instructor communication via computer conferencing. *Higher Education, 32,* 217–241.

Myers, C., & Jones, T. B. (1993). *Promoting active learning: Strategies for the college classroom.* San Francisco, CA: Jossey-Bass.

Neal, J. S. (1994, January). The interpersonal computer. *Science Scope, 17* (4), 24–27.

Negroponte, N. (1995). *Being digital.* New York, NY: Vintage.

Neuwirth, C. M., & Wojahn, P. G. (1996). Learning to write: Computer support for a cooperative process. In T. Koschmann, (Ed.), *CSCL: Theory and practice of an emerging paradigm* (pp. 147–170). Hillsdale, NJ: Lawrence Erlbaum Associates.

Nixon, M. A., & Leftwich, B. R. (1998). Leading the transition from the traditional classroom to a distance learning environment. *Technical Horizons in Education, 26* (1), 54–57.

Nofsinger, R. E. (1999). *Everyday conversation.* Prospect Heights, IL: Waveland.

O'Donnell, A. M., & O'Kelly, J. (1994). Learning from peers: Beyond the rhetoric of positive results. *Educational Psychology Review, 6* (4), 321–349.

Olcott, D., & Wright, S. (1995). An institutional support framework for increasing faculty participation in post-secondary distance education. *The American Journal of Distance Education, 9* (3), 5–17.

O'Loughlin, M. (1992). Rethinking science education: Beyond Piagetian constructivism toward a sociocultural model of teaching and learning. *Journal of Research in Science Teaching, 29* (8), 791–820.

Palloff, R., & Pratt, K. (1999). *Building learning communities in cyberspace: Effective strategies for the online classroom.* San Francisco, CA: Jossey-Bass.

Parks, M. R., & Floyd, K. (1996, Winter). Making friends in cyberspace. *Journal of Communication, 46* (1), 80–97.

Pea, R. (1993). Seeing what we build together: Distributed multimedia learning environments for transformative communications. *The Journal of the Learning Sciences, 3* (3), 285–299.

Pearce, W. B. (1989). *Communication and the human condition.* Carbondale, IL: Southern Illinois University Press.

Pearce, W. B., & Cronen V. E. (1980). *Communication, action, and meaning: The creation of social realities.* New York, NY: Praeger.

Peters, T. J., & Waterman, R. H. (1982). *In search of excellence: Lessons from America's best-run companies.* New York, NY: Harper & Row.

Porter, L. W., & McKibbin, L. E. (1988). *Management education and development: Drift or thrust into the 21st century?* New York, NY: McGraw-Hill.

Quasthoff, U. (1993). Ethnozentrische Verarbeitung von Information: Zur Ambivalenz in der Funktionen von Stereotypen in der interkulturellen Kommunikation. In P. Matusche (Ed.), *Wie verstehen wir Fremdes? Aspekte zur Klaerung von Verstehensprozessen* (pp. 37–62) [How do we understand the 'foreign': Towards an explanation of the processes of understanding]. Munich, Germany: Goethe Institut.

Quinn, T. (Ed.). (1999). *Quotable women of the twentieth century.* New York, NY: William Morrow.

Rao, N. (1993). Verstehen einer fremden Kultur. In P. Matusche (Ed.), *Wie verstehen wir Fremdes? Aspekte zur Klaerung von Verstehensprozessen* (pp. 110–121) [How do we understand the 'foreign': Towards an explanation of the processes of understanding]. Munich, Germany: Goethe Institut.

Rheingold, H. (1993). *The virtual community: Homesteading on the electronic frontier.* New York, NY: Harper Collins.

Riel, M., & Fulton, K. (2001). The role of technology in supporting learning communities. *Phi Delta Kappan, 82* (7), 518–523.

Roberts, C., Edwards, R., & Barker, L. (1987). *Intrapersonal communication processes.* Scottsdale, AZ: Gorsuch Scarisbrick.

Rosenblatt, L. (1983). *Literature as exploration.* New York, NY: Modern Language Association.

Rothwell, J. D. (1998). *In mixed company: Small-group communication.* Toronto, Ontario: Harcourt Brace.

Ruberg, L. F., Moore, D. M., & Taylor, C. D. (1996). Student participation, interaction, and regulation in a computer mediated communication environment: A qualitative study. *Educational Computing Research, 14* (3), 243–268.

Russo, T., & Campbell, S. W. (2001). *Perceptions of mediated presence in an asynchronous online course: Interplay of communication behaviors and medium.* Paper presented at the annual meeting of the National Communication Association, Washington, DC.

Russo, T., & Chadwick, S. A. (2001). Making connections: Enhancing classroom learning with a virtual visiting professor. *Communication Teacher, 15* (3), 7–9.

Russo, T. C., Campbell, S., Henry, M. P., & Kosinar, P. (1999). An online graduate class in communication technology: Outcomes and lessons learned. *The Electronic Journal of Communication, 9* (1) [Online]. Available: http://www.cios.org/getfile\Russo_v9n199

Saba, F. E. (1999, November 1). New academic year starts with controversy over the use of technology. *Distance Education Report, 3* (21), 1–2.

Salomon, G., & Globerson, T. (1989). When teams do not function the way they ought to. *International Journal of Educational Research, 13,* 89–99.

Savery, J. R., & Duffy, T. M. (1995). Problem-based learning: An instructional model and its constructivist framework. *Educational Technology, 35,* 31–38.

Savery, J. R., & Duffy, T. M. (1996). Problem based learning: An instructional model and its constructivist framework. In B. G. Wilson (Ed.), *Constructivist learning environments: Case studies in instructional design* (pp. 135–148). Englewood Cliffs, NJ: Educational Technology Publications.

Scharlott, B. W., & Christ, W. G. (1995, Summer). Overcoming relationship-initiation barriers: The impact of a computer-dating system on sex role, shyness, and appearance inhibitions. *Computers in Human Behavior, 11* (2), 191–204.

Schlosser, C., & Anderson, M. (1993). *Distance education: Review of the literature.* (Available from Research Institute for Studies in Education, College of Education, E005 Lagomarcino Hall, Iowa State University, Ames, IA 50011.)

Schmidt, J. (1994). Partnering with your client. *Project Management Network, 8* (9), 27–30.

Schutz, A. (1967). *The phenomenology of the social world* [G. Walsh & F. Lehnert, Trans.). Evanston, IL: Northwestern University Press.

Schwartz, D., Xiaodong, L., Brophy, S., & Bransford, J. D. (1999). Toward development of flexibly adaptive instructional design. In C. M. Reigeluth (Ed.), *Instructional design theories and models: A new paradigm of instructional theory* (Vol. III, pp. 183–215). Hillsdale, NJ: Lawrence Erlbaum Associates.

Shapiro, N. S., & Levine, J. H. (1999). *Creating learning communities: A guide to winning support, organizing for change, and implementing programs.* San Francisco, CA: Jossey-Bass.

Shedletsky, L. (1993). Minding computer-mediated communication: CMC as experiential learning. *Educational Technology, 33* (12), 5–10.

Shedletsky, L. J. (1989). *Meaning and mind: An intrapersonal approach to human communication.* Annandale, VA: Speech Communication Association and ERIC Clearinghouse on Reading and Communication Skills.

Shedletsky, L. J., & Aitken, J. E. (2001, July). The paradoxes of online academic work. *Communication Education, 50* (3), 206–217.

Shepperd, J. A. (1993). Productivity loss in performance groups: A motivation analysis. *Psychological Bulletin, 113,* 67–81.

Sherry, L. (1996). Issues in distance learning. *International Journal of Educational Telecommunication, 1* (4), 337–365.

Sitko, B. M. (1992). Writers meet their readers in the classroom: Revising after feedback. In M. Secor & D. H. Charney (Eds.), *Constructing rhetorical education* (pp. 278–294). Carbondale, IL: Southern Illinois University Press.

Slavin, R. E. (1991). Synthesis of research on cooperative learning. *Educational Leadership, 48,* 71–82.

Smith, K. A., & MacGregor, J. (2000). Making small-group learning and learning communities a widespread reality. *New Directions for Teaching and Learning, No. 81* (pp. 77–88). San Francisco, CA: Jossey-Bass.

Smith, P. L., & Tillman, J. R. (1999). *Instructional design* (2nd ed.). Upper Saddle River, NJ: Prentice-Hall.

Smith, R. C., & Eisenberg, E. M. (1987). Conflict at Disneyland: A root metaphor analysis. *Communication Monographs, 54,* 367–380.

Southern Association for Colleges and Schools, The Commission on Colleges. (2000). *Distance education: Definition and principles* [Online]. Available: www.sacs.org

Sprague, J. (1993). Why teaching works: The transformative power of pedagogical communication. *Communication Education, 42* (4), 349–366.

Sproull, L., & Kiesler, S. (1991). *Connections: New ways of working in the networked organization.* Cambridge, MA: MIT Press.

Stanton, A. L. (1990). An ecological perspective on college/university teaching. In J. A. Daly, G. W. Friedrich, & A. L. Vangelisti (Eds.), *Teaching communication: Theory, research and methods* (pp. 39–52). Hillsdale, NJ: Lawrence Erlbaum Associates.

Staton-Spicer, A. Q., & Wulff, D. H. (1984). Research in communication and instruction: Categorization and synthesis. *Communication Education, 33* (4), 377–391.

Stice, J. E. (1987). Using Kolb's learning cycle to improve student learning. *Engineering Education, 77,* 291–296.

Stinson, J. E. (1990). *Integrated contextual learning: Situated learning in the business profession.* (ERIC Document Reproduction Service NO. ED 319 330)

Stinson, J. E., & Milter, R. G. (1996). Problem-based learning in business education: Curriculum design and implementation issues. In W. Gijselaers & L. Wilkerson (Eds.), *New Directions in Teaching and Learning in Higher Education, No. 68.* San Francisco, CA: Jossey-Bass.

Stith, B. (2000, March). Web-enhanced lecture course scores big with students and faculty. *T.H.E. Journal, 27* (8), 20–23.

Stoll, C. (1996). *Silicon snake oil.* New York, NY: Anchor Books/Doubleday.

Stout, N., & Mills, L. (1998). *Ft. Hood and the Texas A & M University System: Collaboration and distance learning.* Paper presented at the Annual Distance Education Conference, Austin, TX.

Strine, M. S. (1993). Of boundaries, borders, and contact zones: Author(iz)ing pedagogical practices. *Communication Education, 42* (4), 367–376.

Swartz, J. D., & Biggs, B. (1999). Technology, time, and space or what does it mean to be present? A study of the culture of a distance education class. *Journal of Educational Computing Research, 20,* 71–85.

Tannen, D. (1990). *You just don't understand: Women and men in conversation.* New York, NY: Ballantine Books.

Thach, L., & Murphy, L. (1994). Collaboration in distance education: From local to international perspectives. *The American Journal of Distance Education, 8* (3), 5–21.

Tommerup, P. (2001). Learning to see academic culture through the eyes of the participants: An ethnographic/folkloristic approach to analyzing and assessing the cultures of alternative institutions. In B. L. Smith & J. McCann (Eds.), *Reinventing ourselves: Interdisciplinary education, collaborative learning, and experimentation in higher education* (pp. 368–390). Bolton, MA: Anker.

Trentin, G. (2000). The quality-interactivity relationship in distance education. *Educational Technology, 40* (1), 17–27.

Turoff, M. (1995, March). *Designing a virtual classroom* [Online]. Available: http://www.njit.edu/Department/CCCC/VC/Papers/Design.html

Turoff, M. (1999). Education, commerce, communications: The era of competition. *WebNet Journal: Internet Technologies, Applications & Issues, 1* (1), 22–31.

vonGlasersfeld, E. (1989). Cognition, construction of knowledge, and teaching. *Synthese, 80,* 121–140.

Vygotsky, L. S. (1978). *Mind in society: The development of higher psychological processes* (M. Coles, V. John-Steiner, S. Scribner, & E. Souberman, Trans.). Cambridge, MA: Harvard University Press.

Walther, J. B. (1992). Interpersonal effects in computer-mediated interaction: A relational perspective. *Communication Research, 19* (1), 52–90.

Walther, J. B. (1996, February). Computer-mediated communication: Impersonal, interpersonal, and hyperpersonal interaction. *Communication Research, 23* (1), 3–43.

Walther, J. B., Anderson, J. F., & Park, D. W. (1994, August). Interpersonal effects in computer-mediated interaction: A meta-analysis of social and antisocial communication. *Communication Research, 21* (4), 460–487.

Walther, J. B., & Boyd, S. (1997, May). *Attraction to computer-mediated social support.* Paper presented at the annual meeting of the International Communication Association, Montreal, Canada.

Webb, N. M. (1982). Student interaction and learning in small groups. *Review of Educational Research, 52* (3), 421–445.

Webb, N. M., & Palincsar, A. S. (1996). Group processes in the classroom. In D. C. Berliner & R. Caffee (Eds.), *Handbook of educational psychology* (pp. 841–873). New York, NY: Macmillan.

Wepner, S. B. (1998, Spring). Your place or mine? Navigating a technology collaborative. *Journal of Computing in Teacher Education, 14* (3), 5–11.

Wernet, S., Olliges, R. H., & Delicath, T. A. (2000, July). Postcourse evaluations of WebCT (Web Course Tools) classes by social work students. *Research on Social Work Practice, 10* (4), 487–504.

Whittington, C. D., & Campbell, L. M. (1999, February). Task-oriented learning on the web. *Innovations in Education & Training International, 36* (1), 26–33.

Wildner-Bassett, M. (2001, Fall). Multiple literacies, CMC, and language and culture learning. *Academic Exchange Quarterly, 5* (3).

Wildner-Bassett, M. E., & Meerholz-Haerle, B. (1999). Positional pedagogies and understanding the other: Epistemological research, subjective theories, narratives, and the language program director in a 'web of relationships.' In L. K. Heilenman (Ed.), *Research issues and language program direction* (Vol. 9, pp. 203–243). Boston, MA: Heinle & Heinle.

Wulff, D. H. (1993). Tales of transformation: Applying a teaching effectiveness perspective to stories about teaching. *Communication Education, 42* (4), 377–397.

Yordon, J. E. (2002). *Roles in interpretation* (5th ed.). New York, NY: McGraw-Hill.

Zuss, M. (1994). Value and subjectivity in literacy practice. In B. Ferdman, R. M. Weber, & A. Ramprez (Eds.), *Literacy across languages and cultures* (pp. 239–272). Albany, NY: State University of New York Press.

INDEX